THE GREATER- GOOD DEFENCE

The Greater-Good Defence

An Essay on the Rationality of Faith

Melville Y. Stewart

Professor and Chair of Philosophy
Bethel College, Minnesota

St. Martin's Press

First published in Great Britain 1993 by
THE MACMILLAN PRESS LTD
Houndmills, Basingstoke, Hampshire RG21 2XS
and London
Companies and representatives
throughout the world

This book is published in Macmillan's
Library of Philosophy and Religion series
General Editor: John Hick

A catalogue record for this book is available
from the British Library.

ISBN 0-333-57556-3

Printed in Great Britain by
Antony Rowe Ltd, Chippenham
Wiltshire

First published in the United States of America 1993 by
Scholarly and Reference Division,
ST. MARTIN'S PRESS, INC.,
175 Fifth Avenue,
New York, N.Y. 10010

ISBN 0-312-08095-6

Library of Congress Cataloging-in-Publication Data
Stewart, Melville Y.
The greater good defence: an essay on the rationality of faith /
Melville Y. Stewart.
p.   cm.
Includes bibliographical references and index.
ISBN 0-312-08095-6
1. Good and evil.   2. Religion —Philosophy.   3. Free will and
determinism.   4. Ethics.   I. Title.
BJ1401 . S83   1993
216—dc20   92-6281
                                                     CIP

To Donna,

Dave, Dan, Steve, Linda, and Glenn

I believe that God can and will bring good out of evil, even out of the greatest evil. For that purpose he needs men who make the best use of everything. I believe that God will give us all the strength we need to help us to resist in all times of distress. But he never gives it in advance, lest we should rely on ourselves and not on him alone. A faith such as this should allay all our fears for the future. I believe that even our mistakes and shortcomings are turned to good account, and that it is no harder for God to deal with them than with our supposedly good deeds. I believe that God is no timeless fate, but that he waits for and answers sincere prayers and responsible actions.

Dietrich Bonhoeffer
Letters and Papers from Prison

Contents

Preface

This book is a study of several defences viewed as specifications or 'offspring' of the parent, greater-good defence. Numerous formulations of two of the defences and critical studies of them abound, but scant attention has been given to their relatedness and common root. In this volume, the 'parent' defence – the greater-good defence – is examined, and several derivations of the defence from tenets of theism are traced. Three specifications, including an original account of what I call the 'Redemption Specification' (incipient perhaps in some way or other in the other two), are critically appraised, and seen as bearing significant 'family resemblances.' I argue that the defences not only sustain a relatedness, but that they need each other, and that they constitute an apologetic complex that successfully defeats the inconsistency strategy and significantly undermines the probabilistic strategy based on evil.

The first chapter provides a brief conceptual landscape in terms of which selected key issues meaningfully fall into place. How the issue of evil is to be construed is one of the central concerns. Chapter 2 examines the omni-attributes central to the debate. Consideration of counterexamples result in adding qualifiers until definitions evolve which are mutually compatible and 'fit' key notions integral to the theist's system of beliefs. Chapters 3 and 4 cover various greater-good defences and greater-good derivations, respectively. The fifth chapter examines the modal free will defence of Alvin Plantinga, and the sixth, the soul-making defences of Keith Yandell and John Hick. The Fall, in the final chapter, is teleologically construed as a *felix culpa* (happy fault), because it gives meaning to the notion and act of redemption.

The manuscript evolved through two main stages, the first of which satisfied a terminal degree requirement at the University of Minnesota. Burnham Terrell supervised the study, and Jasper Hopkins was a strong influence and encouragement. I am grateful to both for their advice and friendship. During a sabbatical leave in 1986, an extensive revision was initiated. I am grateful to Bethel College for granting the sabbatical so that I could write at Oxford University. Richard Swinburne kindly wrote letters of introduction to the Bodleian and Radcliff libraries, and graciously consented to read two drafts, one while at Oxford, and another later. His many comments at both stages led to numerous significant improvements. As it turned out, Oxford proved to be an ideal environment for the project. Much of the writing took place in a corner at Pusey Library of St. Cross College.

Many others have helped sharpen the ideas and arguments. Alvin Plantinga responded to questions that I had regarding his free will defence, and granted permission to refer to materials he presented as part of a lecture series at Bethel College. James Sennett drew my attention to several imprecisions in an early account of that defence. An early draft was read by Bruce Reichenbach, and some of his criticisms were very helpful, and a greater-good defence he suggested is included in Chapter 3. Thanks are also due Eleonore Stump for reading and commenting on the manuscript. The section on omniscience in Chapter 2, was read as a paper, to which George Mavrodes offered comments and helpful examples, some of which appear in Chapter 2. C. Anthony Anderson offered a number of helpful suggestions regarding the definitions that appear in Chapter 2. I am grateful to several anonymous readers for having offered many helpful suggestions which led to revisions *passim*.

Along the way, colleagues at Bethel College, Stan Anderson, Alan Padgett, Don Postema, Paul Reasoner, Greg Boyd, and Roger Olson, critically responded to sections of the manuscript read at philosophy department seminars. My T.A., Andrea Winquist, carefully read a late draft, which resulted in some changes for the better, and Robert Franks and Lamont A. Crook helped in proof reading.

The discussion of omnipotence in Chapter 1 appears in slightly different form as an article in *Explorations* under the title, 'On Defining Omnipotence' (Vol. 9, No. 3, Spring, 1991, 77–94), and the seventh chapter, 'O Felix Culpa, Redemption, and the Greater Good Defence,' is a revision of an article under that title that appears in *Sophia* (Vol. 25, No. 3, October, 1986, 18–31). I am grateful to both publishers for permission to include these materials in this study.

The final copy has been meticulously prepared by Janine McFarland, who patiently typed revisions, promptly met deadlines, and kept a watchful eye on detail and fine points of style.

Finally, I owe more than I can ever express in mere words to my wife and children, to whom this volume is dedicated. They patiently endured my many absences and times of stress, in order that I might complete the study. Thanks to their many encouragements and steadfast support, this inquiry has reached this final form.

Table of Logical Symbols

⤳	'ϕ ⤳ ψ,' 'if ϕ, then-probably ψ,' two-place probability functor
∇	' ∇ ϕ,' 'it is probable that ϕ,' one-place probability functor
.İ.	'so-probably' of inductive inference
→	'$\phi \rightarrow \psi$,' 'if ϕ then-materially ψ'
$\bar{\phi}$	'not ϕ'
(/)	'ϕ/ψ,' 'probability of ϕ given ψ'
□	' □ ϕ,' 'necessarily ϕ'
◊	' ◊ ϕ,' 'possibly ϕ'
ICa	'individual concept of Adam'
Ia	'individual Adam'
sa	'set(s) of actions'
ssa	'set(s) of logically possible states of affairs'
T(W)	'true in world W'

1

Introduction

Is the existence of evil in the world compatible with the existence of the God of Christianity?[1] Detractors of theism have generally tended to argue that both existence claims cannot be true. Some have argued that there is a logical contradiction perhaps not directly, but if one or two propositions are added which some judge to be compellingly true, since the first belief is obviously true, if the added propositions are compellingly true, it is false that God exists. Others have taken the more modest line, given the amount of evil that there is, it is strongly probable that some of it is gratuitous, and the strong probability that there is gratuitous evil in the world makes it strongly improbable that God exists. Various rather sophisticated theistic defences have been formulated in response to both lines of attack in the current philosophy of religion literature.[2] Implicit in those defences which have received the most attention is what might be called the 'Greater-Good Defence.' Part of my task is to look at this defence in preliminary form as it is presented by Keith Yandell since he has offered a straightforward and extended account of this strategy.[3] Then variant accounts of the Defence are formulated and examined, and selected contemporary defences which may be viewed as significantly incorporating a greater-good notion are critically appraised. I shall contend that the greater-good defence (hereafter the GGD), or some variation of it, is derivable from essential tenets of theism, that the redemption specification of the GGD which I offer is a significant addition to theistic apologetics, and finally, that the three specifications are incorporable into a greater-good complex of arguments which provide a secure place for the theist to stand against the inconsistency charge.

1

1. FORMULATING THE PROBLEM OF EVIL

It is important, as we begin, to give attention to the matter of how
to characterize the problem of evil, since the way in which a philosophical problem is formulated can and usually does significantly
influence the manner and method of its attempted resolution. At
least three separate and distinct construals of the problem may be
found in the literature.[4] Regarding the first, according to Lactantius,
an apologete for Christianity circa 260 A.D., the problem is rather
incisively posed in question form by Epicurus:

> God either wishes to take away evils and he cannot, or he can and
> does not wish to, or he neither wishes to nor is able, or he both
> wishes to and is able. If he wishes to and is not able, he is feeble,
> which does not fall in with the notion of god. If he is able and does
> not wish to, he is envious, which is equally foreign to god. If he
> neither wishes to nor is able, he is both envious and feeble and
> therefore not god. If he both wishes to and is able, which alone
> is fitting to god, whence therefore, are there evils, and why does
> he not remove them?[5]

Two millennia after Epicurus, David Hume in his comprehensive
and on some estimates devastating attack on Christianity, draws
attention to Epicurus' question and judges that theists have failed
to answer it, and on that account thinks that the Christian hypothesis
faces a challenge it cannot survive.

Roughly the same lofty concept of God which is at the center and
gives such forcefulness to Epicurus' and Hume's question plays
a central role in J. L. Mackie's attack on theism in 'Evil and
Omnipotence.'[6] It is Mackie's main contention in this key essay
that the theist is committed to a set of beliefs that is inconsistent.
According to Mackie's account of the charge, the theist faces a
logical problem:

> The problem of evil, in the sense in which I shall be using the
> phrase, is a problem only for someone who believes that there
> is a God who is both omnipotent and wholly good. And it is
> a logical problem, the problem of clarifying and reconciling a
> number of beliefs: it is not a scientific problem that might be
> solved by further observations, or a practical problem that might
> be solved by a decision or an action.[7]

Thus for Mackie the issue of evil as it relates to the theist's set of beliefs generates a problem of a different genre from those which are either practical or scientific. One significant differentiating feature of the first sort of problem has to do with the way whereby one attempts its solution. Solutions of the first sort of problem involve a clarification and reconciliation of the set of beliefs in question, not 'decision' or 'action,' as with the practical, or 'further observation,' as with the scientific.

Formulations of the problem of evil in terms of questions do not pose a serious challenge to theism, notwithstanding Epicurus' and Hume's claims to the contrary, since even if the theist does not or cannot come up with anything in the way of a significant answer to the question, it does not follow from this failure that God does not exist, or that there is not a helpful and relevant answer available. All that we may legitimately infer from such a failure is some sort of conclusion regarding the respondent's ignorance or ineptness at answering the question.

Mackie's approach which views the theist as facing a logical problem, however, merits a closer look, because of its current popularity, and discussion of it provides something of an introduction to a third sort of formulation of the problem of evil suggested by George Mavrodes. Mavrodes claims that framing the problem as Mackie does, i.e., formulating it as a logical problem, is a misguided effort.[8] Setting it up this way, Mavrodes believes, generates several difficulties. First, Mackie's discussion appears to use the terms *belief* and *proposition* interchangeably. Mavrodes points out rightly that there are significant differences between these terms in the context of the alleged difficulty Mackie raises. *Inter alia*, regarding propositions, logical relations exist between or among propositions *qua* propositions. The notion of belief, on the other hand, brings psychological information into the picture relative to the persons who have them. Hence, if we have a logical problem as Mackie suggests, whether the propositions in question are believed by some person or not has nothing to do with the logical relations that may exist between or among the propositions in question.

Further, Mavrodes questions whether Mackie's notion of 'the reconciliation of beliefs' is on target. In his criticism of Mackie on this point Mavrodes draws an analogy between the 'reconciliation of beliefs' notion generally and the 'reconciliation of two enemies.' Regarding the latter, reconciliation can be brought about if there is a change in beliefs, attitudes, etc., but the identity of the individuals reconciled is preserved. In the case of beliefs which are logically inconsistent, the original set – those contemplated for reconciliation – cannot be reconciled by means of alteration, since the alteration involves a move away from the original beliefs.

Matters are made worse when Mackie suggests that there are 'adequate solutions' to the problem, *one* of which might involve jettisoning a subset of beliefs in a set because of its incompatibility with the remaining members of the set. What we have here is a procedure with decision as its main ingredient, and in this respect it is not unlike the practical sort of problems mentioned that might find solution through action or decision.

Mavrodes' analysis of Mackie's formulation of the problem serves well to point out some important weaknesses in Mackie's framing of the problem. At the same time Mavrodes sees something of value in Mackie's construction that he (Mavrodes) wants to retain as an element in his own formulation of the issue, which is the third possible construction of the problem of evil. In his discussion of evil, Mackie sometimes moves back and forth indiscriminately between propositions and beliefs, but in the process he offers the insight that the central issue under study involves *beliefs* of persons. Mavrodes works with the notion of belief, refines it and sees it as having a key role in a proper and helpful structuring of the issue of evil.

For Mavrodes, *belief* is something that is 'person-relative' and 'person-variable.' Regarding the first concept, whereas propositions involve objective sorts of concepts and as such do not convey psychological content, beliefs involve subjective sorts of concepts and as such do convey psychological information. A belief is a proposition with regard to which a person may be said to be 'in a certain psychological state.' Thus beliefs are 'person-relative' in the sense that the beliefs are held by some person or group of persons.[9] He uses the following notation to express it more formally thus: (where p stands for some proposition, ϕ stands for some psychological state with regard to p, and N stands for the person who is in psychological state ϕ), 'p is ϕ by . . . N.'[10] Concerning the notion 'person-variable,' he points out that subjective concepts do not have the same opposites as objective ones do. Regarding propositions, the opposite of 'true' is 'false.' If we have in mind a certain proposition, say P, then 'P is true' is logically incompatible with 'P is false.' But we do not have an opposite with this sort of feature for 'believed.'[11] According to Mavrodes' construction, there is no *one* problem of evil for all persons. Theistic sets of beliefs (which include for example the belief that there is evil) may differ according to those who hold them, and if certain sets of beliefs include propositions which in fact or only putatively confront the holder with some sort of logical incompatibility, then because those sets that present the real or alleged difficulties differ, in all likelihood there will be correspondingly different problems of evil. For Mavrodes, an incompatible set held by an individual constitutes an 'epistemic dilemma.' An epistemic dilemma is defined by Mavrodes as follows:

> A person faces an epistemic dilemma if and only if he believes (or is inclined to believe) a set S of propositions (the 'core' of the dilemma) plus an additional proposition Is (the 'rider') which is, 'S is inconsistent.'[12]

In the above, the larger set which includes the core and the rider is inconsistent. If the rider is true, then some one or more of the core is (are) false. But if all of the core are true, then the rider is false.

Two sorts of epistemic dilemmas, hard and soft, are distinguished by Mavrodes. A hard epistemic dilemma involves belief in a set of propositions which are genuinely contradictory. A soft epistemic dilemma, on the other hand, concerns belief in a set which contains propositions that are only apparently contradictory. Closer inspection or plausible and hopefully appropriate interpretations show them to be compatible. Those who wish to mount a rational defence for theism by offering a justification pattern (or patterns of justification) for evil, would generally be inclined to concur that theists are at the very worst confronted with only soft epistemic dilemmas. If Mavrodes' construction of the issue at hand is correct – and I think that it is in the main – then there would be a final proof against a theist just in case one can show that a theist faces a hard epistemic dilemma. And that case would stick only for the theist in question, since the beliefs in question are person-relative and person-variable. Regarding evil, it will be part of my task to show that the theist at the worst faces only a soft epistemic dilemma, by showing that the tenets in question are consistent.

(a) The Inconsistency Strategy

There are at least two ways of charging the theist with inconsistency relative to his system of beliefs. The first calls into question the

consistency only of the religious set of beliefs which are held basic
or essential to Christian theism, (hereafter I shall use the shorter
expression 'theism' in place of 'Christian theism,' and I shall use the
expression 'ISI' to refer to the first sort of inconsistency strategy),
and constitutes an *ad hominem* argument. The second strategy is
broader because the set of beliefs challenged is more inclusive. In
this case, the theist is thought to be in jeopardy because his set
of religious beliefs combined with another set which consists of
obvious truths constitutes a set judged to be inconsistent, which
is again an *ad hominem* type argument (hereafter I shall refer to this
strategy as ISE).[13] If the atheist can succeed with either strategy, that
is, if he can show that the religious set of beliefs is inconsistent by
itself (ISI) or in conjunction with a set of obvious truths (ISE), then
the theism that embraces the religious set collapses.

Any number of routes may ease the theist out of either the ISI
or the ISE. He may resort to an alteration of one or more of the
tenets of theism. Some theists, for example, have rejected the *God
is omnipotent* thesis, and have opted for a finitist position regarding
God's power.[14] It is not clear, however, that the benefits of such a
move overbalance or even counterbalance its liabilities.[15]

The theist could develop a 'consistency strategy' in response to
the inconsistency challenge. Consider the set of beliefs J. L. Mackie
presents in his construction of the problem of evil in 'Evil and
Omnipotence':[16]

(1)   God is omnipotent,
(2)   God is omnibenevolent, and
(3)   There is evil in the world.

For the sake of argument, let us say that the atheist grants that
(1) and (2) are consistent, but that when (3) is added, the atheist
judges the resultant set to be inconsistent. By using the consistency
strategy, the theist can nullify the atheist's attack just in case he can
show that (1) and (2) together with another statement, say (4) entail
(3).[17] This further statement must be self-consistent and consistent
with (1) and (2). The task that then faces the theist, is coming up
with some sort of justification for evil which will be a specification
of (4) that will show (1), (2) and (3) to be consistent. More than one
specification may be available, and any consistency strategy that
specifies (4) could count as a defence for theism.

Another route involves exploring some belief or set of beliefs which the theist for some reason or other might be thought to hold in addition to his initial set of essential tenets of theism, and which when combined present at least a prima facie case of inconsistency against the theist. The purpose of the maneuver is to see whether there might be some genuine cause for worry for the theist. The theist may develop his response to a prima facie account in any one of several ways, as suggested above. He might decide either that prudence lies with a revision of the belief or set of beliefs in question, or with the consistency strategy. Or he might judge that the belief or set of beliefs under consideration does not carry the threat it appeared to contain on first inspection, or that there is (are) no reason(s) that compel(s) him to hold the belief(s) in question.

(b) The Probabilistic Strategy

Disenchanted with the inconsistency line, some atheists have turned to an argument they consider to be more promising, viz., the probabilistic argument against God's existence based on evil. In rough terms, it is to adduce the reality of evil as evidence for the probability that God does not exist. The argument runs something like the following (I shall refer to it as PA):[18]

PA (1) If there is a great abundance of evil in the world, then it is probable that some of it is gratuitous.

(2) There is a great abundance of evil in the world.

(3) Therefore, it is probable that some evil is gratuitous.

(4) If it is probable that some evil is gratuitous, then it is probable that God does not exist.

(3) It is probable that some evil is gratuitous.

(5) Therefore it is probable that God does not exist.

The inference pattern is rather straightforward. That is, by two operations of Modus Ponens, (3) follows from (1) and (2), and (5) follows from (4) and (3).

Several matters are of chief concern to any serious consideration of this strategy. The first has to do with the truth of premise (1). Theists, at least a lion's share of them, are reluctant to acknowledge that there are such things as gratuitous evils,[19] though few, if any, would cavil with the claim that there is a great abundance of evil in the world. Gratuitous evil is discussed at length in Chapter 3, and there is no need to enlarge upon it here.

Second, as with any argument taken in earnest, it is important to provide as clear and favorable account as is practically possible. How the probability mode figures in the probabilistic strategy and how probability itself is to be unpacked are pivotal. Three allegedly different interpretations of probability have been distinguished. The first, the 'personalist' sense, runs roughly as follows. A person S is spoken of as having a 'credence function,' such that S assigns to every proposition about which S has an opinion a real number ranging from 0 to 1, depending on the degree of belief S entertains relative to a certain hypothesis A (which is being considered). If B is S's total evidence on the matter, then if we take $P(\ /\ )$ as the probability function, the formula, $P_s(A/B)$ will have a value from 0 to 1, which will indicate how likely A would be for S, given B.[20] This version of probability centers attention on information relative to the bias of some person, and so tends to be 'autobiographical' in nature.[21] For this reason, any objection to theism based on this sort of probabilistic claim would have relevance only for persons who entertain a similar sort of bias.

Two other senses of probability that have been distinguished have a greater bearing on the strategy in question. Following Rudolf Carnap's practice, I will refer to them as probability$_1$ and probability$_2$. Probability$_1$ is a 'logical concept, a certain logical relation between two sentences (or, alternatively, between two propositions).'[22] Its purpose is to 'account for the inductive use of "probability."'[23] The probability calculus on this interpretation does not work with properties but with statements, and more particularly with statements in their logical relation.[24] Brian Skyrms points out as an additional feature of this sort of probability that 'probability ascription statements . . . are analytic,'[25] i.e., their truth value is not dependent on empirical data. He adds, 'the value of Pr $(q$ given $p)$ depends solely on the meaning of "probability" and the meanings of the statements "p" and "q" . . . . '[26] Probability$_1$, often referred to as 'inductive probability,' informs us then of the strength of the evidence the premises 'provide' for the conclusion.[27] It is this sort of probability John Hick has in mind in *Faith and Philosophy* when he writes,

On this view a proposition is probable, not in isolation but in relation to other evidence-stating propositions. A judgment of probability thus presupposes a corpus of (actual or hypothetical) items of information (p,q,r) such that belief in these prior propositions authorizes belief in a further proposition (x); and the strength or confidence of the belief thus authorized is the measure (although not a measure capable of precise numerical statement) of the probability of x in relation to p, q and r.[28]

The probabilistic inference relation can be expressed either of two ways, in terms of a probabilistic argument, or in terms of a corresponding conditional. I am assuming that just as with a deductive argument containing finitely many premises, there is a corresponding conditional, where the antecedent is the premises taken conjunctively, and the consequent is the conclusion, so in a similar fashion, a probabilistic argument with finite premises can be expressed in a corresponding conditional, where the premises taken conjunctively form the antecedent, the conclusion is the consequent, and the logical connector is a probability functor. If we let a and b be variables ranging over statements, and '.İ.' be a probabilistic inference sign, and ' $\rightsquigarrow$ ' be a two-place probability functor, such that '$a \rightsquigarrow b$,' we can represent the probabilistic argument form and the corresponding conditional thus.

ARGUMENT FORM   CONDITIONAL

$$a$$
$$.\dot{I}.b$$

$$a \rightsquigarrow b$$

The inference from a to b symbolized by '.İ.b' reads as, 'a, therefore-probably b.' The corresponding conditional, '$a \rightsquigarrow b$,' translates as, 'If a, then-probably b.'

A second interpretation of probability, probability$_2$, focuses on the relative frequency of events. Two leading exponents of this interpretation are Hans Reichenbach and Wesley Salmon. They start with the idea that probabilities are ratios or properties of events of one kind in relation to events of another kind. *Probability* is defined as, 'the limit of *frequency* within an infinite sequence.'[29] The general idea is that probabilities have to do with the relative frequency of events of one kind in relation to events of another kind within an infinite series. Hick applies the theory to the probability of causes, and Alvin Plantinga broadens the definition of the term *event* so as to include classes of possible worlds.[30] This move allows

Plantinga to apply the frequency theory to statements. When the probability functor applies to some statement, we have what is called, 'epistemic probability.' In the case of our earlier argument PA, the probability mode applies to the statements which serve as premises and conclusion to the argument, not to the inference itself. A formal rendition of the argument would thus employ one-place probability functors.[31] If we let ' ∇ ' be a one-place probability functor, we can express probability$_2$ relative to variable a as ' ∇a,' which translates as, 'probably a,' or, 'it is probable that a.'

That probability has a number of distinct meanings is not the consensus. Max Black, for example, challenges Carnap's distinction, charging that his argument, if closely examined, is 'based solely upon the different modes of verification of two probability assertions.'[32] He argues that 'there seem to be no compelling reasons for recognizing radically distinct senses of probability.'[33] Whether there are distinct sorts of probability need not detain us here. But on the side of Black, our first sense of probability, viz. the personalist sense, might be viewed as a species of probability$_1$, since the probability mode applies to the inference made not to propositions. And even if there is only one main sense of probability, its application in probability$_1$ is different from its application in probability$_2$, since in the former the mode applies to an inference, and in the latter it applies to propositions. However distinct in concept and/or application, there is an important relation between the two, i.e., epistemic probability is inductive probability relative to total available evidence.

A discussion of probabilistic arguments against God's existence would be incomplete without some attention given to Bayes' Theorem. The theorem has general use as a formula for calculating the value of a conditional probability, which involves a determination of the value of the converse of the conditional probability along with certain other values. Discussion of the theory usually takes place in the context of consideration of an hypothesis for confirmation. In the case of probabilistic arguments against God's existence based on evil, the argument is used to show that, given the evidence and background information, then-probably God does not exist. The basic strategy in this case is to move from 'prior probabilities' which are presumably known, to a 'conditional or forward probability' which one wants to establish.

Two sorts of questions arise in connection with the Theorem:

(1) Should the Theorem be used when prior probabilities are not known? (2) Does it (the Theorem) work with all sorts of probabilities (assuming that there are different sorts, or at least a variety of possible applications)? The former question raises concerns that need not concern us here, and the latter we can answer, at least in a preliminary way. Since we can take a probabilistic inference as having a corresponding conditional, and since Bayes' Theorem applies to conditional probabilities, the Theorem can be applied to probability$_1$. As for probability$_2$, the Theorem applies to probabilities 'construed as relative frequencies,'[34] and if so, then perhaps also to propositions, if the relative frequency theory can be applied to propositions.

In order to get a handle on how the Theorem can be applied to the atheologian's probabilistic strategy, let us begin with a simple case. Suppose that at a Cadillac factory in Detroit, call it 'Willow Run,' only Cadillac cars are produced on March 1, 1990. Suppose further that we know that of the cars assembled that day, 90 percent have stereo radios, and 10 percent of this number have moon roofs. Suppose further, that among the 10 percent of those that do not have stereo radios, 20 percent are equipped with moon roofs. What is the probability that a Cadillac with a moon roof is also a Cadillac with a stereo radio?

Working with Bayes' Theorem, we can find the answer. If we let $P(p)$ = the probability that a Cadillac is equipped with a moon roof, and $P(q)$ = the probability that a Cadillac is equipped with a stereo radio, then we have the following values,

$$P(q) = 0.9 \qquad\qquad P(p, \text{ given } q) = 0.1$$
$$P(-q) = 0.1 \qquad\qquad P(p, \text{ given } -q) = 0.2$$

The probabilities to the left above are the prior probabilities, and those to the right above are the forward or conditional probabilities. Since we have only two variables, we can work with a simplified version of the Theorem that works with variables p and q. The simplified version runs as follows:

$$P(q, \text{ given } p) = \frac{P(q) \times P(p, \text{ given } q)}{[P(q) \times P(p, \text{ given } q)] + [P(-q) \times P(p, \text{ given } -q)]}$$

Given the above values for the prior and forward probabilities, we have the following:

$$P(q, \text{ given } p) = \frac{0.9 \times 0.1}{(0.9 \times 0.1) + (0.1 \times 0.2)} = \frac{0.09}{(0.11)}$$

In our example, the probability that a Cadillac with a moon roof is also equipped with a stereo radio depends on the prior probability that a Cadillac is equipped with a stereo radio and the conditional or forward probability that a Cadillac with a stereo radio is also equipped with a moon roof. Our answer is 9/11.

The application of the Theorem to the issue of evil is, at least on some accounts, more complex. That is because the discussion works with three variables; background information, evidence and the hypothesis. The following is roughly how it goes. Given propositions A, B, and C, where A is the hypothesis, B is the evidence, and C the background information, and the probability function P (/), the theory can be stated thus:[35]

$$P(A/B\&C) = \frac{P(A/B) \times P(C/B\&A)}{[P(A/B) \times P(C/B\&A)] + [P(\bar{A}/B) \times P(C/B\&\bar{A})]}$$

The various combinations of symbols in the formula can be given the following meanings.

$P(A/B)$ = the prior probability that the hypothesis A is true, given the evidence B.

$P(\bar{A}/B)$ = the prior probability that the hypothesis A is false, given the evidence B.

$P(C/B\&A)$ = the probability of the background information C given the evidence B and hypothesis A is true.

$P(C/B\&\bar{A})$ = the probability of the background information C given the evidence B and hypothesis A is false.

$P(A/B\&C)$ = the probability that the hypothesis A is true, given the evidence B and background information C.

If we apply the Theorem to the probabilistic strategy of the atheologian based on evil, A is God does not exist, the prior probability $P(A/B)$ is, the probability that God does not exist, given the amount of evil we find. The prior probability $P(\bar{A}/B)$ is, the probability that it is not the case that God does not exist, given the amount of evil that we find. The probability of the background information C, which is the sort of world we have (that is, it is a world that can be characterized as containing various sorts of creaturely inhabitants, and as exhibiting certain laws of nature, etc.), given the amount of evil we find, and that God does not exist is true are meanings that may be assigned to C, B and A respectively, in the formula, $P(C/B\&A)$. The probability of the background information, that is, the sort of world we have, given the amount of evil we find, and that it is not the case that God does not exist, are the meanings given to $P(C/B\&\bar{A})$. Finally, $P(A/B\&C)$ is the probability that God does not exist, given the amount of evil we find and the sort of world we have. The theist, of course, could mount a similar strategy offering arguments for different values for the hypothesis, *God does exist*.

Three probabilities in the Theorem need to be determined if the atheologian is going to be able to calculate the probability of $(A/B\&C)$: she needs the prior probability $P(A/B)$. If the atheologian knows this, she knows the other prior probability, $P(\bar{A}/B)$, since the probability of the two add up to 1. She also needs to know the probability of $(A/B\&C)$, which is the probability that such and such an effect would occur given the evidence and if it is assumed that God does exist.[36]

In order to establish the prior probability (A/B), she must show that the evidence makes it more probable that God does not exist than that he does. How she reads the world will obviously effect how she determines the values. She will likely discount the teleological argument,[37] as well as other apologetic devices contrived by the natural theologian. Contrarywise, the theist will likely try to make use of such data as evidences for $\bar{A}$. Both sides will likely have different values for crucial variables in the Theorem. A computer is no more reliable than its input. Bayes' Theorem helps us compute probabilities relative to values assigned to the various formulas constitutive of the Theorem – values which at least indirectly reflect the bias of the person calculating the values. Even the most earnest effort to preserve objectivity is going to yield at crucial points to bias. Decisions have to be made as to what is going to count, and how much as evidence. Hence, any sort of Bayesian analysis is going to require a lot of preliminary argument to show what the values of the probabilities which enter into Bayes' Theorem are. Those arguments will be working with assumptions which will reflect at least indirectly the belief system of the analyst. In his critical Bayesian analysis of theism, for example, J. L. Mackie insists that the theistic hypothesis does not 'fit' with the 'background information,' but his analysis is confined to explanations which are scientific. If theism works with another model, say, the 'action of an agent' model,[38] then Mackie is stacking the deck against theism from the start. But so does Swinburne in his defence of theism. He formulates his own Bayesian analysis with his own account of background information, which includes *inter alia* free will, and his view of personal explanation.[39] In order to tabulate results, one is going to have to scrutinize the arguments behind the data filling in the 'blanks.' Issues that divide the theist from the atheist in the inconsistency strategy figure in the probabilistic argument, only the name of the argument has changed. The atheologian's contention that, given the evil that there is, then-probably God does not exist, or, given the evil that there is, it is probable that God does not exist, faces countermoves similar to those offered in response to the inconsistency strategy. The theist can counter, given the evil that there is, then-probably God does exist, since he might argue that evil is a consequent of creating a world populated with free moral agents.

2. KINDS OF EVIL

There is evil in the world is an essential tenet of theism and an obvious truth about the world. Examples of evil in the world are legion: cancer, heart disease, floods, earthquakes, volcanic eruptions, fires (and other sorts of natural phenomena which have a negative impact such as suffering or pain), humans inflicting pain for its own sake on others, taking human life for pleasure, etc. These sorts of things provide clear examples of what we mean by evil, and they make plain evil's reality. Commonly, at least two kinds of evil are distinguished.[40] The first class of evils include those which result from the misuse of freedom of choice, and the second is a catch-all for the remaining evils. Different justification patterns have been formulated to handle the various sorts of evil. The free will defence, for example, is tailored to justify moral evil resulting from the misuse of free agency.[41]

3. ORDERS OF GOOD AND EVIL

A contrast between moral and natural goods might be drawn that has an affinity with the distinction made earlier between moral and natural evils. Moral goods include both good actions and their intended consequences, i.e., actions and intended consequences that result from the appropriate use of free agency. The precise force of 'appropriate' in this context is not necessary for present purposes. All other goods not included in this first class may be subsumed under natural goods. The twofold distinction between natural goods and natural evils, and moral goods and moral evils corresponds roughly to Mackie's account of first and second order goods and evils. First order goods and evils are passive experiences. Examples of the former are pleasure and happiness,[42] and of the latter, pain and misery.[43] By contrast, second order goods and evils are actions done in the light of first order goods or evils, and logically require the occurrence of the former. Second order evils such as cruel and abusive treatment of others, cowardly behavior in the face of danger, etc., involve a misuse of free agency. This is the more important of the two orders of evil, because with regard to the latter, evil is viewed as increasing in measure by reason of the fact that it involves a choice of the agent. Second order evil compares roughly to what I have called moral evil. When there is a heightening or increase of first order goods such as happiness as a result of an appropriate use of creaturely free agency we have a second order good, which compares to what I have called 'moral goods.' One might say, for example, that there is a potentially higher sense of happiness experienced by an agent when he shows sympathy toward a cancer victim, or manifests fortitude when faced with severe pain. As for higher order goods or evils, they are done in the light of goods or evils of the next lower order, and logically require them. Mackie suggests that third order evils involve beings of an higher order than humans. On this view, evils of this sort would include such things as malevolent influences and activities brought about by the agency of evil spirits designed by them to mitigate, so far as God will ultimately and sovereignly allow, full-orbed human responses to divine benevolence. He sees third order goods as resulting from God's will to 'maximize second order goods.'[44] It is not clear, however, that Mackie has the matter right. For human actions such as forgiving others would typically be third order goods. That is, the good of forgiveness could not occur, unless there were episodes of moral evil in some other agent needing forgiveness.

4.   THE GREATER-GOOD DEFENCE

Without the sophisticated garb it sometimes acquires in polemic contexts, the GGD involves the claim that evils that exist in the world are either counterbalanced or overbalanced by goods which require them (the evils, or something like them). And though this general pattern of argument is to one extent or another utilized in some of the main theistic arguments in response to the challenge of inconsistency, or the probability argument against God's existence based on evil, Keith Yandell stands out as one of the few who has provided a detailed account of this particular defence. According to Yandell, not only is some formulation of the defence an important part of the theist's apologetic, but the GGD is an entailment of essential tenets of theism. Both contentions will receive serious attention later.

5.   A COMPLETE JUSTIFICATION

Some theists (Yandell, Plantinga, and Swinburne, for example) seriously question whether the theist can come up with an IFF for justified evils.[45] Some argue that since creatures do not share God's *sub specie aeternitatis* vantage point, it would be presumptuous to think that the theist could realistically formulate such a comprehensive scheme. M. B. Ahern, in *The Problem of Evil* makes the point thus:

> To state and to answer definitely all of the concrete problems of evil, a God's eye view of the world which saw not only everything evil and good of the past, the present and future, but also how they are inter-related would be necessary. This view would need to span the whole history of the world and its final outcome, as a whole and in its parts. If certain theist claims are true, it would need to take into account supernatural facts, the significance of Jesus Christ and the reality and nature

of an after-life. Human beings cannot lay claim to omniscience of this kind.[46]

In more general terms, John Hick avers that there are limitations on human explanatory powers regarding divine motives, and there is an 'element of mystery' which may be construed as an integral part of a world designed by God for soul-growth.[47]

If the theist takes a line like Ahern's, he might thereby be vulnerable to a question-begging charge. There are two ways to counter such a move. He can offer a *defence* the more modest of the two options which is an attempt to specify a reason or justification for evils of a certain kind. Generally this more modest approach does not involve the claim that the reason or pattern of justification offered is *God's* reason or pattern of justification. Further, as a defence, it is usually incomplete, and commonly there is a recognition that a final justification for all evils requires a divine perspective on things.

In contrast to the more modest *defence*, a *theodicy* is an attempt to specify God's reasons or patterns of justification for evils. At least it is hoped that the reasons or patterns of justification given approximate what might be divine reasons or patterns of justification, assuming that God exists, and that he has patterns of justification. Furthermore, a theodicy usually involves a comprehensive justification for all evils, or at least a complement of patterns for all the different kinds of evils. Thus, in a defence the theist relinquishes the task of providing justification patterns for all evils or all evil-kinds, and so developing a defence is easier than formulating a theodicy. If the theist can provide a possible reason or pattern of justification, he can argue that some evils are thus justifiable, and he thereby defuses the inconsistency charge. He might go on to argue that we cannot *know* that a particular evil is not justifiable, since not having a justification ready at hand, does not mean that there is no such pattern. If the atheist presses the claim that there are gratuitous evils, the theist can either challenge the probabilistic argument in support of the atheist's claim, call his bluff and ask for examples of gratuitous evil, or admit to gratuitous evils and work out a defence which allows such evils (see Chapter 3).

In this chapter we have taken a brief look at some of the main issues of concern relative to setting the conceptual stage necessary to understanding and discussing the GGD. First, as to the matter of evil, it was decided that formulating a problem of evil in terms of an 'epistemic dilemma' is superior to either of the other constructions considered – formulations in terms of questions and logical-problem formulations. It was also concluded that it is very unlikely that there is *one* problem of evil, but rather there are various epistemic problems or dilemmas relative to the persons who have them. Two sorts of inconsistency strategy were distinguished, ISI and ISE, both of which were characterized as *ad hominem* (the former was more narrowly confined to theistic beliefs proper, the latter was broadened to include obvious truths along *with* the set of theistic beliefs) in the sense that both are directed against the theist *qua* theist.

In addition to the inconsistency strategy, a second sort of challenge to theism was sketched, viz., the probabilistic argument against God's existence based on evil. Different sorts of probability were discussed and attention was given to different construals of the probability mode.

Preliminary distinctions were made between two kinds of evil, moral and natural, and three orders of goods and evils were discussed. Finally, the GGD was presented in preliminary form, and it was suggested that the theist would be better advised to take the 'low road' of defence rather than the 'high road' of theodicy.

In Chapter 2 our task is to examine the content of the tenets of theism that give rise to the charge that theism is untenable because it involves incompatible beliefs. The inconsistency strategy charges that a contradiction obtains in the system of beliefs of the theist, and the probabilistic strategy claims that the abundance of evil makes it probable that there is gratuitous evil, and this makes the existence of God improbable, since the God of theism would not allow gratuitous evil. It is important now to look more closely at the Christian conception of God – the God who putatively would not allow evil, and so whose existence is incompatible with evil, or, whose existence is improbable, given the existence of gratuitous evil.

2

Omnipotence, Omniscience, and Omnibenevolence

Currently, one could probably learn more about the attributes of God from philosophers of religion than from Christian theologians.[1] Philosophical interest in the divine attributes is due in part to the role the omni-attributes have in theodicy formulations.[2] One of the main atheological attacks based on evil is against the theist *qua* theist. After all, isn't the existence of evil incompatible with the existence of an omnipotent, omniscient and omnibenevolent God? If the attack has bite, a central reason is the fact that the theist holds that all three predicates are central to the nature of God. Take any one away the charge fizzles. If God is not omnipotent in some sense, then although he might know of every occurrence of evil in the world and desire to remove them all because he is perfectly good, his lack of *power* might stand in the way of his doing so. Or, God may possess the power and desire to remove all evil from the world, but if he does not have omniscience in a significant way, he may fail to remove every manifestation of evil in the world because he may not be cognizant of every evil. If he is not perfectly good in some straightforward sense, then he may have it in his power to act and know of every instance of evil in the world, but he may not remove every evil because it is not according to his *desire* to do so. The denial of any one of the omni-descriptions theists hold appropriate to God would be sufficient then to defuse the inconsistency charge, but concomitantly, denial of any one of the attributes would weigh heavily against his being worshipworthy.[3] Thus either way the theist might be in a bind.

Relative to the divine attributes there has been a longstanding dispute as to whether or not God has a nature or essence.[4] That is, is God essentially omnipotent, omniscient, and perfectly good, or are these only contingent properties? How one comes down on

19

this significantly affects the theist's response to the inconsistency strategy.[5] Suppose, for example, the theist were to argue for a variant of the Cartesian thesis that God is in absolute control over every truth – that he is absolutely omnipotent in this sense.[6] On this account God would have no nature because there would be no property God could not be without, since it is within his power to 'bring it about that he lacks that property.'[7] Since it would be up to God whether a proposition is made true or false, there would be no necessary truths. Descartes' discussion of 'eternal truths' is particularly germane. One such truth is, *The three angles of a triangle are necessarily equal to two right angles* (let us refer to it as *P*). On one interpretation of Descartes – 'universal possibilism' – God's control over the truth of propositions extends to making 'contradictories true together.'[8] With this kind of control over the truth of propositions, if he wanted, he could have made *possible* logically 'impossible propositions' such as *P and not-P*, and if he could have made such propositions possible, surely there is nothing standing in the way of his making them true. Or, he could have made not-*P* (which is a contradiction, since *P* is an 'eternal' or 'logically necessary truth') true. It is not hard to see how this Cartesian doctrine might aid the theist. If God can cause even contradictory propositions to be true, then the theist need not dispute the charge of inconsistency at all. That is, the theist can make the universal possibilism move that contradictory states of affairs can be divinely allowed or caused, thereby checkmating the inconsistency strategist. But this line does not mean that no problem of evil at all exists. That is, while God may allow or cause logically incompatible states of affairs, the issue of why a divine being would allow evil might still be in need of some sort of explanation. But when, where and for what reason(s), if he in fact could, would the theist call an end to this holiday from consistency? And, does this sort of tampering with consistency not put *omnipotence* itself into jeopardy? Hopefully, there will be an unravelling of some of these issues in the discussion that follows. As for those who have only disdain for such excursions, holding they are too costly, and who take the task of making faith coherent seriously, an attempt is made to flesh out in at least preliminary fashion a consistent picture of the omni-attributes central to the dispute.

1. DEFINITIONS OF OMNIPOTENCE

Regarding God's power, a fairly wide spectrum of options has been proposed and defended, ranging from a finite or limited-God thesis all the way to some form or other of the Cartesian absolute-omnipotence suggested above. Though the former view might hold some philosophically interesting ideas and nuances relative to the issue of evil, since it is generally agreed that the thesis in question does not represent what traditional theists have been inclined to embrace concerning the extent of God's power, it is left unexplored.[9] Clearly, theists (of the Christian variety) have tended strongly to the view that God is omnipotent or all-powerful. In fact, as we have already intimated, some of those who favor the stronger notion hold that God is absolutely omnipotent in some way similar to Descartes' 'absolute omnipotence' doctrine.[10] On this view God is somehow supralogical and hence can, 'if he wants,' nullify or set aside the canons of logic and make true a contradictory proposition or do something that would be contradictory for him to do. Why are some theists attracted to this Cartesianism, and what can be said in its defence?

Historically, the leading proponent of the view is Descartes. He defended the view primarily because he saw its defence as essential to the preservation and protection conceptually of God's absolute sovereignty. Exactly what Descartes had in mind is not clear since there is a question as to just how he intended to preserve this sovereignty in the face of truths of logic. Two positions have been distinguished in his writings, universal and limited possibilism. The former is the view that Descartes' 'eternal truths,' e.g., the truths of logic, mathematics, etc., are *not* necessary truths.[11] The latter position by contrast affirms that eternal truths are necessary, but they owe their necessity to divine decree.[12] P. T. Geach takes Descartes as holding the latter thesis, at least with regard to the truths of logic and mathematics.[13] Plantinga judges that though Descartes 'makes two quite distinct suggestions about eternal truths,'[14] his (Descartes) discussion at times runs the two together and so he does not appear to have been entirely clear on the matter.

It is transparent that Descartes believed that God cannot have any limits – he is infinite. According to Plantinga's reading of Descartes, God is without limits because he is the absolutely sovereign being upon whom everything distinct from him depends.[15] That means that he cannot be limited by necessary truths. The universal possibilism reading of Descartes poses no threat to God's sovereignty because this interpretation assumes that he denies that there are necessary truths. Limited possibilism preserves God's sovereignty but with a more modest claim. Under limited possibilism God is in control over what propositions are necessary, but once he makes them so, they are then necessary. The marked emphasis of Descartes on God's absolute sovereignty in his writings[16] leads Plantinga to lean toward a universal possibilism interpretation. In its (universal possibilism's) defence Plantinga offers the following argument in Descartes' behalf:

(1)   God has infinite power;
(2)   If God has infinite power, there are no necessary truths; therefore,
(3)   There are no necessary truths.[17]

Though Descartes would most certainly hold the argument valid (it is a substitution instance of Modus Ponens), he need not concede that the argument's corresponding conditional is a necessary truth.[18] Further, he need not be at a loss as to providing an explanation of how he arrived at the conclusion. He can offer the standard response that an argument is valid if it is a substitution instance of an argument form which has no instances where the premises are true and the conclusion false.[19] There are problems with such a view, but as Plantinga says Descartes is not forced to give up standard first-order logic and identity on account of universal possibilism. He could hold that none of the truths of logic are necessary. Plantinga sees this account of Descartes as not incoherent in any straightforward sense; rather 'the most we can fairly say, here, is that his view is strongly counterintuitive.'[20]

If, on the other hand, Descartes is taken as not denying that there are necessary truths, but only as denying that it is necessarily true that they are necessary (i.e., he is only denying the characteristic axiom of S4), then the problem of evil would not be resolved so easily. For then the propositions in the set that generate the problem of evil really will be inconsistent. God might have made it true that the propositions in question are not inconsistent, but he has not.

Perhaps if a theist, with a penchant for something resembling universal possibilism, wanted reinforcement from a contemporary philosopher, he could for starters look to W. V. Quine's discussion of so-called 'necessary truths.' In Quine's judgment the laws of logic and mathematics may be open to revision 'despite all "necessity."'[21] They are true, he avers, 'by virtue of our conceptual scheme.'[22] This is a long way yet from universal possibilism, but one might see it as paving the way. Conceptual schemes are things we bring about and create. Removing necessity opens the door beyond a crack to the claim that there are no necessary truths.

Whether the theist sides with Descartes, the human element in such matters is important to recognize. Though it is generally recognized (Quine included) that there is a rigidity about those canons which set the very boundary of meaningful thought and verbal expression, we need to remember that their formulation is the result of human understanding and perception, hence any construction of them at best will be less then complete and fallible, and worse, in some significant aspect flawed. In the final analysis we might have to allow, as Quine suggests, for clearer and better grasps of the canons, which might in turn affect their rigidity. Maybe *possibility* itself as a concept will correspondingly carry a different, perhaps richer sense than the content currently conveyed by reason of present boundaries given the term by contemporary possible-worlds ontologists and logicians. Here, the cautious and prudential route might be to leave these matters guardedly and somewhat open-ended.

The two sorts of possibilism discussed above require two definitions of omnipotence. However, our main concern is to examine Cartesian possibilism and how it might contribute to the theist's cause. Since God is not bound by logical necessities on the universal possibilism reading, it will be sufficient for our purposes to consider a definition of omnipotence that corresponds to this stronger reading of Descartes. In our definition we will quantify over individuals and propositions.[23] Let x be a variable ranging over individuals, and p over propositions. The definition might run something like the following (I shall refer to it as omnipotent$_1$, and succeeding definitions as omnipotent$_2$, omnipotent$_3$, etc.).

Omnipotent$_1$ For any individual x, and any proposition p (the content of which *may* or *may not* be coherent), x is omnipotent IFF x can make p true.[24]

The definition allows that an omnipotent being can bring into existence a non-compossible state of affairs, say a round-square, which satisfies the proposition, 'Object O is a round-square.' Thus as we have seen, the logically impossible is made possible by a being that is omnipotent in this way.

There are at least two critical problems facing the view. If the theist is to be a 'consistent Cartesian,' if God is in some way or other absolutely omnipotent and absolutely sovereign, then not only must *de dicto* necessity be excised as in universal possibilism, but *de re* necessity must go as well.[25] On the view that God is absolutely sovereign, he cannot be said to have any attribute necessarily, because having an attribute necessarily stands in the way of his being sovereign in respect to his having or not having the attribute. But this generates something of a paradox. That is, relative to the notion of absolute omnipotence, there is a meta-level restriction that says, God *must not* possess any one attribute or combination of attributes necessarily, for if he did, then he would not be free to have or not have the property in question, and so would not be sovereign in the possession of properties. But even if he were sovereign in this way, i.e., even if he had no property or combination of properties necessarily, he would not be absolutely sovereign, since the meta-level restriction requires that 'he *must not* possess any one or combination of properties.' That is, God could not cause it to be the case that he had some property or combination of properties necessarily. Thus in spelling out the doctrine, a restriction that seems unavoidable interferes with his being absolutely sovereign. To be sovereign relative to property possession then, he must be free in respect to the mode of his having them, but to be free in respect to the mode of his having them, he *must not* possess one or any combination of them necessarily.

Secondly, if *existence* is taken as a predicate,[26] then since God may be said to have existence only contingently, conceivably he could decide not to. This sort of sovereignty allows that the God of Christian theism might not exist now, though he might have in the past.

The theist could respond to the first by saying, since God could have no good reason for relinquishing sovereignty, he would not do so. A somewhat similar response could be offered with regard to his relinquishing existence. Still the possibility for both remains, however remote. Whatever other difficulties there might be with the view, there is one distinct advantage attaching to the omnipotent$_1$ definition. On this view, God can bring about non-compossible states of affairs satisfying contradictory propositions. Hence bringing about or allowing evil, whether horrible, gratuitous, or even contradictory (even with God's nature), is a live option for a being with this sort of power. Presumably there would be no genuine conflict with divine omnibenevolence either, since God is not limited in *any* way by *any* sort of contradiction.

If Descartes failed to offer an adequate account of omnipotence,[27] he is not lacking for company in this endeavor. In his early work, *God and Other Minds*, Plantinga abandons his search for a totally satisfactory definition of the term,[28] and in *The Nature of Necessity*, he offers only a rough definition, similar in tone to those tendered by Anthony Kenny and Richard Swinburne, because their definitions quantify over logically possible powers and not over logically possible actions. In his discussion of omnipotence, the latter explores four preliminary candidates before settling on a final definition that makes provision for his notion of God's 'perfect freedom.' A brief survey of those preliminary definitions can be helpful and instructive toward understanding some of the issues which besiege any who might take on the challenge.

Our second definition quantifies over *sets* of logically possible actions.[29] A person may be said to be omnipotent$_2$, IFF he can do any member of any set of logically possible actions. If we let x be a variable ranging over individuals, and *sa* be a variable ranging over sets of actions, we can formalize the definition as follows.

Omnipotent$_2$ For any individual x, and any set of logically possible actions *sa*, x is omnipotent$_2$ IFF x can do any member of *sa*.

Clearly, a being that is omnipotent$_2$ cannot create a round square, since the description of the action in question is not coherent. But this limitation does not detract from an agent's omnipotence, since a logically impossible action 'is not an action.'[30] However, the following shows the definition deficient. For example, 'Making true the logically possible statement *Nixon's autobiography is authored by Nixon without Nixon being caused by God to write it*' is an action that is logically impossible for God to perform.[31] God cannot perform the action since the statement logically precludes God from doing it.

A revised definition that quantifies over sets of logically possible states of affairs covers such counterexamples as those that troubled omnipotent$_2$. In our new definition, a person is omnipotent$_3$, IFF he can bring about any member of any set of logically possible states of affairs. Or more formally, if we let x range over individuals, and *ssa* range over sets of contingent states of affairs, we have the following.

Omnipotent$_3$ For any individual x, and any set of contingent states of affairs, *ssa*, x is omnipotent$_3$ IFF x can bring about any member of *ssa*.

Despite the revision, omnipotent$_3$ is defective because it does not rule out an omnipotent$_3$ agent from bringing about *past* states of affairs. Since bringing about past states of affairs is logically impossible, a definition such as the following is required which covers these sorts of counterexamples. A person is omnipotent$_4$ at a certain time, IFF, for any set of contingent states of affairs, that person can bring about any member of any set of possible states of affairs at the time in question. If we let x range over individuals, and *ssa* range over sets of contingent states of affairs, and t range over possible times, we have

Omnipotent$_4$ For any individual x, and any set of contingent states of affairs, *ssa*, and any time t, x is omnipotent$_4$ IFF x can bring about any member of *ssa* after t.

In addition to handling the sort of counterexamples mentioned above, the new definition handles problems of the following sort. For any member of any set of logically possible states of affairs an agent, say A might be said to bring about after t, A's bringing about any member of any set of logically possible states of affairs after t must also be consistent with what has happened at or before t.[32] It might be logically possible (apart from consideration of sets of logically possible states of affairs prior to t), to bring about a particular member of a set of logically possible states of affairs, say the member of set ssa_1 which is, *Bertrand Russell is married*, but it would *not* be possible for A to bring about the member of ssa_2 which is, *Bertrand Russell is divorced at* or *after t*, if *before t*, the member of the set of possible states of affairs ssa_3 had been brought about, which is, *Bertrand Russell had never been married*. An omnipotent$_4$ being could not bring about the member of ssa_3 in question after t, if before t the agent had brought about the member of ssa_3 in question, because the member of ssa_3 is not a logically possible state of affairs after t given that the agent has brought about the member of ssa_2 before t.

Two difficulties count against the omnipotent$_4$ definition. First it allows that an omnipotent$_4$ being bring about 'logically necessary states.'[33] So to be omnipotent$_4$ a being would have to be able to bring it about that *if x is a body then x is extended*. But no agent can do this, since of necessity all bodies are extended in all possible worlds, and so all bodies will of necessity be extended quite independent of any agent's bringing it about. Thus those sets of possible states of affairs the members of which an omnipotent being could be thought to bring about must be confined to contingent sets of logically possible states of affairs.

Second, a being that is omnipotent$_4$ is supposed to be able to bring about an uncaused state of affairs, or a state of affairs not brought about by the agent in question, both of which are not logically possible. Once again we need to add qualifications to our definition to cover problems of the sort mentioned. Our new definition is, a person is omnipotent$_5$ at time *t*, IFF the person in question is able to bring about any member of any contingent and logically possible states of affairs after *t*, the description of which does not entail that the person in question did not bring about the member in question after *t*. No new notation need be introduced to formally express the definition.

Omnipotent$_5$ For any individual *x*, and any set of contingent states of affairs, *ssa*, and any time *t*, *x* is omnipotent$_5$ at *t* IFF *x* can bring about any member of *ssa*, the description of which does not entail that *x* did not bring about the member in question after *t*.

Our revised definition handles the counterexamples omnipotent$_4$ failed to. It has been argued that a similar definition also enables the theist to reckon with the much-discussed Paradox of the Stone.[34] Though accounts of the Paradox vary, roughly it begins with the question, Can God make a stone (so heavy) that he cannot then lift? If one answers, 'Yes,' then he is not omnipotent, since he cannot then lift the stone, and if one answers, 'No,' then he is not omnipotent since he cannot create such a stone. If the power or capacity to bring about members of sets of contingent and logically possible states of affairs is confined to time *t* before an omnipotent$_5$ agent, say *P*, creates a stone that *P* cannot then afterwards lift, then the theist can affirm that *P* can create such a stone. Of course, once *P* does bring about the stone, *P* ceases thereby to be omnipotent. But as

Swinburne points out, that P can create such a stone does not carry the implication that P will. However, final resolution to the Paradox is not yet in hand. The argument turns on the assumption that omnipotence is a contingent, not necessary property. In his chapter on omnipotence in *The Coherence of Theism*, Swinburne leaves open the question as to whether God is necessarily omnipotent. However, in his discussion of 'A Necessary Being,' and in particular, his focus on God as 'the personal ground of being,' he argues that were such a being to lack omnipotence, that would evidence that he 'had never been a personal ground of being.'[35] Thus for Swinburne, God's omnipotence is a necessary property. If omnipotence is taken to be a necessary attribute of God, then an argument which claims that God, being omnipotent can create such a stone commits the fallacy of contradictory premises,[36] since a 'rock that God cannot lift' is logically incompatible with God's being necessarily omnipotent. On this account, definitions omnipotent$_3$ and those which follow, cover the Paradox, since a 'stone that God cannot lift' is not a logically possible state of affairs, given that God is necessarily omnipotent$_5$.

Swinburne offers another definition that makes provision for the 'perfect freedom' of God. God 'chooses freely,' means that regarding his actions there is no 'full explanation – of any kind, whether of the kind described by scientific explanation or of the kind described by personal explanation.'[37] This freedom is *perfect* in the sense that he 'cannot do actions which he believes to be morally wrong.'[38] Actions are morally wrong, if there are 'overriding reasons' for refraining from doing them (the actions). A definition of omnipotence that reflects this account of God's 'perfect freedom,' is constructed as follows.

Omnipotent$_6$ For any individual x, and any set of contingent states of affairs, *ssa*, and any time t, x is omnipotent$_6$ at t IFF x can bring about any member of *ssa*, the description of which does not entail that x did not bring about the member in question after t, and x does not believe that it would be better to refrain from bringing about the member in question.

The new qualification in omnipotent$_6$ takes into account the claim that God is in some sense free. Some theists might argue to the contrary that God is not in any significant sense free, and further, that since God is necessarily good, the good he does, he does of necessity. This move might create a problem with regard to ascribing moral predicates such as 'good' and 'praiseworthy' to God, since if whatever good he does, he does necessarily, might mean that he cannot be properly said to be good or praiseworthy. Some of these and related matters will be discussed shortly in connection with God's omnibenevolence or perfect goodness.

Omnipotent$_5$ eliminates the possibilities that an omnipotent agent could bring about members of sets of possible states of affairs *not* brought about by the agent in question. But it does not cover an agent's bringing about logically possible states of affairs that might be logically impossible for the agent in question because of the agent's nature. In omnipotent$_6$ a condition is added which excludes as options those things incompatible with an omnipotent agent's character. But as omnipotent$_6$ stands it is too broad, since it does not prevent a very limited agent, such as for example, one who can scratch only his ear, from being appropriately described as omnipotent$_6$, since all of the conditions of omnipotent$_6$ apply to this agent. The example is posed originally by Plantinga,[39] and the agent is given the name McEar by Richard La Croix.[40] The definition is clearly deficient, since the theist would not want to ascribe omnipotence to an agent who can perform only one sort of act, viz., scratch his ear, because all other acts are logically incompatible with his nature. To cover this sort of counterexample, one further qualification is needed. What if we added, 'no being *y* greater in power than *x* can be conceived?'[41] Does this prevent such limited beings from being eligible for the attribute thus defined? Perhaps it does, but the phrase 'greater in power' is ambiguous since its *range* over possible states of affairs is not clear. Humans have it in their power, or have the capacity to bring about states of affairs such as, choosing a moral evil; whereas God does not, at least directly. Humans are capable of making mistakes in judgement; God cannot. A citizen of the United States can run for President; God cannot, since he is not a citizen of the United States. Neither can he become a pilot for Northwest Airlines. The list goes on. In at least these significant ways, humans might be said to be beings with greater power than God, at least greater in the sense that humans *can* do these things, and God cannot. On the other hand, God can bring about some possible world, say *W*, whereas humans cannot. The crucial issue here is the range of 'greater in power.' And though humans may have it in their power to bring about certain sets of logically possible states of affairs God cannot directly, God's overall range far exceeds that of humans. Furthermore, most theists have maintained that human powers are derived, whereas God is self-subsistent. If we change Reichenbach's qualifier to read as follows, 'no being y greater in overall power than x can be conceived,' the above difficulty is resolved. However, the added qualifier needs further specification, because it disallows that we can conceive of a being y greater in overall power than x. But we can, because we can conceive of y as capable of bringing about any number of sets of states of affairs that x cannot because x is confined by a morally restrictive clause, 'does not believe it would be better to refrain from bringing about the member in question.' We eliminate this potential difficulty if we revise our initial qualifier so as to read as follows: No being y greater in overall power and moral excellence than x can be conceived. We can now formulate omnipotent$_7$, adding variable y as ranging over individuals.

Omnipotent$_7$ For any individual x and any individual y, and any set of contingent states of affairs, ssa, and any time t, x is omnipotent$_7$ at t IFF x can bring about any member of ssa, the description of which does not entail that x did not bring about the member in question after t, x does not believe that it would be better to refrain from bringing about the member in question, and no being y greater in overall power and moral excellence than x can be conceived.

Omnipotent$_7$ might need revision if the theist were to make use of Plantinga's free will defence, or something like it. Whereas the definition in question quantifies over sets of logically possible states of affairs, Plantinga's free will defence talks about God's freedom and power in terms of world-making, and so the focus is upon logically possible *worlds*. A possible world is a set of possible states of affairs, but not every set of possible states of affairs is maximal or complete. Stage one of Plantinga's modal free will defence, which trades on his distinction between strong and weak actualization of possible worlds, shows that while God is omnipotent he cannot strongly or even weakly actualize just any possible world.[42] If the theist were to take such an argument seriously, then he could add a further clause to Omnipotent$_7$, so as to make provision for this point in Plantinga's argument. Let x range over individuals, y range over individuals, ssa range over sets of contingent states of affairs, t range over possible times, and w range over logically possible worlds. The new definition runs as follows.

Omnipotent$_8$　　For any individual x and any individual y, and any set of contingent states of affairs, ssa, and any time t, and any logically possible world w, x is omnipotent$_8$ at t IFF: (1) x can bring about any member of ssa which is such that (a) the description of that member does not entail that x did not bring about the member in question after t, (b) x does not believe that it would be better to refrain from bringing about the member in question, (c) that member is included in a logically possible world which (given the counterfactuals of freedom which actually obtain) x can strongly or weakly actualize; (2) no being y greater in overall power and moral excellence than x can be conceived.

There are two necessary conditions to omnipotent$_8$, the first covers sets of logically possible states of affairs, and the second logically possible worlds. The new definition is necessary, if the theist is going to argue along the lines of the modal free will defence of Plantinga, since the latter involves the claim that God cannot bring about just any possible world that he pleases. Further justification for the added condition regarding God's strong or weak actualization of possible worlds will be forthcoming in our discussion of this defence in Chapter 5.

Suppose that an omnipotent being were to bring about a logically possible world populated with morally free agents. Suppose further that in order to preserve the freedom of these agents, he imposes limits on the range of his actions. Is this not a variation of the 'rock-that-he-cannot-lift' problem? If the theist holds that God is contingently omnipotent, then he can create such creatures, but his doing so *will* bring an end to his being omnipotent. If, however, the theist holds God is necessarily omnipotent, then is it consistent to think that he could bring about such a set of states of affairs where agents are free? It is important to note here that none of our definitions quantify over *power*, and so there is no condition requiring that an omnipotent agent have all power directly under his control. Morover, if bringing about such agents is a limitation, the limitation is not a result of imposition from external powers, but rather comes from within. Thus there does not seem to be any violation of the conditions of omnipotent$_8$.

Eight readings of omnipotent have been considered. Some counterexample may be lurking somewhere 'out there,' which might show omnipotent$_8$ to be deficient in some way. Still it or something like it may be very close to what the theist needs.

There are, of course, those who think that the task of providing an IFF for omnipotence is misguided, because they hold that there is no 'reasonable interpretation' of the thesis that God can do everything.[43] For P. T. Geach, for example, prudence lies with setting the concept of omnipotence aside altogether and working with the concept of *almightiness*.[44] This move only trades one set of problems for another.

2.   DEFINITIONS OF OMNISCIENCE

Philosophical interest in the divine attributes is due in part to the role the omni-attributes, omnipotence, omniscience, and omnibenevolence have in theodicy formulation. Omniscience generates a family of problems at least as perplexing as those facing the other two divine predicates.

Whether *omniscience* can be coherently defined, and how the attribute effects human freedom, are two central issues that continue to trouble and divide those concerned. As to the *first* worry, presumably an agent that is omniscient is so at some time or other.[45] Suppose that an agent, say A, is omniscient at time t_1. Then at least in a minimal sense we may say A is *omniscient* if A knows all true propositions at t_1. Suppose further that as the theist holds God is immutable, A is immutable – that he does not change in any way with regard to say, his being, power, knowledge, and any other attribute that may be appropriate to A. Now consider propositions whose truth depends (in part) on indexical expressions they contain being satisfied by particular correspondingly-indexed states of affairs. Take the indexed proposition, 'It is 4 P.M., March 1, 1990 in Boston' as an example of this sort of proposition.[46] Call it proposition P. Let the time t_1 (the same time that A is said to be omniscient) be the time (4 P.M., March 1, 1990 in Boston) at which

P is true. Since P is true only at t_1, by a fairly standard definition of knowledge (*knowledge* as 'justified, true belief'), P can be known by *any* knower only when the time indicated by p corresponds to t_1. That means that no agent, not even an omniscient one, could properly be said to know P before or after t_1. Since A is omniscient, he knows all true propositions, and so he must know P, but he cannot, *before* t_1 or *after* t_1. Hence, any being that knows P, must go through a change in respect to knowing P,[47] even if the being is omniscient. Any omniscient being who is properly said to know P, moves from *not knowing* P before t_1, to *knowing* P at t_1, to not knowing P after t_1.

There is another sort of counterexample that has been raised that some think stands in the way of a coherent understanding of omniscience. It has been argued that the concept in question is not coherent when knowledge claims regarding human self-consciousness are taken into account. If, for example, while giving a first-person report of the following sort, 'I am this thing here,'[48] the reporter points to himself, then this sort of first-person knowledge claim is not something to which God has access in the way that the person in question does, precisely because it is a first-person claim. God might be said to know *when* a human agent 'knows this,' and *that* the human agent knows what he knows, if he in fact does know, but he (God) cannot be properly said to know in the first-person way what the human agent knows. He also would have his own first-person reporting to do (should he choose to so share it) relative to knowing 'I am this thing here,' so far as it might make sense for him to make such an utterance, and were he to do so. Thus it might be argued that there are some things, viz. a whole set of first-person report statements relating to creaturely self-consciousness which he (God) may not be properly said to know. Thus there are at least these two sorts of counterexamples which need to be reckoned with if the theist is going to succeed in giving a coherent account of *omniscience*. I shall argue in the following that there is a definition of omniscience that is at once compatible with human freedom, and that enables the theist to deal decisively with both sorts of counterexamples.

J. R. Lucas, in *The Freedom of the Will*, cites Ambrose's poignant remark to Origen, "'If God knows the future beforehand, and it must come to pass, prayer is in vain.'"[49] Some argue that such prescience has not only grave implications for prayer, it also completely undercuts human freedom. That is, if God's knowledge includes everything that will come to pass, down to the smallest possible detail, then it follows that everything that God foreknows happens of necessity. If the theist holds that persons are in some significant sense free, then he is going to have to 'scale-down'[50] his view of *omniscience*, or show how such knowledge is compatible with human freedom.

Quite apart from the difficulties outlined above, defining omniscience is problematic partly because it is notoriously difficult to provide an IFF for the non-prefixed concept 'knowledge' (or 'knowing'), in particular the concept *propositional knowledge* or *knowledge that p*. Problems of a different sort arise if, as some theists believe, God is a radically different knower as compared to human agents. Some have contended that there is a quantitative and qualitative difference between human and divine knowledge.[51] Regarding the mode of divine knowledge, traditionally theists have maintained that God knows everything that he knows immediately and intuitively, not discursively, as it is with humans. More recently, it has been argued that it might be that God knows all true propositions not intuitively, but in their logical-connectedness all at once.[52] Another set of problems arise when we ask the question, Are the conditions for God's knowing that *p*, the same or different from those for human knowledge? As interesting and tempting as these issues might be, serious discussion of them would take us too far afield. However, as to the conditions of God's knowing, some matters must be briefly addressed because of their importance to at least a preliminary understanding of the non-prefixed notion in question.

First, the *truth* condition must hold for God, that is, for any proposition *p*, *p* must be true, if God can be properly said to know *p*. And, since all contradictory propositions are necessarily false (Cartesian universal possibilism excepted)[53], God cannot be properly said to know any contradictory propositions. Further, for any proposition *p*, where *p* is contradictory for God to know, God could not be properly said to know *p*. For example, he (God) could not know *God does not exist*. If we let *x* range over individuals, and *p* range over propositions, a preliminary definition of omniscience may be stated thus (let us refer to it as omniscient$_1$, and succeeding definitions as omniscient$_2$, omniscient$_3$, and omniscient$_4$).

Omniscient$_1$　　　　For any individual *x*, *x* is omniscient$_1$ IFF, for every proposition *p*, if either *p* is true or it is possible for *x* to know *p*, then *x* knows *p*.

The definition clearly excludes three sorts of propositions from being possible candidates for God's knowledge: (1) for any proposition p, if p is false, then God cannot know p; (2) for any proposition p, if p is a contradiction, then since p logically cannot be true (Cartesian possibilism excepted), God cannot know p; (3) for any proposition p, if p is contradictory for God to know, then God cannot know p. Thus far, our concern has been with the truth of propositions God knows.

For any proposition God knows, does he also *believe* it? That is, does God satisfy the belief condition in his knowing a proposition? Nelson Pike seems to think so, since in spelling out the necessary conditions of omniscience he lists two: (1) such a being must believe all true propositions, and (2) such a being must believe no false propositions.[54] If we assume that God satisfies Pike's conditions, as I think he (God) does, then there is the question, Does God's believing a proposition count as a sufficient condition for that proposition's being true? Presumably God could have no false beliefs. God would not believe *Tokyo is the capital of the Soviet Union*.[55] It seems correct to say that if God believes p, then p is true. But if we assume God's believing a proposition *is* a sufficient condition for its being true, might such a view not pose a threat to human freedom similar to the one posed by omniscience? If God believes all true propositions, might this not interfere with human free agency, since any proposition he believes cannot fail to be true?

First, the theist need not deny, in fact many want to affirm that God has beliefs about many future events, none of which are false. For example, he holds true beliefs about courses of action that he wills and carries out in a first-person way. He *knows* what will happen in such instances because he wills it thus, and since his will on this account is never frustrated, his *beliefs* about such choices and their outcomes (where his will alone is the direct cause) are never mistaken. Many want to add that he also holds true beliefs about future events that follow natural law and the psychological tendencies of persons, individually and as they (persons) function in collective ways, as in institutions and nations. On the view that says God is perfect, he never errs in his calculations and projections, so he never mistakenly believes propositions about predictable truths. More about this shortly.

But what about cases where created moral agents enjoy libertarian freedom, say where individual M freely chooses to do x instead of

y at some future time, say t_1? Does God know before t_1, that M will freely choose x instead of y, and does he also inerringly believe that M will freely choose x and not y at t_1? The former is another way of putting the question, Does God know in advance which counterfactual conditional of freedom will be actualized by a created free agent – does he have middle knowledge? The second question is, does God have 'middle beliefs,' say a true belief that such-and-such counterfactual conditional of freedom is going to be the case (hereafter, I will refer to counterfactual conditionals of freedom as CF's)? If the theist answers both affirmatively, then does God's having such knowledge and the corresponding beliefs interfere in any way with the freedom of created agents? Then there is the question, Might the theist hold that God has beliefs about such choices, and sometimes is mistaken, i.e. he holds to beliefs that later fail to correspond to actual choices? If the theist says yes, can she hold *God is perfect* in a meaningful way?

As to whether, if the theist holds that God has middle knowledge, and perhaps also middle beliefs relative to CF's, such knowledge and beliefs interfere with free choice, a compatibilist line might run roughly like the following: (1) God's knowledge, and so also his middle beliefs, do not enter into the causal path of free choices; (2) what God knows and believes in such cases are contingent truths. Since issues relating to compatibilism come up again shortly, I will not expatiate on them further here.

At least as nettlesome as the dilemma posed above is the question, Does God have middle knowledge? Does he know CF's?, and more to the point of our inquiry, Does God ever believe p, where p is a CF? And, if he holds beliefs about CF's, Does he hold only true beliefs about them? Obviously, if the theist holds God does not have beliefs at all, then he (God) does not have beliefs about CF's. So our concern is with the theorist who allows God has beliefs. Further, since much of the current discussion focuses on *middle knowledge*, and because middle beliefs are so closely related to the former, what we say about the former will give us some indication as to the direction the theist might take with the latter.

Since God satisfies the truth condition for knowledge, he cannot be said to know a CF, if it is either false, or does not have a truth value. Accounts of CF's range all the way from a Russellian-type analysis, which says that all such conditionals are true, (since the antecedent is contrary to fact, and so false, which makes the material conditional trivially true, since the only case when a material conditional is false, is when the antecedent is true and the consequent false), to the Adamsian analysis which says that all CF's are false, with the analysis which says that those CF's are true which are true in the 'closest possible world' falling somewhere in between. Linda Zagzebski judges that defenders of middle knowledge are right in their contention that at least certain CF's are true, such as for example, '(23) If Adams were to ask me to go climbing at Tahquiz Rock the next time I come to California, I would gladly (and freely) accept.'[56] She goes on to point out, rightly so, that even if one were to grant that certain select CF's are true, this is not sufficient to establish the theory of middle knowledge or to lend it plausibility.[57]

Questions about CF's inevitably lead to questions about the ontological status of possible worlds, at least for those who hold that the condition of a CF's being true is that it correspond to the closest possible world. As to possible worlds ontology, the menu ranges far and wide, running from Lewis' 'extreme' realism which says that 'nonactual possibles and worlds exist, in exactly the same sense as that in which our world and its denizens exist,'[58] to the denial of possible worlds ontology altogether.

If we simplify the semantics, and so avoid some of the rather sophisticated garb that often clothes the issues, perhaps we can sketch in rather broad strokes a tableau of how the theist might take the matter. Attention is directed to a few key terms that are notoriously troublesome and rather typically get skimpy analysis. Consider 'real' and 'exist.' Both have a rather straightforward sense when we speak about the actual world – the world that is present, which is 'blooming and buzzing.' A mother might say, *That tree is tall*, pointing as she speaks to a tree in the back yard. It is the sort of thing that children play under, or climb, or where birds can nest. If, on the other hand, a woman were to write a story about children playing under a tree, one could easily distinguish the tree in the story, which is fictive, from the tree in the back yard, which is real – part of the actual world. 'Real' as used in the non-fictive context resists analysis in some ways perhaps, since the term conveys a basic idea in terms of which more complex categories are often understood. By contrast, when speaking about 'nonactual possibles' and 'possible worlds,' the terms in question undergo a modal shift as to meaning, from real in the straightforward sense to real in the possibility mode. We may speak of a 'real' nonactual possible, but the entity in question is not real in the sense that it is actual – it is a nonactual entity that is possible. When speaking of the former, we mean 'real as actual,' such that if the entity in question were material, we might think of being able to lift it, or trip over it, or some such thing. This is real in the sense of 'real$_1$.' 'Real' in the possibility mode, is real in the sense that, were it to be actual, we *might* be able to lift it or trip over it. Real in this sense is 'real$_2$.' A similar sort of analysis can be given for 'exist.'[59]

Correspondingly, contingent propositions may be said to be true, just in case their truth-conditions are satisfied by some state of affairs in the real$_1$ world.[60] On at least one interpretation of CF's, they (CF's) may be said to be true relative to some possible world. In the former sense of 'true,' we have in mind 'simply true,' or, 'satisfied by an actual state of affairs,' or 'true$_1$,' whereas in the latter sense of 'true,' we have in mind, 'true in some possible but nonactual world,' or, 'satisfied by some possible state of affairs,' or 'true$_2$.' A basic notion is shared, viz. 'satisfied by a state of affairs.' What is different is the former has a referent that is actual, while the other has one that is only possible. What does all this have to do with CF's?

A CF may be said to be true$_2$ relative to some possible world, and God may be said to know the CF in question, but this does not qualify as middle knowledge, since the latter is knowledge as to which CF becomes actualized, or is true$_1$. The question is, Does God have knowledge as to which CF's are going to be actualized?

It is precisely here that the libertarian notion of free will poses a difficulty for the middle knowledge theorist. On Plantinga's account of free will, how is the theist going to give account of how it is that God has such knowledge, or, what grounds does he (God) have for making such claims? *Inter alia*, the choices about which the knowledge claims might be made do not follow as a matter of necessity or even probably from antecedent causes and conditions. A Plantingian could argue that there is no explanation except the one that goes, Agent M freely chose to actualize CF$_1$. On this view, the model of explanation is, the will is the first cause in a series of causes, and there is no explanation for the first cause in the sense that one can identify antecedent causes and conditions that necessitated it (the first cause). However, this does not give God much to go on as to grounds for belief or knowledge.[61] What other way could the theist go to make sense out of his claim that God knows CF's? Some are attracted to a Boethian strategy, which affirms that God enjoys a timeless eternity. Then God can know which CF is actualized freely at some future time because for God, the past, present and future are somehow *present* to him. However, several weighty objections have been raised against this view, among which involves the criticism that a timeless being could not be a person.[62] Still others argue that God is able to explain how he knows that certain CF's are true in advance of their being actualized, but present models of explanation fail to give us a clue as to how his model works. None of the above appear to be satisfactory, and that leaves us with the option that denies that God has middle knowledge, and that has the corollary that he does not have middle beliefs either.

If one holds that God does not have middle knowledge (and so not middle beliefs about CF's), then can God know what sort of world he is getting when he creates one populated with free moral agents answering Plantinga's description? How one answers the question turns in part upon how often, and how much freedom God actually confers. Historically, even those who have contended that persons are contracausally free, have maintained that persons ordinarily act out of character. That is, regarding most of their choices and actions, persons are determined – they make choices as a result of antecedent causes and conditions. God has a significant role here, but so do humans, and perhaps other created agents. As for when persons are free in the libertarian sense, perhaps only God knows. Some of these concerns are discussed further in connection with Plantinga's free will defence in Chapter 5.

Near the beginning of our discussion of God's beliefs regarding future events, divine infallibility regarding calculations and projections was mentioned. Further comment is in order regarding his knowledge and beliefs relative to 'predictable truths,' since there might be a question as to just how sure God can be about predictables, given the freedom allowed. Can God be mistaken after all on such matters? For Lucas, God may be genuinely mistaken; it is not a mere 'hypothetical possibility.' So on his view, God may have mistaken 'forebeliefs' about future free choices of created agents. How might the theist avoid this sort of conclusion? The theist could argue that since God causes persons to be free, he also has control over *when* persons are free, i.e. he causes a person to be free at a time. The created agent is still free, but free in the sense only that there is an openness as to the direction the will takes, not as to when it (the will) is free. At all other times (other than those times when

God causes a person to be free), a person's choices are predictable. About such predictables, or 'would-probably conditionals,' God has a probable knowledge. Such conditionals are 'grounded in the subject's propensity to act in a certain way, in the light of his character and circumstances.'[63] Since God causes *when* the agent is free, he knows when the agent will not be predictable. Hence his projections with regard to would-probably conditionals are always accompanied by the appropriate degree of doxastic assurance.

Perhaps a few distinctions could be introduced for further clarification. God's *natural knowledge*, as it has been called, includes knowledge of what is necessary and possible, whereas his *free knowledge* is of 'what is actual.'[64] Between the two, according to the Molinist, is middle knowledge, or knowledge about CF's. Where foreknowledge fits into the picture, turns in part on one's position on middle knowledge, and what is read into actual knowledge. Some things that God foreknows he is certain about, whereas he is less than certain about some things. The former is certain foreknowledge, the latter probable foreknowledge. Correspondingly, there are certain forebeliefs and probable forebeliefs. Suppose, for example, that we say that God held to such-and-such forebelief, say F_1 (we are not talking about middle beliefs about CF's). Presumably, he held F_1, which is a belief about an agent's choice that *can* be explained in terms of antecedent causes and conditions, up to the time when the choice is made by the agent in question, say agent A_1. For any time prior to the choice of A_1, God held F_1. Take any moment in eternity past, prior to A_1's choosing, say t_a. Suppose further, that F_1 is the belief that Adam will choose to plant a garden at some future time, say t_1, and that F_2 is the belief that Adam will choose not to plant a garden at t_1. Regarding such beliefs, God holds or rejects them to the degree that the evidence warrants. Suppose that the probability attaching to F_1 (epistemic probability) is .88. Suppose further that God believed F_1 at t_a, where t_a is a time prior to t_1 (it could be any time prior to t_1), and that God held F_1 with the appropriate degree of doxastic assurance (given the background evidence). Suppose further, that A_1 actualizes F_2 at t_1, instead of F_1. God no longer believes F_1 but F_2 at and after t_1, hence there is a shift in the divine mind from F_1 to F_2. However, this shift need not be taken as indicating that God was mistaken at t_a. That is because different epistemic concepts are paired. At t_a, we have 'correct' versus 'incorrect,' or 'probably true' and 'probably false,' and at t_1, we have 'true' versus 'false.' Given the evidence *prior to*

t_1, it was *correct* to believe F_1, and incorrect to believe F_2, *ceterus paribus*. On this view, at an earlier time, God may be said to have a correct belief, which later becomes a truth about which he cannot be mistaken – it becomes part of his 'free knowledge.' Of the former, he was not mistaken at t_a, since he only held it to be probably true, and given the evidence, it *was* probably true, and so he was *correct* in holding the belief in question.

What about free choices and divine belief and knowledge? Perhaps the theist can allow that God has beliefs as well as knowledge about CF's relative to possible worlds only, that is, God knows CF's are true$_2$ but not true$_1$, which is to deny that he has middle knowledge. It does not appear to me that (23) counts as an example of a true CF, since Plantinga judges it true on certain grounds – grounds relating to his character or what is predictable.

If the theist were to opt for a divine fallibility thesis such as the one entertained by Lucas, she might not have to give up the notion of divine perfection altogether. At least Lucas thinks that there is a sense in which God can still be thought to be perfect. He says, 'God cannot, so long as He has created us free and autonomous agents, infallibly know what we are going to do until we have done it.'[65] But this is a departure from the view proffered by traditional theists.

While I tend to side with Hasker and Adams in rejecting middle knowledge, I do not think that this leads to the conclusion that God is to be thought of as the 'bookie than which none greater can be conceived.'[66] The gift of human freedom *is*, because it must be, consonant with divine sovereignty instantiated in the divine nature and divine ends. A free will thesis of some sort is necessary, or God becomes the '"manipulator than which none greater can be conceived."'[67] I have tried here to strike a course that does not deny divine sovereignty, but also does not sacrifice the freedom of created moral agents. Middle knowledge is not required for God to be sovereign, but if divine middle knowledge is denied, then some sort of limit has to be set with regard to the frequency and perhaps measure of creaturely free agency, or God might turn out to be that bookie who takes infinitely costly risks.

In the above we have argued that an omniscient being could not hold false beliefs or believe falsely. Infallibility of belief is reflected in our second definition.

Omniscient$_2$ For any individual x, x is omniscient$_2$ IFF, (1) for every proposition p, if either p is true or it is

possible for x to know p, then x knows p; (2) x
does not falsely believe any p that x knows.

What of the justification condition? Does God have to satisfy the
'having-of-reasons-for-believing-p' condition in order to be properly
said to know? Theists appear divided. Pike's definition omits it. If
one assumes that God cannot be mistaken in the beliefs that he
has, then the theist could take this as satisfying the third condition
for propositional knowledge, and so satisfaction of the infallibility
qualifier in omniscient$_2$ would be tantamount to satisfaction of the
third condition, and so omniscient$_2$ can stay as it is.

With some understanding of how the non-prefixed concept,
knowledge might apply to God, I turn now to the first main
problem the theist must face in defining *omniscience*, viz. whether
or not *omniscience* can be coherently defined. Two general sorts of
counterexamples have been cited, the first of which were viewed as
presenting a potential hazard for the theist who maintains that God
is both omniscient and absolutely immutable. As for the second,
one sub-class of counterexamples were considered, viz. first-person
knowledge claims about self-consciousness. The latter were initially
construed as not within the province of what God might be properly
said to know.

Of the two sorts of counterexamples mentioned above, the first
is more nettlesome than our initial account might be thought to
suggest, and so requires a closer look. We observed earlier that
proposition P, 'It is 4 P.M., March 1, 1990 in Boston.' is true only
when in Boston it is 4 P.M., March 1, 1990. However, in reporting
the time, a Bostonian would likely say, 'It is 4 P.M.,' or, 'It is now
4 P.M.' The 'now' in the latter locution is merely a redundancy, so
our attention will be directed to the former, and I will refer to it as
proposition Q. Obviously Q is more ambiguous than P because of
the reduction in indexical specification. Whereas P is true only at t_1,
Q is true in Boston each day of the year at 4 P.M., and in every other
time zone when it is 4 P.M. each and every day of the year. Some
have argued that Q expresses an eternal proposition, or different
propositions when expressed at different times. Yet another perhaps
more satisfactory construal takes Q as expressing one and the same
proposition at different times, only the truth value changes from
time to time. If this reading is taken, then there is no *one* time at
which Q is true, since it must be true at least seven times a week
within a single time zone.

The picture of Q's indexicality is more complex yet. Suppose a conference call takes place involving people in Boston, Chicago, Denver, and San Diego, all of whom say (more or less simultaneously) 'It is 4 P.M.'[68] It does not seem possible that more than one of them could be speaking the truth. That is because Q is also understood as being geographically indexed. We can make the geographic indexicality of Q explicit by inserting 'here.' So if we say that Q is true only at certain times, then we should also say that Q is true only at certain places.

Given the above analysis of temporal and geographic indexicality relative to Q, it would seem that to know what time it is requires that the knower have geographic location. Hence God could know what time it is only if he has geographic indexicality. But I can know what time it is in Boston without being there. All that is necessary is that I do the addition or subtraction required by the time zone difference, if there is such a difference. If an ordinary knower can know what time it is in Boston without being there, surely God also knows without being there. But as Mavrodes observes, *Knowing what time it is in Boston is not the same thing as knowing what time it is*. I can know what time it is in Boston without knowing what time it is, because I may not know where I am relative to Boston, or know the time here (where I am) is correlated with the time in Boston. I may even know what time it is in every time zone in the world, and still not know what time it is, because I may not know where I am. So, if God is to know what time it is, it cannot consist in his knowing such things as, 'It is 4 P.M. in Boston.'

Some theists have argued that God has no geographical location. If in order to know what time it is, the knower must satisfy a geographic indexical requirement, at least in the sense that the knower must know in a relevant way where he is, then it appears that God would not know what time it is. Though he might know that someone in Boston had said Q, that it was exactly 4 P.M. in Boston when the person uttered Q, and that the person had asserted a truth, still he would not know what truth the person had asserted, on the account that says he has no location, and given the above analysis of the indexical requirements for knowing what time it is.

Others have argued that God is everywhere present simultaneously. If so, then when it is 4 P.M. in Boston, God may know Q. But curiously, since he is also present in Chicago, Denver, and San Diego, among other places, he will also simultaneously know 'It is 3 P.M.,' 'It is 2 P.M.,' and 'It is 1 P.M.' How might the theist avoid such paradoxical results? Perhaps there needs to be some rethinking of the way(s) in which we employ such indexical expressions, and the knowledge they represent. More about this shortly, but for the moment I should like to turn our attention to a general proposal for handling such expressions.

Both sorts of counterexamples discussed contain indexical or quasi-indexical expressions such as 'I,' 'you,' 'now,' 'today,' etc. The terms serve to pick out a person or time relative to the speaker. Thus, as we have seen in the second sort of counterexample, a first-person knowledge claim can be known in a first-person way only by the individual satisfying the indexical requirement of the knowledge claim in question. God may know that some person had made such a first-person claim, and that the person had asserted a truth, but he would not know what truth the person had asserted, since he could not (logically could not) satisfy the indexical requirement of the knowledge claim. The proposal is, if appeal is made to a principle offered by Hector-Neri Castenada, both sorts of difficulties (presented by the two sorts of counterexamples) can be resolved. The principle is as follows (I shall refer to it as I):

I   If a sentence of the form 'X knows that a person Y knows that . . . ' formulates a true statement, the person X knows the statement formulated by the clause filling the blank ' . . . '[69]

The way out of the difficulty regarding indexical requirements and knowledge claims, is to offer additional indexical expressions in order to clarify and make explicit the proper subject and object references. If, for example, person A knows on March 1, 1990 the proposition *It is now March 1, 1990*, it seems possible to also affirm that another person, say B, can know at another time, say March 2, 1990, that A knew *It is now March 1, 1990* on March 1, 1990. All that we need do is add indexical references so as to eliminate ambiguity as to the subjects and objects in question. Hence according to (I), B can know on March 2, 1990, that a day earlier, A knew that it was March 1, 1990 on March 1, 1990.[70]

As to indexical references which pick out a particular subject, a similar move is suggested. If Reagan knows that he is in the hospital, for example, surely another, say Regan, can know that Reagan knows that he (Reagan) is in the hospital. The fleshing out is similar to the program followed for tensed propositions.

However, the proposal does not work. The addition of temporal indexical references to tensed propositions for example, might allow the agent to know a tensed truth at another time, but the added indexical reference is an alteration of the original proposition, and so it is really a different proposition that is known. There is a change then in respect to the object known.

Similarly, when adding indexes relative to first-person knowledge claims, this move involves a change with regard to the agent, and so here too we have a difference as to the propositions which are claimed to be known. The counterexamples with regard to first-person reports of self-consciousness, are not adequately taken care of by appealing to (I). The actual bits of self-conscious knowledge had by other knowers is not part of the divine epistemic repertoire, nor indeed could they ever be, unless one were to maintain somehow that God's consciousness is not distinguishable from human consciousnesses, say in some panpsychistic way.

The theist need not get bent out of shape when faced with such difficulties. For starters, he can take R. K. W. Paterson's advice, and 'scale-down' his view of God's immutability.[71] The loss is a vestige perhaps of neo-Platonic immutability that is perhaps better abandoned for this and other concerns.[72] He can allow then that God might not know certain propositions at certain times. That's because they cannot (logically cannot) be known, when they are not true.

What about temporal and spatial indexing, and knowers? Perhaps the theist might allow that such indexical expressions might apply in different ways, or maybe not at all, when taking God into account. The theist's account of God's omnipresence is pivotal here. If the theist holds that God is straightforwardly everywhere present, then we have the paradoxical results that since God is simultaneously in Boston, Chicago, Denver, and San Diego, when if it is 4 P.M. in Boston, it is simultaneously 3 P.M., 2 P.M., and 1 P.M. for God, since he is simultaneously in each of the cities. Notice, however, that for each time registered in the divine consciousness, there is a correspondingly different geographic index. This might help to explain an otherwise curious knowledge claim. Whether these suggestions are helpful or not, there is another pressing concern. On such a view, God might be thought to not know the time, since he has no particular or single geographic reference, since all geographic indexes are properly his on the view in question. That is, there is no single 'reference point' in terms of which he views the disparate markings of time. Here it could be argued that God could either create some special location (say his throne in heaven, assuming heaven is a place),[73] or he could arbitrarily select some point in space to serve as a 'reference point' in terms of which he might view all places and be able to answer the question, What time is it?

An alternative to the above is to argue that God has no location in space or in time – that he is atemporally eternal regarding the latter. Whatever advantages such a view might be thought to have, this move seems to only exacerbate some of the difficulties raised with the other views discussed.

Alternatively, the theist could argue that God is in time and that he can be properly spoken of as being omnipresent but in a less-than-straightforward sense. That is, God is omnipresent in the sense only that he causally effects things in space, creates things in space, and knows things in space.[74] Statements like, 'God is here,' or, 'God is present,' can be taken to mean, 'God knows what is going on at location x,' or, 'God can act at location x.' As to our immediate concern, God could know that someone in Boston just said, 'It is 4 P.M.,' and that it was exactly 4 P.M. in Boston when the person in question said it, and further, know the truth of what was asserted, because God satisfies in his unique way the spatial indexical requirement, since he is 'there.' As to whether he might know what time it is, the theist could adopt the earlier proposal tendered in connection with the view that God exists in time and space. That is, conceivably there is some special spatial reference point on earth or in the heavens, in terms of which he views all other reference points, or he could select one. Or perhaps it is not too far off the mark to say that for God there is no marking of time by zones. In this regard, the theist might say he knows 'what time it is' in terms of his *present*, which like ours is flanked by the past and future. His *present* or *now*, on at least a temporal view of eternity, is conceivably at least roughly simultaneous with the *now* of created beings in different time zones and perhaps in different universes. Since we, unlike God are at least in this life bound by space, we mark time according to a certain time zone, and our knowledge claims reflect this in claims that are temporally indexed. What is now for us, is also now for God, though the latter may lack straightforward geographic indexicality. However, this lack need not stand in the way of his either knowing what time it is in terms of his now, or what time it is for any one of his creatures anywhere in creation. We may conclude then that there does not seem to be insurmountable difficulties standing in the way of claiming that God might satisfy certain indexical conditions in his own special way. Hence he might be said to know both the truth of what is asserted when a person in Boston says, 'It is 4 P.M., March 1, 1990' and to be able to answer the question, 'What time is it?' With regard to the former, he knows the proposition in question, *only* when it is true that 'It is 4 P.M., March 1, 1990.'

In view of our above discussion, the theist will have to admit both that God does not know certain propositions at certain times, if the propositions in question are temporally indexed, and further that he might not know certain bits of knowledge which belong only to individuals who have them in a first-person way. But in neither case, need the theist think that God's omniscience is thereby detracted or diminished. That God cannot know first-person knowledge claims or temporally indexed propositions at certain times, are claims that, like knowing a contradiction, lie outside the realm of logical possibility. We are now ready to offer a definition of *omniscience* which handles both sorts of counterexamples. If we let x range over individuals, i range over possible indexical expressions, and p range over propositions, our new definition may be formulated as follows.

Omniscient$_3$ For any individual x, x is omniscient$_3$ IFF, (1) for every proposition p, if either p is true or it is possible for x to know p, then x knows p; (2) x does not falsely believe any p that x knows; (3) the indexical requirements i in p that can be satisfied by x in knowing p, are satisfied.

It has been argued that theological determinists have as their 'chief theological argument' for determinism the argument from divine omniscience.[75] If God's knowledge includes in detail everything that will come to pass, then it follows that everything that God foreknows must happen.[76] Hence all of history, in all of its complexity and detail, flows inexorably. Detractors of theism argue that such knowledge destroys the possibility of human freedom. Theists are divided on the matter; some hold that persons are not free, while others hold that determinism is compatible with freedom.[77] Still others hold that divine foreknowledge and human freedom are perfectly compatible. As a staunch representative of the first position, Luther asseverates, 'God foreknows nothing contingently, but that He foresees, purposes, and does all things according to His own immutable, eternal and infallible plan. This bombshell knocks 'free will' flat, and utterly shatters it.'[78] For Luther, if the expression is appropriate at all, it applies only to God. As a reply to Luther, Mavrodes says that the theist could argue that God knows all things, including those things which will be done by human free will, *but he knows many of those things contingently*. In particular, he knows contingently those things which depend on human free will. It may, indeed, be a necessary truth that he knows every truth, and that he knows everything I will do. But for a particular truth, p, about what I will do, the fact that God knows p, rather than knowing not-p, is contingent, because it is contingent that it is p rather than not-p which is true. And because of this, it seems to him, that the Lutheran bombshell is a logical-misfire which leaves free will undamaged.

By contrast, Augustine and Calvin held to a compatibilism, that God's predestination and foreknowledge are compatible with human agents being in some sense free.[79] In *The City of God*, Augustine says that 'As Christians and philosophers, we profess both – foreknowledge, as a part of our faith; free choice, as a condition of responsible living.'[80] Calvin takes a similar line.[81] There is difference of opinion as to how one might show how God's knowledge is compatible with, or does not interfere with human freedom. According to Augustine, God in his omnipotence is the Cause 'of all causes,'[82] and he foreknows all that comes to pass. But neither this causing nor the knowing interfere with the freedom of human choices because neither enter into the causal path of the agent when the agent chooses freely. 'Our choices . . . are our own.'[83]

There is another worry with omniscience. According to many theists, God's omniscience includes middle knowledge, i.e., he knows all counterfactual conditionals, in particular, counterfactual conditionals of freedom. If one maintains a contra-causal freedom in the sense that Plantinga does, then persons, at times, are supposed to experience a freedom of choice such that their choices are free from causal laws and antecedent conditions.[84] Against such a position George Botterill's claim that Plantinga's possible-world metaphysic cannot give account of God's foreknowledge because Plantinga cannot explain how it is that God can know counterfactual conditionals might be cogent.[85] The theist might argue that he does not know how it is that God knows such conditionals, he (God) just does, or he might opt for a backward causality thesis, and argue that humans are free in their choices, and such choices have a backward effect with regard to God's foreknowledge, neither of which appear to be satisfactory responses.

Perhaps a more promising way of handling the difficulty confronting middle knowledge is to opt for some sort of 'attenuated omniscience' notion, defended by William Paley, 'well argued' for by J. R. Lucas in *The Freedom of the Will*, and endorsed as the most plausible view by Swinburne. Not only is the notion plausible and congenial to human free agency, it appears to be quite compatible with the Biblical account of God's knowledge.[86] Simply stated, it is the view that in order to preserve the freedom of agents he created, and in order to preserve his own freedom, God has limits as to his knowledge of the future.[87] One might look at it this way. Suppose the theist were to draw a distinction between actual and potential omniscience, (we will refer to the former as omniscient$_a$, and the latter as omniscient$_b$) such that a being that is omniscient$_a$ might satisfy all of the conditions say of omniscient$_2$ at some time, say t. In the actual mode, the being in question has before his consciousness all those propositions the range or domain of which is specified in omniscient$_3$, excepting the set of counterfactuals of freedom which are not true in the actual world unless and until they are actualized by human free choice. Respecting this set, God is only potentially omniscient, that is, potentially omniscient in the sense that he can and does know all such conditionals but only when their truth conditions are met. But when the truth conditions are met, they are no longer counterfactuals.

Drawing a distinction between actual and possible omniscience is one way of taking attenuated omniscience. A definition of omniscience which reflects this direction can be formulated in the following way. Let x range over possible individuals, i range over possible indexical expressions, and p range over propositions. Our final definition of omniscience is:

Omniscient$_4$ For any individual x, x is omniscient$_4$ IFF, (1) for every proposition p, if either p is true or it is possible for x to know p, then x knows p; (2) x does not falsely believe any p that x knows; (3) the indexical requirements i in p that can be satisfied by x in knowing p, are satisfied; (4) x knows counterfactual conditionals of freedom p only when p's truth conditions are met.

No doubt there are yet rough edges and a few loose ends. Our purpose here is mainly to suggest and discuss several important understandings of omniscience. I should like to touch on two further concerns relative to an attenuated omniscience thesis.

First, if we suppose God exists and that he is omniscient$_4$, could he be mistaken? He need not be, since the attenuated omniscience thesis does not imply fallibility with regard to what is known, but allows that a limit has been set with regard to the propositions known. It is a limit that is self-imposed, in order that some measure of freedom for those agents he has created in his image might be preserved. Regarding propositions that relate to human free choice, i.e., propositions which describe the outcomes of human free choice, one might have to allow at best a probability even for God. But he need never be mistaken with regard to them, at least in respect to what he claims for them, and the measure of certainty that he attaches to them, since he knows our motives and *all* the other causes that enter into the causal picture. But does this not imply that God can *not* know which possible world will become actual? Perhaps in a limited sort of way. The theist can still maintain a measure of theological determinism. That is, he can affirm that God predetermines the main course of history, and he continues to be active as an agent in the world through providence. And so God can be said to exercise some measure of control as to what possibilities will become actual. But the theist can also affirm that created agents, in respect to their choices, have effects on outcomes. The main lines and course of history are directed by God, and the fleshing out of various details and particulars are directed and actualized by the choices of created agents to the extent that God wants to preserve and uphold creaturely freedom.

Does this sort of proposal not have the corollary that there will be evils resulting from creaturely free agency which God might not foreknow, and so there might be evils for which God would have no justification, at least in advance of their happening? One *general* justification pattern that might be appealed to here is the free will defence. Evils of this sort, one could argue, come about as a result of misused free agency, the latter of which is a value that God in creation and providence wishes to preserve and sustain. Many more questions arise that cannot be given a hearing in this context, because of constraints the focus of this study quite naturally impose.

In conclusion, the conditions specified in omniscient$_3$ handle both sorts of counterexamples viewed as posing a threat to a coherent account of God's omniscience. If it can be established that divine omniscience understood as including complete and detailed knowledge of the future and counterfactuals of freedom interferes with human free agency (a thesis I have only suggested), then the theist has recourse to an attenuated omniscience thesis, as specified in omniscient$_4$, or something like it. The shift is not only congenial to free agency, but it appears quite compatible with the Biblical account of divine knowledge.

3. OMNIBENEVOLENCE

Historically, theists have held that God is also omnibenevolent, or as some say, perfectly good. A question of particular interest here is, Can valuation terms like *good* and *benevolent* be applied to God in a way similar to the way these terms apply to humans? Certain 'negative' theologians representing both Western and Eastern philosophical traditions hold the view that propositions which take the form 'God is ϕ' (where ϕ stands for any positive property) are unknowable.[88] Dionysius the Areopagite, for example, opines that for any property P, P must be both denied and affirmed of God. On one reading, we have a straightforward contradiction, but we do not if P is literally false of God, but analogically true of him. Most 'negative theologians' combine the way of negation with some account or other of symbolic or analogical attribution. Swinburne and Yandell are of the opinion that the view in question prevents such predicates as *good* in *God is good* from being meaningfully ascribed to God. On such a view, God is neither good nor evil, neither just nor unjust.[89]

Swinburne and Yandell think that a positive approach is possible and superior. Swinburne thinks that when the theist affirms *God is good* that the term *good* is used in a straightforward ordinary sense. If there is anything extraordinary, it has to do with the infinite measure with which the term applies to God *vis-à-vis* humans. A model the theist can appeal to in order to give sense to divine omnibenevolence is that of a good earthly father. The theist can reason that a good father will refrain from lying to his children so far as he is able. By analogy, God (being good) will never lie since his omnipotence means he has the power to refrain from doing so.[90] Further, just as a good father will not allow his children to suffer any more than he has to, God, because he is omnibenevolent will not permit his children to suffer if he can prevent it, and since he is omnipotent he always can.[91] Here, the theist should not overlook what some would argue is a marked difference between omnipotence when applied to truth telling and omnipotence when applied to the elimination of suffering. Some theists, for example, would contend not only that God would not lie because he is omnipotent and omnibenevolent, but that he also could not lie because he is essentially truthful. At the same time they hold that for some justifying reason he could allow suffering, even though he is omnipotent and omnibenevolent. In any case, there are quantitative *and* qualitative differences as to predicate ascription between the creature and the Creator, the former has to do with *good simpliciter*, the latter with *all-good* or *perfectly good*. On the quantitative difference side, whatever makes the good earthly father good, God has without limit in respect to his power and knowledge.[92] As to the qualitative difference, only God can be appropriately described as 'all-good.' The picture is brief enough, but it provides some indication as to the direction a theist might go with value terms as they apply to God and creatures. The meaning a value term has when it applies to a human being must be univocal, in some respect, with the meaning it has when it applies to God, if the term in question is to be meaningfully ascribed to God.[93]

Swinburne takes the discussion a step further and allows that in addition to the ordinary sense some terms might have in describing God, there are other terms, which if they are taken in their ordinary sense, will generate incoherent descriptions.[94] This leads Swinburne to allow that such terms as 'person,' and 'knows,' when used to talk about God, must be taken analogically.

The analogical route has tended to work with either or both of two important rules that relate to analogy as it is used in so-called 'religious discourse': the analogy of attribution and the analogy of proportionality. The former is a rule for analogy that gives account of certain important 'functions' that relate to language used to talk about God, in particular, to describe him. According to this rule, God does not possess a property 'formally' but only by attribution.[95] According to James Ross, he (God) has it 'on account of His causal or conserving relationship to our experiencing certain effects.'[96] The more important of the two rules, however, is the rule of analogy of proportionality. Here, as Ross says, 'it is assumed by the conditions for this sort of analogy that there are similarities between God's relationships to His actual and possible operations and man's (or some other creature's) relationship to his actual or possible operation.'[97] The term *good*, for example, 'is employed in speaking of God just because we recognize the similarity of His relationship to the relationship we call "being good" with respect to the creature.'[98] Ross' description of the analogy of proportionality rule, and his account of 'being good' lines up with what we have been saying about God's being good and an earthly father's being good. What we have sketched is a cognitivist rather than a noncognitivist thesis regarding religious discourse. Here I should note that at work in the material mode of speech – that mode which gives us information about real properties (in this context, properties possessed by God) – is Thomas Aquinas' principle of *analogia entis* (analogy of being), an interpretation of which Ross attempts to defend, and which has been sharply attacked by neo-orthodox and reformed theologians.[99] Theologians representing both traditions claim that the *analogia entis* idea fails to reckon with the depraved condition of postlapsarian humanity and the ontological chasm that exists between the finite creature and the infinite God. They believe that it is impossible for a finite characteristic to be identical in sense with an infinite one.[100] Some think that the way out of the putative difficulty is to work with a formal view of the analogy of proportionality, where, according to Frederick Ferré, analogy offers the rule:

> A word may be borrowed from ordinary speech for use in theological discourse only if it is constantly borne in mind that the word can apply to 'God' exclusively in the manner (unimaginable to us) permitted by the fundamental axioms and entailment-rules governing the entire system of theistic talk about God.[101]

Whatever the merits of the formal mode of the analogy of proportion, I see no need for confinement to it, since it is not clear that the finite-infinite distinction drawn between the Creator and the creature generates the difficulties with regard to predicate ascription that the theologians in question imagine.

Before we leave the concept of omnibenevolence, another ingredient some have included in it should be touched upon. Omnibenevolence means among other things that 'God wills that each man attain his greatest good.'[102] Put another way, if God caused or allowed an event which hindered a man from attaining his greatest good (i.e., man's greatest good), and if this hindrance was not in some way a just punishment from God, then God would not be omnibenevolent.[103] Or the point can be expressed in still another way: if God could have caused or allowed events which would have helped a person toward attaining his (the person's) highest good and God failed to do so, and if withholding this help was not a consequence of some evil act on the person's part, then God is not omnibenevolent. We can safely assume that for Yandell, humanity's greatest good is salvation (which includes everlasting life). On Yandell's reading of omnibenevolence, it seems that for many (if not most) humans God could have caused the world to be more conducive to man's achieving the greatest good. He could have performed more miracles, revealed himself more frequently and clearly, etc.

Peter Abelard might have tried to answer the above difficulty by saying that God cannot act differently from the way he in fact does.[104] But Yandell wants to deny this of God, and it is not clear just how he could or would want to go about handling the difficulty. Perhaps he could say were God to do more than he in fact does, that doing more might impinge on the sort of freedom that God wants to preserve for created agents. So much for the content of God's omnibenevolence, at least for present purposes.

In this chapter we have examined in some detail predicates central to the Christian theistic conception of God and pivotal to atheological formulations of the inconsistency and probabilistic strategies. Omnipotent$_7$ might be the definition the theist is looking for, but if he wants to work with anything like Plantinga's modal free will defence, then omnipotent$_8$ reflects Plantinga's contention that even though God might be omnipotent, he cannot strongly or weakly actualize just any possible world. Further minor adjustments might be needed if the theist holds that God can impose limits on his omnipotence in order to make room for human and non-human creaturely freedom.

A final definition of omniscience was offered, omniscient$_3$, which takes into account indexed propositions. If the theist thinks that God can limit his knowledge, then omniscient$_4$ might be attractive. In respect to both attributes, the theist might have to consider a scale-down if such a move is necessary to certain values God might wish to preserve, such as, for example, freedom of choice.

God is perfectly good or *omnibenevolent* involves predicates that have either a qualifier or a prefix. The prefixed or qualified form is taken analogically in order to avoid confusions that might otherwise come about if an ordinary sense is given such terms when ascribed to God. But non-prefixed and unqualified predicates might be understood in a rather standard ordinary-language use.

These understandings of the divine predicates in question, are not viewed as logically incompatible, so they can belong to one and the same being. In fact, it can be argued that if God is going to be omnipotent in any significant way, he must also be omniscient. In order to be able to bring about members of sets of logically possible states of affairs, a being must first know the set of logically possible states of affairs. In order to be omnibenevolent, a being must have a knowledge of all the ways in which he can be benevolent, and all the needs and desires of agents in behalf of which he might be benevolent, etc. We will assume that there is a coherent sense that can be given to each and that the attributes are logically compossible. Whatever problems remain are judged to be minor, needing only minor revisions at most. Having sketched a conceptual picture of the God of Christian theism, we turn next to the greater-good defence itself.

3

The Greater-Good Defence

Most if not all theistic attempts to resolve the problem of evil make use in some way of the greater-good defence (hereafter the GGD₁).[1] Few if any philosophers have given more concentrated attention to this defence than Keith Yandell.[2] In simple terms the defence runs as follows.

GGD₁   For every evil that God permits, there is a good state of affairs (or good states of affairs) which counterbalances and which logically could not exist without the evil in question (or some other evil of at least equal negative value), and some evil is overbalanced by a good state of affairs (or good states of affairs) which logically require the evil in question (or some other evil of at least equal negative value).[3]

It has been argued that the GGD follows from basic Christian tenets. The tenets are:

(1)   God exists.
(2)   God is omnipotent, omniscient, and perfectly good.
(3)   God created the world.
(4)   There is evil in the world.

By way of quick review the above set of beliefs sketch God and the world in the following way. There is a God whose power to actualize states of affairs is limited only in that he cannot make a contradictory statement true, and he cannot do something which would be contradictory for God to do.[4] This God is also all-knowing, i.e., God knows every true statement that is logically possible for God to know. He is also perfectly good. Terms like *good* and *just* apply to him univocally. So when the theist says

'God is good,' the predicate *good* is univocal in some way when it applies to God as when it applies to humans. 'He is perfectly good,' means at least this; he wills that each individual achieve his (the individual's) greatest good compossible with the greatest goods of other human beings. The fourth statement is a tenet of theism and a fact about the world, *there is evil in the world*. Hurricanes, earthquakes, floods, etc., which result in pain and suffering, and moral acts such as rape, murder and torture are examples of the reality of evil.

1. THE GGD AND THE BEST OF ALL POSSIBLE WORLDS

What sort of world would a god, answering to the above description create? One might be tempted to think that the tenet

(2)   God is omnipotent, omniscient, and perfectly good.

implies that if God chooses to create, he will of necessity create or bring about the best of all possible worlds, as Leibniz thought. That is, given that he is omnipotent, surely he can bring about or create just any possible world that he pleases. And since he is perfectly good, if he brings about any world at all, he will bring about the best. The main inference may rest on two mistakes. If Plantinga is correct in his analysis of possible worlds that God can actualize, then God cannot bring about just any possible world that he chooses.[5] Second, there is serious doubt that Leibniz's notion 'best of all possible worlds' is coherent. The first issue is discussed at some length later.[6] As for the second, I should like to turn attention for a moment to a different but relevant thesis defended by Thomas Aquinas, viz., that *for any world God creates, he could create a better one*. This doctrine is proffered in response to the principle defended by Augustine in the *Enchiridion* that '"each thing that God has made is good, and, taken all together they are very good, because in them all consists the wondrous beauty of the universe."'[7] In response Aquinas affirms that in the existing universe, the things that now exist could not be better, 'on account of the most noble order given to these things by God . . . . '[8] More directly to the point he adds: 'Yet God could make *other things*, or add something to those things that are made, and then the universe would be better.'[9] In his customary style, he enlarges upon the idea that *God can do better than he does* under the heading, 'The Omnipotent God.' As a preface to his 'Reply,' he cites a Biblical passage, and then proceeds to enlarge upon the topic under discussion, viz. ways in which God can do better than he does. Apparently, he saw the statement *for any world he creates, he can create a better one* as a corollary to *God is omnipotent* – which he took to be explicit in the canon of Scripture. Thus he regarded the former statement as a necessary truth, following from God's omnipotence.[10]

If Aquinas is right, then God could not, as Leibniz argued, create or bring about the best of all possible worlds (assuming there is no problem with the concept 'best of all possible worlds'), since for any world which might be thought to be the best, God could, as Aquinas argued, create a better one. Let us set aside for the moment Aquinas' contention, and return to Leibniz's view that God can create the best of all possible worlds, and more particularly, to the concept, 'best of all possible worlds.' Two senses of the expression have been distinguished (hereafter I shall refer to them as BPW_1 and BPW_2).[11] A world instantiating BPW_1 would have all *possible* goods. Suppose that we say that world W_1 is such a world, and that W_1 has 10,000 bens of good.[12] We can conceive of another world say W_2, which has 10,001 bens of good, and so we can conceive of a better world than the best of all logically possible worlds; hence world W_1 would not be the world with the greatest number of possible goods. Thus for any world containing n bens of good, one may conceive of another world which exceeds the first by at least one ben. The difficulty contemplated is similar to the one confronting anyone who thinks that he can come up with the greatest conceivable number.[13] Just as we cannot identify the greatest conceivable number, we cannot conceive of the best logically possible world in the sense of BPW_1. This is similar to Aquinas' contention that for any world God creates, he can create a better, only there is a possible worlds twist. There is no 'logical upper limit' on the number of goods a logically *possible* world can have, and so there is no best logically *possible* world.[14]

BPW_2 quantifies over 'compossible goods,' so that the phrase *best of all logically possible worlds means* 'a world containing all compossible goods.' For example, it may be a good that human choices be guaranteed to be right ones, and good that all human choices be made freely, but because the goods in question are not compossible there can be no world which instantiates both.

The strengthened definition, however, is defective in a way similar to BPW_1. That is, even if there are only a finite number of compatible goods, there may be no limit to the number of instances of kinds of compatible goods, and so there may be no upper limit to the number of goods a world can have, and so no best logically possible world. Aquinas' point once again applies.

Perhaps there is a qualified best-of-all-possible worlds notion that falls somewhere in between the 'better-world' idea of Aquinas, and either BPW_1 or BPW_2. As a way of fleshing this out, I should like to draw six points, the first three to help clarify the conceptual landscape and the last three sketch the concept in rough outline. First, the actual world is 'all that is the case,'[15] or is the 'maximal possible state of affairs that is actual.'[16] So, though there may be *many* possible worlds, there can be only *one* actual world.

Second, there might be any number of equally good possible worlds, and further, there might be any number of equally good best-of-all-possible worlds (assuming that the 'best-of-all-possible worlds' notion is not problematic). The first suggestion appears straightforwardly true, but the second might raise an eyebrow. Suppose that 'best-of-all-possible worlds' is in some way or other a coherent notion (say by some limitation or qualification), and suppose that God has a conceptual picture of 'the' best-of-all-possible worlds; there does not seem to be anything standing in the way of there being any number of such possible worlds, say W_1, W_2, W_3, etc.[17] Such worlds would be maximally complete possible states of affairs.[18] Perhaps the worlds are alike in every respect, except that they are conceived as being brought into existence at different times. That is, W_1 is identical to W_2, except W_1 is conceived as being actualizable at t_1 rather than at t_2, and W_2 is conceived as being actualizable at t_2 rather than at t_1.[19] It is assumed that temporal indexing does not affect the goods contained in each of the worlds. Thus there is not just *one* best-of-all-possible worlds. Perhaps the most that can be claimed is that there might be a best-of-all-possible-world kinds.

In Chapter 2 we saw (according to the definition of omnipotent$_3$) that God does not bring about logically necessary states of affairs (Cartesian possibilism excepted). For example, all blue objects are necessarily colored objects. If, as some theists hold, God has his existence necessarily, then he exists along with all other logically necessary states of affairs in all possible worlds. Strictly speaking then, if God exists necessarily, he does not bring about all that is the case in bringing about some possible world. Rather, for any world *W* that God brings about, he brings about only those possible states of affairs in *W* which are not logically necessary.[20]

Fourth, for any time *t* God could create or bring about only one possible world, but he could and so might create or bring about at time *t* many possible universes, say U_1, U_2, U_3, etc., where *universe* whether possible or actual connotes a limited domain – a 'system' of states of affairs, which, if actual, is less than all that is the case, and which if possible, is less than all possible states of affairs in some possible world.[21] All possible universes of some possible world make up all possible states of affairs of that possible world, and all actual universes make up 'all that is the case.' Possible universes can be differentiated in terms of possible properties present in one and maybe absent in another, while some possible universes might enjoy a limited 'transworld identity,' i.e., they might have membership in more than one possible world. Conceivably, some combination of possible universes contained in some possible world, might be *one* of perhaps any number of possible worlds which are instances of the best-of-all-possible world-kinds for expressing some motive God might have in 'world-making.' As to actual universes, one might think of this earth as part of a larger universe, and the theist might argue that this universe serves some divine purpose and design similar (or different) in respect to purpose and design to other universes that might be 'out there.' In this universe, call it U_1, there is a planet where evil exists. It might be that there are other universes (or even planets in this universe) which have at least one planet populated with moral agents who (as Mackie suggests) freely choose to do only the good and where there is no evil. There have been hints of this suggestion in the history of the Church. In the present 'world,' evil is present, moral agents can choose to do good or evil. Many theists hold that there is another realm, an intermediate state, where the spirits of departed believers dwell. And though there is no agreement as to whether such existence allows for moral choices, many have held that moral evil is left behind since such believers are in the presence of Christ. If there are free choices, and moral evil is left behind, then presumably we would have moral agents freely choosing to do only the good. We have thus a picture similar to the one suggested above, where one possible universe populated with creatures who freely choose to do only the good is contrasted with another possible universe populated with creatures who freely choose to do good and evil. Whichever way the possible universes are put together, contemporaneously or in temporal sequence, it is arguable that a possible world containing at least two such contrasting possible universes might be a better whole than a possible world populated with creatures who do only the good. If a 'better whole,' then we might have one example of perhaps any number of possible worlds which are instances in this way of the best-of-all-possible world-kinds.

Fifth, 'best' in 'best-of-all-possible worlds' is ambiguous. Several questions arise. Best in terms of what, and for whom? To be the best, does the possible world in question have to be intrinsically and instrumentally the best, or only intrinsically or only instrumentally the best? Perhaps 'best in every relevant respect and for every relevant agent in terms of which a possible world might be ranked,' is a start toward addressing some of the issues the above questions raise. But there remains a crucial ambiguity about the term itself. What does the term in question mean when we consider a possible world that God might consider actualizing? Suppose we give 'best' the somewhat Pickwickian sense of 'perfect,' that is, perfect as in 'complete,' or 'without omission,' rather than the stronger sense of 'without defect' or 'flawless.'[22] The suggestion provides us with a fairly standard sense of 'perfect,' and one that is compatible with the following. Suppose for any possible world, say W^*, that there are two possible universes contained in W^*, say U^* and U^{**}. Suppose further that God has different and distinct purposes and values corresponding to the possible universes contained in W^*, i.e., that he has purpose P^* and value V^* for U^*, and purpose P^{**} and value V^{**} for U^{**}. Conceivably, U^* might allow for a complete actualization of P^* and V^*. The same may be said, *mutatis mutandis*, for U^{**}. Of course there may be any number of possible universes like U^* and U^{**} in W^*, which allow for the actualization of the values in question without omission or completely. Hence, as with the 'best-of-all-possible worlds' concept, the most that could be hoped for is a best-of-all-possible universe-kinds with regard to (a) certain purpose(s) and (a) certain value(s). The contention is, it is possible, perhaps likely, that in creating a possible world, God might want more than one value (or one set of values) and more than one purpose (or one set of purposes) actualized or actualizable. Drawing a distinction between possible universes and different possible values and purposes for respective possible universes, allows God the option of actualizing states of affairs where redemption, for example, is meaningful, *and* states of affairs in some other universe where redemption is not necessary. And the *whole* of such a possible world that includes different possible universes might make possible a fuller expression of divine values and purposes. Such a whole is arguably at least as good, or might even be better than a world where no evil occurs.

Sixth, (in support of the claim expressed in the above that a possible world containing evil might be at least as good as a world not containing evil), adding an evil to a good state of affairs might on balance make things better, and adding a good to an evil state of affairs might make things worse. In 'God and Evil,' John Wisdom holds as true the first of two principles, viz., that '(i) A perfect and all powerful being would allow only the best logically possible world.'[23] The second principle, '(ii) A world containing evil could not be the best logically possible world,'[24] he rejects. Wisdom examines and appraises two arguments offered for the second principle and rightly rejects both. The first, the 'Subtraction Argument,' is formulated in rough terms thus: 'A world containing evil could always be improved merely by subtracting the evil.'[25] The argument fails because 'every evil may be contained in, and thus logically necessary to, a whole good enough as a whole to balance the evil.'[26] The point is, bringing about a state of affairs where an evil necessary to a certain whole is also brought about may make matters better, for the evil in mind makes logically possible the whole which is good. The second argument, the 'Substitution Argument,' is briefly stated as follows: 'A world containing evil could always be improved by substituting something else [a good] for the evil.'[27] The substitution of a good for an evil may thus remove the possibility of some of the best wholes. Thus adding a good could make matters worse. For example, substitution of an evil (or some evil like it) necessary to soul growth or mature moral character might result in making matters worse, so would elimination of the 'possibility' of evil, if it is viewed as a necessary condition of freedom.

What has been gained from our experiment with the limited best-of-all possible world-kinds and universe-kinds? First, a viable, albeit qualified sense has been given to best-of-all-possible world-kinds and best-of-all-possible universe-kinds. Regarding the former, there might be a best-of-all-possible world-kinds, if that possible world-kind is *best* (perfect, i.e., complete) which includes at least one possible universe populated with at least one free moral agent who is not in any way morally flawed and who never makes an evil choice, and at least one possible universe where evil makes redemption a meaningful divine act. But then don't we have a similar problem to the one facing BPW_1 and BPW_2? That is, there seems to be no logical upper limit to the number of possible universes of both kinds God might instantiate or bring about and so no best-of-all-possible world-kinds. That is, God could always add more universes and so make the world better. One might ease his way out of the difficulty by contending that a possible world is perfect or complete if there is at least one of each, and adding on others does not make a possible world more complete, if the alleged divine reason(s) for creation are actualized. That is, all that we have in the proliferation of such possible universes is more of the same, not something more perfect. Conceivably, the theist could leave this matter open, since he might want to allow that God could bring about any number of such universes. But then he would have to abandon at least this best-of-all-possible-world-kinds notion.

Second, there is of course for the traditional theist at least, a universe which is perfect in the strong sense, comprised of the divine *ménage à trois*, if the members of the Trinity are held to be free and choose only the good.[28] If so, why should it be thought impossible for God to bring about a world with *creatures* who also freely choose only the good? Many traditional theists come down on the side of Mackie, at least in the case of the doctrine of the Incarnation. The human nature of Christ according to many theologians is at once free and chooses only from the highest and purest of motives. If God thus *brings into existence* a *human nature*, we have God bringing into existence a universe which includes a morally free creature who chooses only the good. If he can do it for the human nature of Christ, why can he not do it for other humans? Mackie points out that there are other doctrinal beliefs which would seem to require that God be able to do this.[29] Since it is logically possible (and not implausible) that no other agent than Jesus would always, if created, choose only freely and rightly, it is far from clear that Mackie is right in thinking that there 'seems to be no reason why an omnipotent, omniscient, and wholly good god would not have preferred this alternative . . . . '[30] We have given consideration to another option, namely that world which has the two sorts of universes outlined, and in some measure to reasons God might have for preferring to allow evil.

2.   THE GGD AND COUNTERBALANCING AND OVERBALANCING GOODS

Yandell's GGD breaks down into two main components, the first deals with a good that counterbalances evils, and the second with a good that overbalances evils. The pivotal terms counterbalance and overbalance are to be read in the following way:

> A good G counterbalances an evil E IFF G *exists* entails E *exists* and if an agent who creates or permits E for the sake of G performs a morally neutral action (is neither praiseworthy nor blameworthy). A good G overbalances an evil E IFF G *exists* entails E *exists* and an agent who creates or permits $G[E]$ for the sake of $E[G]$ is thereby morally praiseworthy.[31]

I shall look at *counterbalance* first. Two conditions must be satisfied in order for a good G to counterbalance an evil E. First, G *exists* must logically entail E *exists*; i.e., G cannot (logically cannot) exist without some evil E. Second, when an agent creates or allows E for the sake of G, the action involved is morally neutral, and so the agent is neither praiseworthy nor blameworthy.

Regarding *overbalance*, again two conditions must be met. The first condition is identical with the first condition of *counterbalance*. The second condition, like the second condition of counterbalance, appears free of quantitative sorts of notions. A good G is said to *overbalance* an evil E just in case creating or allowing E for the sake of G makes the *agent* morally praiseworthy.

Three points bear mentioning with regard to the above account of the terms in question. First, presumably regarding *counterbalance*, there are no *other* logically possible courses of action open to the agent which would, on balance, effect a greater balance of good over evil. Though the definition does not explicitly disallow this, I assume it is understood. Second, *counterbalance* and *overbalance* are quasi-quantitative terms, but the definitions seem to be devoid of quantitative notions. The ordinary meanings of *counterbalance* and *overbalance* convey the basic idea of some sort of measurement taking place, such as the weighing or measuring of the positive value, say, of G against the negative value of E. The locutions, *an agent who creates or permits E for the sake of G* and *an agent who creates or permits G for the sake of E is thereby morally praiseworthy*, however, appear to be formulated so as to avoid quantitative analysis. But then the question arises, What makes one action morally neutral and another praiseworthy or blameworthy? Perhaps an analysis could go in either a quantitative direction, or a qualitative one. A quantitative analysis would allow some sort of calculation in terms of measurable quantities. However, a qualitative comparative analysis can be given. For example, 'Kant is a better philosopher than Locke' or 'The first Critique is even heavier than the Groundwork,' are locutions that make use of comparative terms, yet in such a way that is not quantitative. Yandell is inclined toward favoring the latter route. Regarding the notion of *counterbalance* it is not clear to me that there are such things as morally neutral actions for God, at least as he has been pictured by theologians in the mainstream of Christian theism. It has generally been held that God is praiseworthy in everything that he does and allows because everything he does and allows manifests his moral goodness. Hence the praiseworthiness of God is supervenient on the inherent moral goodness of God's nature. Third, regarding *counterbalance* it is not clear whether the agent or the action is described as 'neither praiseworthy nor blameworthy.' It is fairly clear in the definition of *overbalance* that the *agent* is in view in the ascription of the predicate 'morally praiseworthy.' In my account of *counterbalance* I have assumed that, as with *overbalance*, the agent is in view.

3. THE ENDS-JUSTIFIES-THE-MEANS PRINCIPLE

The three most popular defences formulated to handle the problem of evil, the free will defence, the soul-making defence, and the greater-good defence, work with some form or other of the ends-justifies-the-means principle.[32] In some way a counterbalancing or overbalancing good is viewed as justifying some evil means, and this means (or some other evil of at least equal negative value) is logically necessary to the justifying good. Interestingly, notwithstanding the Principle's wide currency in theodicy literature, the role that it has in these theodicies is rarely discussed.[33]

More generally, the Principle has a rather common and natural place in ordinary life. A person suffering from an illness that requires surgery, is usually willing to undergo the pain and suffering that often attends surgical treatment in order to attain the end of long-term health. Another with a toothache might go to a dentist, knowing that he will follow a procedure that will likely incur some measure of pain, but the patient has the expectation that his toothache will come to an end and that the cause will be eliminated. In such cases, the means are causally necessary to the end contemplated. In a formal fashion the principle at work can be stated as follows (I will refer to it as EJM_1, and later definitions which follow as EJM_2 and EJM_3).

EJM_1 An end justifies a means IFF, some state of affairs (or states of affairs), say M, is (are) causally necessary to some end state of affairs (or states of affairs), say E, such that E justifies M.

The evil means must be at least causally necessary to the end desired, since if it were not, then the end could be reached without evil, thus making any route which employs the evil means gratuitous.

Though the above principle or something like it might justify these and other such teleological uses of pain, it (the principle) will not work for the theist who wants a justifying mechanism for handling evil, given that God is omnipotent, since an omnipotent being can bypass causal necessities.[34] Means-end need a stronger link of necessity, viz., that of logical necessity. That is, in order for a good end to justify some evil, the evil in question (or some evil like it – of at least equal negative value) must be logically necessary to the good end (Cartesian possibilism excepted, since for Descartes, God is not even bound by logical necessities).[35] To couch it differently, for some evil means M which God may be said to bring about or allow, and some good end desired, say E, E logically cannot exist without evil M or some evil like M. That is, if not-M, then not-E. A revised EJM principle which reflects this stronger tie between means and end may be formulated thus.

EJM_2 An end justifies a means IFF some state of affairs (or states of affairs), say M, is (are) logically necessary to some end state of affairs (or states of affairs), say E, such that E justifies M.

Prima facie, EJM_2 could be thought to be just the definition the theist wants. But is it? In brief form, the logical relationship between means and end is stated as follows (I will refer to the statement as LN).

LN   An evil means M must be logically necessary to a good end E,

which means, 'a *particular* evil (this evil as opposed to some other) is logically necessary to a good end.' The reasoning behind LN runs something like this: if M is only a causally necessary condition, then because God is not confined to causal laws, he could have brought about E without M, which would make M gratuitous. To see the faultiness of the doctrine, we might consider two different ways of attempting to justify evils. First, it is argued that the evils of fear and pain are justified on the ground that they are logically necessary to *courage* and *bearing pain with fortitude*. Some contend that even if the evils in question do not on occasion give rise to virtue, they may be justified merely because they provide an environment necessary for the manifestation of these virtues. Second, there is the argument that moral evil is the price that must be paid if there are to be morally free agents. If agents are to be free in a morally significant sense, then they must be free to do good or evil.

To counter the first argument, bearing pain with fortitude requires (logically requires) that some pain or other exist, but not that some *particular* pain as opposed to some other is a logically necessary condition of bearing pain with fortitude. Some pain or other is required if Gorbachev is to bear pain with fortitude, but not a pain in Gorbachev's foot, say, as opposed to a pain in his neck.

In response to the second argument, no *particular* evil choice is logically necessary to free moral agency, in fact, no *actual* evil is required, only the possibility of some evil or other. Thus in neither case does the invoking of (LN) justify the evil in question.

Another difficulty with (LN) has been pointed out. Suppose that an evil means M is justified if it is logically necessary to an overbalancing good end E. Consider the following universe (suggested by Plantinga), where there are a dozen evils logically necessary to one good G, and the positive value of G is more than the negative value of any one of the evils, but the positive value of G is outweighed by the negative value of any two of the evils. Even though (LN) justifies each evil, we have a universe where evil overbalances the good. This shows us that (LN) is too broad. For this reason, the theist is going to have to develop a sense of justification which will handle aggregate evils.

Since, strictly speaking, the theist might not want to claim that some particular evil, as opposed to some other very much like it, is logically necessary to some good, he needs a revised EJM principle that avoids the error of (LN). Perhaps the following will do.

EJM$_3$ An end justifies a means IFF some state of affairs (or states of affairs), say M (or some state(s) of affairs of equal negative value), is (are) logically necessary to some end state of affairs (or states of affairs), say E, such that E justifies M (or an evil like M).

EJM$_3$ or something very much like it, is an underlying principle in most teleological schemes designed to handle the problem of evil. Whether the link between the evil means and the good end is direct or indirect, depends upon the defence. In some defences, an evil of some sort is a direct logical necessity to the end desired. For example, some sort of pain is logically necessary to a person's bearing pain with fortitude. But in the case of the free will defence, at least current versions of it, usually there is no direct linkage between the evil (usually its possibility) and the good end. It is not claimed that evil is directly necessary to the good end in view, say some moral good, but rather, freedom of choice is logically necessary to the desired end, and freedom makes possible moral evil. Freedom as a first-order good (because the agent *is* free, he doesn't *choose* to be free), is a necessary condition to second-order goods, say goods freely chosen, and as such is a 'mixed' means (a logically necessary condition) to the end, since though freedom is an intrinsic good, its misuse can lead to moral evil. More generally, it is argued that if there is to be a world with moral goods, a necessary condition to making such goods possible is freedom, and with this freedom there is the possibility of moral evil.

Two concluding observations are in order. The EJM principle clearly has a teleological flavor. Some variant of the principle is invoked whenever the theist focuses upon some end that is desired and hopefully realized in consequences which are viewed as justifying some evil means. Instead of a deontological targeting on intrinsic values or objective standards of goodness and meaning, attention is directed toward some end which is hopefully objectified in some measure and manner in outcomes.

In most instances where the EJM principle is employed, an incipient greater good notion is at work, so that an end is understood as justifying a means in the sense that the positive value of the end on balance offsets the negative value of the means. It is now our task to take a close look at variant greater-good defences.

4. VARIANT GGDs

Our purpose here is to explore variant readings of the GGD in order to consider their respective merits, and see what relation, if any, they may have to those theistic tenets listed at the beginning of our inquiry. The first account of the defence, GGD_1, can be read in either of two ways:

GGD_{1a} For every evil that God permits, there is a good state of affairs which counterbalances and which logically requires the evil in question (or some other evil of at least equal negative value), and some evil is overbalanced by at least one good state of affairs which logically requires the evil in question (or some other evil of at least equal negative value).

GGD_{1b} For every evil that God permits, there is a good state of affairs which counterbalances and which logically requires the evil in question (or some other evil of at least equal negative value), and some evil is overbalanced by all the good states of affairs which logically require the evil in question (or some other evil of at least equal negative value).

Since the ambiguity does not significantly affect the discussion which follows, hereafter I shall refer only to the GGD_1 formulation. I shall not attempt to unpack the concepts *counterbalance* and *overbalance*, since attention was given to them in section two, and present purposes do not require adding anything further to that discussion. The first account affirms that every evil has at least a counterbalancing good, and that *some* evils have overbalancing justifying goods. The theist might take yet a stronger line than the above.

Suppose he were to argue that for *every* evil that God allows, he has a justifying overbalancing good. Since GGD_1 says only that *some* evils have justifying overbalancing goods, the second argument involves a stronger claim. We can formulate the GGD so as to reflect this shift thus (I shall refer to it as GGD_2):

GGD_2 Every evil that God allows is such that it (or some evil of at least equal negative value) is logically necessary to some overbalancing good state of affairs (or good states of affairs).

Claiming that GGD_2 is true is one thing, trying to show that it comports with the facts is quite another. What would incline the theist to this more-difficult-to-defend view? We saw earlier in our discussion of *counterbalance*,[36] that an agent that allowed evils which had only counterbalancing goods, *ceterus paribus*, would be neither praiseworthy nor blameworthy. But for every evil allowed that has an overbalancing good, a being would be praiseworthy. Hence if a theist holds that God is praiseworthy in *all* that he does and in *everything* that he allows, more to the point, in *every* evil that he allows, then obviously the GGD_2 variant would be more attractive. It is important to see here, that there are at least two senses in which a being (in this context God) may be said to be praiseworthy. First, he may be praiseworthy because everything he does and allows manifests his moral goodness. In this case God's praiseworthiness is supervenient on his inherent moral goodness. He may also be praiseworthy if GGD_2 is true, i.e., every evil that God allows is such that it (or some evil of at least equal negative value) is logically required by some overbalancing justifying good.

Earlier, in our discussion of the ends-justifies-the-means principle, we said that the free will defence does not claim that evil is directly necessary to the good end contemplated, but rather freedom of choice is, and that freedom makes moral evil possible. Since in the free will defence, evil, or its possibility, is not logically necessary to some good end, we need a GGD that will reflect this refinement. The following has been suggested by Bruce Reichenbach (I will refer to it as GGD_3).[37]

GGD_3 Every evil that God allows is either logically necessary (as in GGD_1) or made possible by a state of affairs which is logically necessary for some great(er) good.

He offers an example, 'My stealing is not logically necessary for any good, but it is made possible by a state of affairs (my having free moral choice) which is logically necessary for some great good (a world with beings capable of doing good is better than a world without such beings).' This variant GGD avoids the (LN) doctrine, since the second disjunct allows that some evils are not 'logically required . . . but still are justified.' One advantage of this version of the GGD is that the second disjunct of GGD_3 covers certain natural evils and evils that result from the abuse of freedom, which GGD_1 does not handle, since as we noted earlier, the evils in question are not *directly* logically required by the good end desired.[38]

Reichenbach's variant takes care of justified natural evils and evils that result from the misuse of freedom, but what about gratuitous natural evils or possible gratuitous natural evils? In *Evil and a Good God*, it is argued that natural evils such as suffering (Mackie's first-order evils),[39] say the suffering of fawns, 'may be pointless or gratuitous, but the possibility of it is a necessary condition of there being that greater good [moral values are the greater good] to which a 'world operating with regularity according to natural laws is a necessary condition.'[40] As freedom is a necessary condition to certain moral goods, so is a world that 'operates with regularity.' As freedom makes gratuitous moral evil possible, so a world that is orderly and predictable makes gratuitous natural evil possible. In both cases, the evils in question are not directly logically required, but their possibility attends conditions necessary to good ends desired. We have seen that GGD_3 handles the former, i.e., gratuitous moral evils, but it also covers gratuitous natural evils, since the second conjunct takes care of evils (whether natural or moral) which are made possible by a state of affairs (or, states of affairs) logically necessary for some greater good.

Suppose that every evil has either a counterbalancing justifying good, or is made possible by a state of affairs (or, states of affairs) which is (are) logically necessary for some greater good. We might still have a GGD variant, that is, if there are evils answering to those mentioned in the second disjunct. It can be formally stated as (I shall refer to it as GGD_4):

GGD_4 Every evil that God permits is such that either there is a good state of affairs (or good states of affairs) which counterbalance(s) and which logically could not exist without the evil in question (or some evil of at least equal negative value), or the evil is made possible by a state of affairs which is logically necessary for some greater good.

The main difference between GGD_4 and GGD_3 is that the former says that every evil that God permits has a counterbalancing good state of affairs which logically requires the evil in question (or some evil like it), whereas the first disjunct of the latter only says that for every evil, there is a good that logically requires the evil. One advantage of GGD_3 is it is weaker than GGD_4, and so perhaps it is easier to defend in terms of providing evidence.

Finally, there is a counterbalancing defence, which is not really a GGD. It allows that there are evils that can be matched with goods that counterbalance the evils, and that there are evils which are made possible by necessary states of affairs if some good or great good is to be possible. The defence may be formulated thus (I shall refer to it as CGD).

CGD   Every evil that God permits is such that either there is a good state of affairs (or good states of affairs) which counterbalance(s) and which logically could not exist without the evil in question (or some evil of at least equal negative value), or the evil is made possible by a good state of affairs which is logically necessary for some (great) good.

Conceivably, the evil in question could also be great, so that the great good only counterbalances it. Given the earlier definition of praiseworthy,[41] God would not be praiseworthy for allowing the evils in question. For this reason, of all the defences thus far discussed, this defence might be the least attractive to the theist.

Relative strengths and weaknesses of the disparate GGD variants have been noted along the way, and their respective connectedness (or lack thereof) to the theistic beliefs with which we began has been briefly indicated. Variants GGD_1–GGD_4 are all more or less compatible with those beliefs. The exception is CGD, but this does not belong to the GGD family. Whether the theist opts for one or another GGD depends largely upon how strong a reading he gives to God's providence. If God is a scrupulously provident being, then perhaps GGD_1 or GGD_2 would register high marks.[42] But then it would not be clear as to how the theist would give account of moral evils. If, however, the theist were to judge that there are gratuitous evils (moral or natural, or both), then he would have to 'soften' his doctrine of providence and opt for GGD_3 or GGD_4. Suppose he favors GGD_3. Suppose further that he agrees with Reichenbach, that freedom makes moral evil possible. But maybe he judges that since God is not constrained by causal necessities, Reichenbach's natural law defence does not go through. Hence so-called gratuitous natural evils are not justified in the way indicated in GGD_3. Then he could particularize GGD_3 so as to eliminate coverage of putative gratuitous natural evils in the following way (I will refer to it as GGD_5):

GGD_5 Every evil that God allows is either logically necessary (as in GGD^1) or made possible by freedom of choice which is logically necessary for some greater good.

A theist might hold that nature can still be an orderly, predictable, place where moral choices can be made, so he might argue that gratuitous natural evil is not thus required, and so he might opt for GGD_5.

Perhaps one final point is in order. It has been suggested that God might be viewed as praiseworthy in the sense that his praiseworthiness is supervenient on the moral goodness of his nature. This perhaps should have the limitation that God is praiseworthy no matter what he creates or allows, providing the evil he allows is not so aggravated, terrible, and prolific, and the good so weak and miniscule by comparison, that the good fades to near 'nothingness.' Theists who allow that there *is* gratuitous evil, or theists who hold that gratuitous evil is not incompatible with God's existence (not that there *are* such evils) hold that the above sort of scenario is not compatible with a loving, compassionate, providential God.

Investigation of the various GGD models has taken us on a long and arduous theodicy odyssey. Two variant GGDs have emerged as strong defences, partly because they allow for the possibility of surd or gratuitous evils.[43] Whether the theist favors GGD_3 or GGD_5 depends on whether or not he finds the natural law argument convincing. Before going on to consider derivations of the GGD, and more particularly derivations of GGD_1, the matter of so-called gratuitous evils needs further attention. Hopefully, the propriety of discussing this sort of evils under the greater-good defence heading will become evident.

5.   GRATUITOUS EVIL VERSUS METICULOUS PROVIDENCE

We have seen that the GGD turns on the claim that for every evil
that God allows, there is a counterbalancing or overbalancing good
which logically requires the evil in question, or some evil like it
that is at least as evil. An underlying assumption to the argument
is the doctrine of meticulous providence – that God would not allow
gratuitous evil(s). Keith Yandell and Michael Peterson argue that
there are gratuitous evils, and that the existence of such evils is not
incompatible with the God of Christian theism, hence they reject the
doctrine of meticulous providence. It is important to explore their
respective arguments, to see what sort of impact, if any, they might
have on the GGD strategy.

Yandell's argument begins with the noncontroversial assumption
that there is evil. To this is added the following proposition:

(N)   Necessarily, if God allows any evil, then He has morally
            sufficient reason for doing so.[44]

Then proposition (N) and its denial are viewed as comprising the
tautology, (N) or -(N). The strategy is then to show that neither
disjunct gives the critic what he wants in order to make good his
claim that the existence of evil is incompatible with the existence
of the God of theism. If we assume the first disjunct, where does
that take the critic? If (N) is true, then for any evil that God allows,
it is going to have the property (P), which is, God has a morally
sufficient reason for allowing it. So if (N) is true, then any and all
evil is going to have the property (P), and so every evil, according
to Yandell, is going to be 'critically cancelled,' with the result that
the critic is *not* going to be able to appeal to evil as counting against
God's existence.[45]

The picture is just as dismal for the critic's attack against theism
if he holds (N) to be false, i.e., if he holds the second disjunct -(N)
is true. It is likely that the critic will hold

(C)   There is an evil that lacks P.[46]

Then the argument for the detractor of theism runs as follows:

(C)   There is an evil that lacks P.

(C1)   If there is an evil that lacks P, then God does not exist.
So: not-(G) God does not exist.[47]

The rationale for the second premise is roughly equivalent to the truth of (N). That is, given God, if he allows evil, he does so only if he has morally sufficient reason. But oddly, (C1) is true because (N) is true. But the critic has assumed (N) is false. So the standard defence for (C1) is undercut.

Yandell then looks at how the defence for -(N) might go. He begins by drawing upon Aquinas' point that God is able to create a better world than any world that he creates. This contention, says Yandell, 'suggests a reason for doubting (N).'[48] The argument goes as follows. Let W^- represent a world such that creating it would not be as good as not creating it. Further, let W^0 represent a world such that creating it is neither better nor worse than not creating it, so W^0 is 'morally neutral.' Finally, let W^+ represent a world such that creating it is better than not creating it, so that W^+ has positive moral worth. Now if for two morally positive worlds, say W^+_1 and W^+_2, we may say of W^+_1 that for some reason or other, it is better that W^+_1 be brought about than that W^+_2 be brought about, then W^+_1 is morally superior to W^+_2. Now it is Aquinas' point that for any positive world that God might create, there is a morally superior one. Further, if it is not a moral deficiency for God to create some positive world W^+, then it is not a moral deficiency in God if he creates a world that has a moral superior. The upshot of the argument at this point is, God's character does not in any way suffer from a defect if he does *less* than he is able.

Yandell applies the above line of reasoning, *mutatis mutandis*, to God's bringing about or allowing evil for which he does not have morally sufficient reason. Suppose that there is a positive state of affairs A which contains evil, and another state of affairs B which does not. Suppose further, that it is better to create A than not, and that B is morally superior to A. Assume that there is no best state of affairs that God can bring about. So, for any state of affairs that God brings about, there is a morally superior one that he could have brought about. And, as long as the state of affairs in question is positive, bringing it about is better than not. Hence, if God brings A about, then he allows evil, and the evil that he allows is not, Yandell says, an evil for which God has morally sufficient reason. He concludes that if God does not have morally sufficient reason for allowing evil, this is not a defect in God nor does it reflect badly on his character, hence (N) is not true.[49] What does this imply for the theist? Bringing about a world with creatures reflecting his image might be better than a state of affairs where God alone exists. But his not bringing about such a world is not evil. Regarding evil, he might have brought about a world without evil, and such a world might be better than a world with it. But were he to bring about the latter, doing so does not reflect badly on God.

This new line of argument has been challenged by Mavrodes.[50] Yandell's crucial thesis in the first part of his argument, when (N) is affirmed, is that an evil that has the property (P) is useless for the atheist, since if (N) is true, then every evil is 'critically cancelled.'[51] First, Mavrodes offers a clarification as to the evils that are putatively 'cancelled.' If (N) is true, then (P) is true only of every *actual* evil, since if (N) is true, only those evils exist which God allows, and God allows only those evils for which he has morally sufficient reason. Here Mavrodes asks, If (N) is true, then (P) is true for every actual evil, but how does this establish that if (N), every actual evil is 'critically cancelled'?[52] Yandell's comment on this point is, 'it seems clear.'[53] Yandell's argument, at least the first part of it (where (N) is affirmed), Mavrodes sees as flawed because (P) is not the property of 'being morally allowable by God' simpliciter, but rather, it is the *conditional* 'being morally allowable by God, if he exists.'[54] That is, if the antecedent of the hypothetical in question is true, then every actual evil is an evil for which God has morally sufficient reason, *and* is an evil the existence of which is compatible with the existence of the God of theism. But if (P) is all that Yandell wants to work with in his new argument, then the conditional will not get him what he wants, viz., a justification of actual evils. If one were to assume that the antecedent of the conditional is false, i.e., if it is not true that God exists, then some actual evils might have the conditional property (P), 'even if they also have the categorical properties of not being morally allowable by God and not being logically compatible with God.'[55] Mavrodes adds, that the 'evidential force' of the property (P) has to do with the 'compatibility' of the property in question with the *existence* of God.[56] Yandell's insistence that he does not want to start with the stronger statement (P) which includes the existence claim in question, according to Mavrodes is fatal to the first part of the argument which affirms (N).

If Yandell's argument against the critic of theism needs rescuing,[57] perhaps the following does the job.[58] Consider three possible properties with regard to any evil, say E_1. The first is, (P) Being morally allowed by God, if God exists. The second is, (P*) Being morally allowed by God, and the third, (P**) Being morally allowable by God. Clearly, E_1 can be said to have (P*) just in case God exists. But E_1 can have the properties (P) or (P*) whether God exists or not. Therefore, the critic of theism cannot know that E_1 lacks the properties (P) and (P**) without knowing also that God does not exist, just as it is the case that a theist cannot know that E_1 has the property (P*) without knowing that God does exist. As the theist cannot justifiably appeal to the 'fact' that E_1 has (P*) in offering an account of the GGD unless she has provided independent reason for thinking that God exists, so the critic of theism cannot justifiably appeal to the 'fact' that E_1 lacks the properties (P) and (P**) unless she has offered independent reason for thinking that God does not exist.

As for Yandell's original argument failing to justify actual evil, the intent was not to establish a claim made by the theist as much as to respond to a critic's argument.

Yandell's discussion focuses on a certain species of gratuitous evil, rather than on completely unjustified evil. Peterson's line is not different in this respect. How Peterson's line fares – offered to support the claim that gratuitous evil is compatible with God's existence – remains for us to see in the following.

6. DEONTOLOGICAL VERSUS TELEOLOGICAL JUSTIFICATIONS OF EVIL

Typically, Christian theists who have sought to counter arguments against God's existence based on evil, have operated with defence strategies which tacitly assume that all evils in some way or other are justified. The theist usually argues something like the following: God is omnipotent, omniscient, and omnibenevolent, hence there would be no evil unless some good end were served. Providentially speaking, God superintends punctiliously over the affairs of human agents and the world in general so as to prevent evils which are without justification from happening. This widely accepted doctrine of scrupulously exact or punctilious providence (I shall refer to it as SP) can be stated formally as follows.

(SP)   An omnipotent, omniscient, and omnibenevolent God
              would not allow genuinely gratuitous evils.[59]

While many if not most theists of a traditional stripe have tended to
accommodate the *experience* of gratuitous evils to the SP doctrine,[60]
some recent theists are inclined to adjust their talk about God to fit
what they judge to be a fact of experience.[61] Michael Peterson sees
both as extremes to avoid, and offers the gambit, acknowledge that
gratuitous evils are a fact of experience and reject SP.

As Peterson tells the story, two 'ethico-theological frameworks'
or schemes, the teleological and deontological, have been used to
support the SP doctrine. In rough terms, a teleological scheme
appraises evils in extrinsic terms, i.e., evils are viewed as a means
to some good end, whereas a deontological framework appraises
evils in terms of their intrinsic nature.[62] A teleological defence of
SP sees every evil as a means to some good end. According to the
greater-good defence, for example, for *every* evil that God permits,
there is a good state of affairs which counterbalances and which
logically requires the evil in question (or some evil like it), and
some evil is overbalanced by a good state of affairs (or good states
of affairs) which logically require the evil in question (or some evil
like it).[63] According to this earlier defence strategy of Yandell, the
'orthodox theist is committed to some version of the greater good
defence.'[64]

By contrast, the deontological approach to evil does not consider
consequences which might be brought about by some evil means
since it rejects instrumental justification altogether. On this view,
'no one, not even God, may do evil that good may come.[65] For any
evil that exists, it is 'regarded as *justified* or *gratuitous* on the basis of
some internal property which it possesses, or fails to possess, or on
the basis of its conformity, or lack of it, to some absolute standard of
goodness or meaning.'[66] Peterson lists Madden and Hare as striking
a similar chord in their contention against theists that there are
certain evils so terrible and aggravated in nature that no future
good(s) could ever be thought to justify them. That there are such
evils Peterson does not question. And part of his counter to those
who argue that God's existence is incompatible with the existence
of gratuitous evil, is to call into question the argument's underlying
assumption, viz., the SP doctrine. More fully, his program is to
affirm the standard Christian theistic picture of God, rejecting
of course the view of providence expressed in SP, and combine

a modified free will defence with a natural-law theodicy and a soul-making justificatory scheme which he thinks are ways of showing that the existence of genuine gratuitous evil belongs in the sort of world the God of theism would create.

In the following I shall argue that: (1) Peterson's gratuitous evils are not really gratuitous, since they are subsumed under one or some combination of three general justificatory patterns; (2) deontological justification, at least Peterson's account of it, turns out to be teleological; (3) the only viable justification procedure for the theist appears to be the teleological one.

According to Peterson, the theist can plausibly argue that God does not always work with an SP mode of providence, and that there are at least three defences for God's allowing genuinely gratuitous evil. The first two are defences against the charge that gratuitous evil is incompatible with God's existence. The first, the free will defence, is an attempt to show that gratuitous moral evil is to be expected in a universe where creatures are genuinely and significantly free, and the second, the natural-law defence, is designed to show that we should not be surprised to find gratuitous natural evil, given the natural order. The third, the soul-making defence, is viewed as having the more positive role of showing that gratuitous evil, natural and moral, might be viewed as lending *truth* to the claims of theism.

As to the first, he is in basic agreement with Plantinga's free will defence, but sees it as not going far enough.[67] He expands the argument so as to include gratuitous evils as among the options actualizable by free moral agents, and this increase in free choice thereby increases the range of opportunities for the agents in question to achieve their highest possible level of meaning and 'human endeavor.' Good and evil must be live options if freedom of choice is to be significant. And if God is going to confer the 'most significant' freedom upon creatures, the range of choices must include the 'highest goods' and the 'most terrible evils.'[68] As to the sense he gives to 'gratuitous evil,' though he stops short of offering a complete or final definition, clearly the prevailing sense he attaches to the expression is, 'pointless' or 'unjustified' evil.[69]

In his natural-law defence for gratuitous natural evil, Peterson like John Hick, argues that for the world to be an environment where moral agents can live with certain expectations and regularities, there has to be the possibility of surd natural evils.[70] But even more important, a natural order must exist if persons are going to be free agents.[71] So, though he acknowledges that this is not the only world that God could have created, or that it is the best of all possible worlds,[72] in order to have the sorts of goods God wants actualized or actualizable, God would have had to bring about or create this world or a very similar one.

His third defence for gratuitous evil, moral and natural, strongly resembles John Hick's soul-making theodicy. Hick holds that states of affairs which give rise to soul-growth involve in one way or another, experiences which are negative (evil episodic properties). 'It . . . does not seem to me,' he says, 'that there is a viable possibility of a soul-making world from which we exclude all risk of severe hardship and injury, with desperate and even suicidal misery as the extreme point of the one continuum, and death as the extreme point of the other.'[73] To this it may be added that the world does not have to contain the particular evils that it does in order to be a soul-making environment, but it does have to have some evils which are real.[74] According to Hick, if evil were to be completely eliminated, the laws of nature would have to be so altered that the resultant environment would not be suited to soul-growth.[75]

Not much space is given to gratuitous evil, but he (Hick) does comment about 'dysteological suffering' thus, 'Such suffering remains unjust and inexplicable, haphazard and cruelly excessive.'[76] This sort of evil, Hick says, may be ultimately present in order to provide opportunity for soul-growth, since 'It challenges Christian faith with its utterly baffling, alien destructive meaninglessness.'[77] For Hick, gratuitous evil may contribute to an 'epistemic distance' between God and human agents, a distance that allows for the free response of faith of the creature. Peterson points out that some of the claims that Hick associates with his epistemic distance doctrine might need to be either revised or excised. Noteworthy is Hick's holding to 'the inevitability of sin' as a corollary of man's epistemic distance.[78] How this squares with his view that persons must be free if they are to perform actions that have moral worth, is not clear.

Though there are variations as to how their respective defences are formulated, Hick, Yandell, and Bruce Reichenbach are in agreement with Peterson's central contention that the theist is mistaken in holding to SP, and agree further that there are moral and natural gratuitous evils. The odd thing is, these putative gratuitous evils are relegated to justificatory patterns. Peterson, for example, offers justificatory patterns for their existence, notwithstanding his use of such descriptive expressions as, 'utterly gratuitous,' and 'really gratuitous.'[79] Just what he means by 'utterly' and 'really' in such contexts is not clear, since the moral and natural evils in question do have at least a general justification of some sort. Keith Chrzan charges Peterson with equivocation on his use of the term, 'justified.' Either an actual evil is justified by some greater good (via one of his three defences), or 'their *possible* existence is necessary for greater good.'[80] Peterson retains his concept of 'gratuitousness' while at the same time expanding on his definition of 'justified.'[81]

Here it might be helpful to draw a distinction between two different ways in which evils may be said to be gratuitous. That is, in addition to actual evils which have counterbalancing or overbalancing goods, there are two sorts of surd or gratuitous evils. There are surd evils (Chrzan calls them 'plethoric' evils) which are so radically gratuitous that not even their possibility are necessary for a greater good.[82] I will refer to this order of evil as $surd_1$ evils. Peterson, Reichenbach, and Yandell do not discuss evils of this sort and so perhaps it may be safe to assume that they hold that there are no such evils. There is another sort of surd evils, $surd_2$ which are supposedly 'pointless,' but *not* without qualification, since they fall under at least one of the general justificatory patterns. That is, in the final analysis, it is arguable that there is a reason for allowing such evils. Though there is no matching of goods which justify individual evils, there is nevertheless a justificatory scheme appealed to. And so as Chrzan says, Peterson 'remains embedded in the greater good tradition.'[83]

Suppose the theist were to try a deontological approach to $surd_2$ evils. That is, suppose he were to show that they are somehow justified, not because they are a means to some good end, but because of some property they have or fail to have. Take for example Hick's notion of 'epistemic distance.' According to Hick's account, the 'surdness' of some evils *contributes* to the element of mystery by making more real the 'epistemic distance' needed if moral creatures are going to be free in their responses to God. In contrast, for Peterson and Frederick Sontag, the 'surdness' of $surd_2$ evils is viewed as possibly providing greater epistemic access to God.[84] In either case, the focus is upon an intrinsic property of $surd_2$ evils, not on consequences. This approach is at its root flawed. An intrinsic feature of $surd_2$ evils is flagged, but this quality or feature about surd evils does not in itself have intrinsic *positive* worth. Rather, its intrinsic *negative* value 'contributes' only as it is *instrumental* to soul growth. If we look at non-surd evils, i.e., actual evils (such as pain) which are justified by overbalancing goods, we see that they too have this intrinsic negative value. It is this negative value about pain that makes pain-bearing fortitude possible. One may hold that such negative elements 'contribute' in this way, but this does not commit one to a deontological approach, since they (the elements) contribute *only* as they are a *means* to some end, and so the putative deontological approach turns out to be instrumental.

Since even surd$_2$ evils are instrumentally justified, and the deontological scheme ultimately turns out to be teleological, it is likely, perhaps unavoidable, that if one is going to embark on the task of justifying evils, the only viable procedure is the teleological one.

4

Derivations of the Greater-Good Defence

It has been contended that the GGD gets its meaning and is derivable from basic or essential tenets of theism.[1] As far as I am aware, the only significant account of how such a derivation might go is offered by Keith Yandell.[2] Though it is only a rough draft, it might be helpful to carefully review and examine that effort to see what use it might have, and look at alternatives open to the theist.

The following is a list of the essential tenets that are assumed.

(1)   God exists.
(2)   God is omnipotent.
(3)   God is omniscient.
(4)   God is omnibenevolent.
(5)   God created the world.
(6)   There is evil in the world.

A rough picture of how tenets (1)–(6) are to be interpreted has already been sketched.[3] Tenet (6) helps give meaning to such theological expressions as, 'repentance and forgiveness, judgment and mercy, damnation and redemption, hell and heaven.'[4] Clearly, there is in this tenet, and in the overall picture, an ethical dimension. For Yandell the overall scheme provides a basis for and 'outline' of theistic ethics comprised of two central theses. The first is the two-fold claim 'that man is created in the *image* of God and that his good is gained through (or comprised by) his *imitation* of God . . . . '[5] The second is this:

> Anything which frustrates (either prevents or diminishes) a man's attainment of his greatest good is evil. To the degree a man's own free actions and choices frustrate his self-attainment, he is evil. If

83

God brings about, or allows, something to occur which frustrates such development, except insofar as permitting men to frustrate their own development is required for the existence of moral agency, or insofar as such frustration is just punishment, He is not all-good.[6]

In the above, a contrast is drawn between *image of God* and *imitation of God* that has rather interesting and significant associations, perhaps even parallels, in the history of theodicy literature – provided that Yandell's concept of *imitation* carries the meaning 'likeness.' Irenaeus (130–202 A.D.), Bishop of Lyons and author of the Christian Church's first systematic theology, makes what is for him an important distinction between the 'image (εικον) of God and the likeness (ομοιωσιζ) of God in man.'[7] For him, the *image* consists of human intelligence and the human capacity for fellowship with God. *Likeness*, by contrast, represents a human being's achievement of his highest good by the Holy Spirit. This distinction is the cornerstone of Irenaeus's entire theodicy.[8] Following this tradition, contemporary theodicist John Hick, in his *Evil and the God of Love*, picks up Irenaeus's distinction and updates and incorporates it into his own soul-making theodicy. The contrast which is initially conceived by Irenaeus and enlarged upon by Hick has a central role in Yandell's account of the GGD. It is, as we have observed (see p. 83), a central thesis in his 'outline' of theistic ethics; and it provides a basis for the development of his notion of *mature moral character* as a specification of the GGD.

The foregoing is a brief picture of how theistic beliefs regarding good and evil relate to the proposition *God is all-good* and to the issue of evil.[9] They also give some content to the GGD and help show its *necessity*. The sort of necessity in mind here is that associated with logical entailment. Yandell argues that the GGD follows from tenets of theism, more particularly those listed above.[10] The derivation begins as follows. The first step in the argument is to derive statement

(7)   For every evil there is, God has a moral justification

from statements (1) through (6). The argument is constructed thus:

(a)   If God exists, then he is omnibenevolent and omnipotent. (This follows from propositions (1), (2) and (4)).

(b)   If God is omnibenevolent, then if he is able, every evil which he brings about or allows is an evil for which he has a moral justification. (This is analytic of the concept, *omnibenevolence*.)

(c)   God exists. (Proposition (1))

(d)   God is omnibenevolent and omnipotent. ((a), (c), MODUS PONENS)

(e)   God is omnibenevolent. ((d), SIMPLIFICATION)

(f)   Then if he is able, every evil which he brings about or allows is an evil for which he has a moral justification. ((b), (e), MODUS PONENS)

(g)   If God is omnipotent, then he is able. (Analytic of *omnipotence*)

(h)   God is omnipotent. ((d), COMMUTATION, SIMPLIFICATION)

(i)   God is able. ((g), (h), MODUS PONENS)

(j)   Every evil which God brings about or allows is an evil for which God has a moral justification. ((f), (i), MODUS PONENS)

The conclusion is equivalent to what we have in

(7)   For every evil there is, God has a moral justification,

if every evil there is, is an evil which God brings about or allows. A basic assumption operative in premise (b), is that for every evil means which God brings about or allows, he must have a morally just end or purpose. Otherwise, his omnibenevolence might be in question. The assumption is a variation of the *ends justifies the means* principle. That is, the counterbalancing or overbalancing good end – the greater good – is viewed as justifying the evil means. But the principle is not invoked without qualification. A good end justifies an evil means just in case the good in question belongs to a sort of good that logically requires evil in order to exist.[11] The basic assumption in (b) that God's moral justification for evil must be teleological might be questioned, at least by those who as Peterson suggests, are open to deontological justifications of evil. I do not wish to discuss this counter at length here, since I think that this proposal is either deficient, or is a teleological move masquerading as a deontological one.

Yandell further points out that if one accepts statement

(8)   There are evils for which God has no moral justification,[12]

then commitment to a consistency principle will compel him to deny statements (1) through (5). Statements (1) through (5), taken conjunctively, are logically equivalent to statement

(9)   God exists, and is omnipotent, omniscient, omnibenevolent, and he is the Creator and Providential Sovereign of the universe.

The following is a reconstruction of Yandell's argument in behalf of the atheist in support of the denial of statement (9).[13]

(a)   There is evil in the world. (Statement (6))
(b)   If God exists, and is omnipotent, omniscient, omnibenevolent, and he is the Creator and Providential Sovereign of the universe, then for every evil there is, God has a moral justification. (Established by the argument which has (j) as a conclusion, see pp. 85, 86)
(c)   There are evils for which God has no moral justification. (ASSUMPTION – Yandell's statement (4))
(d)   Therefore, it is not the case that God exists, and is omnipotent, omniscient, omnibenevolent, and he is Creator and Providential Sovereign of the universe.
       ((b), (c), MODUS TOLLENS)

Thus the atheist accepts statement (8) and the denial of statement (9). The theist, to the contrary, accepts statement (9) and statement (7). We have not as yet arrived at a statement of the GGD.

We catch a glimpse of *moral justification* in the second step of the argument. To begin, it is assumed that evil is logically necessary to some goods. The question at hand is, On what grounds are evils morally justified? The answer, at least in part, is that evils are necessary if certain goods are to be possible or exist. The following is an example.

Thus *Andrew is courageous* entails *Andrew has conquered fear*. If fear is an evil, and courage a virtue (and so a good), then necessarily this virtue exists only if evil exists. It is, of course only *some fear or other*, not any particular fear, that is entailed.[14]

In contending that evils are necessary to some goods the theist should be careful to avoid the 'dogma' held by some philosophers – viz., that some particular evil is logically necessary to a certain good (see p. 67). In the example, fear is reckoned as an evil in the following way. If a person *could* somehow help another avoid experiencing fear, and he did not do so, then that person would be blameworthy. But when he fails to help another avoid fear, he is not held morally culpable, if the cause of his failure is ignorance, some limitation of power, or some moral justification. Since God is omnipotent, omniscient, and omnibenevolent, he can avoid moral culpability with regard to his bringing about or allowing evil just in case he has a morally sufficient reason, or to put it more crudely, if the ends justify the means.

The negative concept, *moral culpability*, is woven together with the concept *justification*. It is not sufficient to justify evil on the grounds that evil is logically necessary to some good. A person could still be morally culpable if the good brought about neither *counterbalanced* nor *overbalanced* the evil in question.[15] For this reason an evil *E* falls under a GGD analysis IFF: '(a) there is a good *G* such that *G* exists entails that *E* exists, and (b) *G* at least counterbalances *E*.'[16]

Two points bear mentioning in this context. Both are rather brief. Presumably, regarding *counterbalance*, there are no *other* courses of action open to the agent which would, on balance, effect a greater balance of good over evil. Though the definition does not explicitly disallow this, I assume that this is understood. Second, in his definition of *counterbalance* it is not clear whether the agent or the action is described as 'neither praiseworthy nor blameworthy.' It is fairly clear in his definition of *overbalance* that the *agent* is in view when he ascribes the predicate 'morally praiseworthy.' In the account given of *counterbalance*, it is assumed that, as with the notion of *overbalance*, so as with counterbalance, the agent is in view, not the action.

Next, the divine being is pictured as *praiseworthy*. The *fact* that God is all-good entails that he is praiseworthy.[17] Moreover, the *fact* that he is providential entails that he acts in a praiseworthy manner toward persons.[18] The first statement focuses on the character of God as all-good, and the second looks at the actions of God as beneficial for persons. God's character is praiseworthy, and so are his actions.

The GGD is formulated in two ways. The first, as stated in (10) below, is expressed in terms of *counterbalance* and *overbalance*.

(10)   Every evil is logically necessary to some good which either counterbalances or overbalances it, and some evil is overbalanced by the good to which it is logically necessary.[19]

The second, as stated in (10') below, makes use only of the concept, *overbalance*,

(10') Every evil is logically necessary to some good, some evil is overbalanced by some good to which it is logically necessary, and *no* evil overbalances the good to which it is logically necessary.[20]

That is, if explicit use is made of the notion of *overbalance* as defined, then (10) may be written as (10'). Since Yandell works with the GGD as it is expressed in (10), I shall confine my comments mostly to (10).

We have thus far seen how statement

(7)   For every evil there is, God has a moral justification

is derived from statement

(9)   God exists, and is omnipotent, omniscient, omnibenevolent, and he is the Creator and Providential Sovereign of the universe,

which (statement (9)) is equivalent to statements (1) through (5). Now the question, is, How may we get from statement (7) to statement (10)? Two routes are considered, the first of which makes no explicit appeal to statement

(11)   God is all-good and providential,

(which contains statement (4), conjoined with *God is providential*). This route is considered to be a trivial logical move, whereas the second appeals to statement (11), and involves a complex and lengthy argument. I shall examine the shorter of the two arguments first.

First it is contended that there is a sense of morally sufficient reason (i.e., God has a moral justification) that allows statement (7) to be rewritten as

(7a) Every evil God allows is such that he is morally praise-worthy or morally neither praiseworthy nor blameworthy for so doing, and there is some evil such that he is morally praiseworthy for allowing it.[21]

Then it is claimed that (7) is merely a verbal variation of statement (10). Statement (10) can be read in either of two ways, depending on how the second conjunct is to be understood.[22] According to the first reading, it is assumed that there is at least one good state of affairs that is good and overbalances the evil in question. The second reading states that the good which overbalances the evil in question involves more than one good state of affairs. I shall call the first reading of (10), (10a), and the second reading (10b).

Regarding statements (7) and (7a), since the expression *morally sufficient reasons* in (7) is roughly equivalent to God's being morally praiseworthy or his not being either morally praiseworthy or blameworthy (which is what we have in the second conjunct of statement (7a)), there is a rough equivalence between conditional (7) and the first main conjunct in (7a). But there is a significant difference between the two statements that should not be overlooked. In statement (7a), the second conjunct goes well beyond what is stated in (7). All that (7) asserts is that all evils which exist are evils for which God has a moral justification. There is no distinction even suggested by Yandell between possible subsets, say E_1 and E_2, where E_1 includes only those evils necessary to goods, for which God is morally praiseworthy, and E_2 includes only those evils necessary to goods such that regarding the net effect God is neither praiseworthy nor blameworthy. Statement (7a) not only makes this distinction, it goes on to claim that set E_1 is not an empty set. It affirms that God is morally praiseworthy for goods which logically require evils. This is clearly going beyond what is explicitly stated in (7).

Furthermore, Yandell's move from (7) to statement (10) (on either reading of (10), i.e., (10a) or (10b)) may not be trivial either. Neither reading of the second conjunct of (10) is equivalent to the second conjunct of (7a). The second conjunct of (7a) says nothing about the necessary conditionality of evil, whereas both conjuncts in (10a) and (10b) do. Another difference may only be verbal: (10a) and (10b) contain references to goods, but (7a) has no explicit reference to goods. However, the expression *is morally praiseworthy* in (7a) may be unpacked in language that resembles the language of (10a) and (10b), i.e., in terms of goods counterbalancing or overbalancing evils. It appears then that the move from (7) to (7a) is not trivial as Yandell claims, and neither is the move from (7a) to (10). But then not much may hinge on the logic of these moves, since if the longer argument (which appeals to statement (11)) goes through, we would still have a derivation of the GGD from tenets of theism.

Before taking up the second derivation, I should note here that a similar so-called 'trivial' move from (7) to (10) is also suggested by Yandell. In place of (7a), he offers the alternative,

(7b)   No evil God allows is such that He is morally blameworthy for allowing it, and there is some evil such that He is morally praiseworthy for allowing it.[23]

But the second conjunct of (7b) is the same as the second conjunct of (7a). Hence the criticisms raised against the first variant apply, *mutatis mutandis*, to this variant.

The longer derivation makes an appeal to statement

(11)   God is all-good and providential.[24]

The appeal to (11), according to Yandell, does not involve just a 'recycling' of (7) to get (10). He says that what is asserted in (10) may be made more explicit in

(12)   Every evil that God allows is logically necessary to some at least counterbalancing good state of affairs, and some evil is overbalanced by the good to which it is logically necessary, where one applicable criterion for a state of affairs being good is that it furthers the growth to moral maturity of some moral agent, and where the evils occurring to each agent are so arranged as to provide him maximal opportunity for moral maturity.[25]

Now the move from (7) to (10), where (12) replaces (10) is the following lengthy argument.

(a)   (7) For every evil there is, God has a moral justification. (Follows from (9), see pp. 86ff.)

(b)   God wills that each man attain his greatest good. (Entailed by (4).)

(c)   Man's greatest good is his realization of his capacities as one made in the *imago dei* and one who is to act always in *imatatio dei*. (Follows from the first of two central ethical theses, pp. 83, 84)

(d)   God controls the course of history so that each man has maximum opportunity to attain his greatest good. (Entailed by the second conjunct of (11), viz., *God is providential.*)

(e)   Logically necessary conditions of attaining moral maturity are: (α) free moral agency, where an agent A is free with respect to a choice x *or not-x* if and only if A can in fact choose x or choose *not-x*; (β) the existence of states of affairs which are evil (in the sense that it would be blameworthy to allow them without morally sufficient reason) and which are logically necessary to states of affairs which are both good (in the sense of being virtues which comprise, or are logically necessary to, mature moral character) and at least counterbalancing.

(Follows from the second ethical thesis, see pp. 83, 84.)

(f)   Some good overbalances the evil to which it is logically necessary. (Entailed by the theistic claim that God's creation of men is a good state of affairs.)

(g)   Therefore, (12) Every evil that God allows is logically necessary to some at least counterbalancing good state of affairs, and some evil is overbalanced by the good to which it is logically necessary, where one applicable criterion for a state of affairs being good is that it furthers the growth to moral maturity of some moral agent, and where the evils occurring to each agent are so arranged as to provide him maximal opportunity for moral maturity.[26]

Admittedly the second is only 'roughly hewn,' it contains 'plenty of loose ends, uninvestigated consequences and undefended assumptions.'[27] Let us look at the logical pieces and how they fit together to see just how 'roughly hewn' the second derivation of the GGD that makes appeal to statement

(11)   God is all-good and providential

is. An account of the justification for

(a)   (7) For every evil there is, God has a moral justification

has already been given. As we have seen, the move from (9) to (7) may need some tidying up, since it turns on a qualified *ends justifies the means* principle.

The next premise

(b)   God wills that each man attain his greatest good

is entailed, says Yandell, by statement

(4)   God is omnibenevolent.

That is, $(4) \rightarrow (b)$. But does it? Do we have strict logical entailment here? If we assume that human beings are not the most important or most valuable of all the creatures God has made, then God might conceivably will that a sub-set (or perhaps even the entire set) of the human species *not* achieve its highest good, *if* this were a necessary condition to God's bringing about some higher good for another conceivably more important species. In this case bringing about the higher good might thus require that the good for the human species be denied. It might also mean that the ultimate fulfillment of some human beings might require that evil happen to other human beings. Given these conditions God might still be omnibenevolent if he denied the human species its highest good. That such a denial might be compatible with divine omnibenevolence is more fully explained in the following. Suppose that there is an order of beings higher (in some order-of-being sense) than that of the human species, and perhaps also higher in the sense that all positive values relating to this higher order are more important to God and so more important for him to actualize or allow to be actualized than those positive values that relate to the human species. Suppose further that the greatest good for this higher species cannot be actualized for at least some of the higher order without denying at least in some instances the greatest good to certain members of the human species. Then, if God willed only compatible goods, and if he willed that each and every member of the higher order attain his greatest good, he (God) could not at the same time will that each member of the human species attain his/her greatest good, and his willing thus would not detract from his omnibenevolence. That there are higher orders of beings is possible. Some theists might hold that angels are such beings. That there would be conflict of greatest goods is pure speculation. But conceivably there might be a conflict of 'greatest goods' with regard to individual members of the human species, that is, the greatest good for one individual, say I_1, might be incompatible in some way or ways with the greatest good for another individual say I_2. If we add a qualifying phrase to (b), the theist could handle both counterexamples. The suggested revision is as follows:

(b¹)   God wills that each person (human or non-human) attain his/her greatest good compossible with the greatest goods of other persons (human or non-human).

Regarding the above suggestion concerning possible higher beings, some theists have recently begun to question the central importance of humanity in creation.[28] This only makes it more obvious that if the theist is going to argue that (b) follows from (4), he first has to show that humans are the focal point of creation and that their well-being and personal achievement is the highest good in the *created order*. Beyond this, does he have to show that the good of human persons has priority over a good of the divine order? Most likely not, because, as far as the present issue is concerned, God's omnibenevolence is in view, and omnibenevolence suggests the idea of God's moving outside himself. Hence the focus is on values relating to the created order not the divine . The main corrective point, then, is statement (4) does not by itself entail (b). The theist would have to add statement

(13)   Creatures created in the image of God are the most important focal point of God's omnibenevolence, and their well-being and personal achievement is the highest good in the created order

or something like it. Furthermore, if, as some writers have argued, humans are not the focal point of God's omnibenevolence, the denial of (13) conjoined with (4) does not entail (b) or its denial.

The third step,

(c)   Man's greatest good is his realization of his capacities as one made in the *imago dei* and one who is to act always in *imitatio dei,*[29]

Yandell says, 'follows' from the earlier of two main ethical theses. That earlier thesis is: 'man is created in the image of God and . . . his good is gained through (or comprised by) his imitation of God . . . .'[30] Humans are created in God's image and they achieve their greatest good through imitation of God. Two concerns emerge. First, the ethical thesis says that humans achieve their greatest good when they imitate God. Statement (c) says that the greatest good for humans involves two things: (1) realization of the human creature's capacities as a being made in God's image; (2) acting in such a way as to imitate God. In all likelihood Yandell holds that the 'realization' talked about in (1) somehow involves the 'imitation' of God in (2). But it has not been made clear just how this is the case. If, as I think Yandell wants to argue, *image of God* and *likeness of God* are two distinct concepts, then how or why does the realization of one lead to or involve achievement of the other? No doubt there is some relation. What is questioned is, the way in which Yandell pictures that relation. Furthermore, whether or not (c) follows from the ethical thesis may depend on just how the relation between (1) and (2) is spelled out.

Second, in the context of his discussion of the thesis, he mentions forgiveness, redemption, and the procurement of heaven as being part of the good which humans are to achieve; but he fails to explain just how these other values relate to the imitation-of-God good.

Step

(d)   God controls the course of history so that each man has maximum opportunity to attain his greatest good

is, on Yandell's account, an entailment of the second conjunct of statement (11), viz., *God is providential.* Whether it is or not, of course, depends on how much the theist is willing to pack into that conjunct. One obvious element included by Yandell is some sort of parity principle relative to the distribution of *maximal opportunity*, since it is claimed that God provides for each person maximal opportunity to reach his highest good. Whatever *maximal opportunity* may mean in this context, each person is supposed to have his share of it. The question is, What does Yandell mean by *maximal opportunity*? If his comments regarding God's omnibenevolence are taken into account, then *maximal opportunity* has at least two qualifications. Humans can be frustrated in achieving their highest good *provided* the frustration is a 'just punishment,' or provided it is 'required for the existence of moral agency.'[31]

In another context, Yandell considers a case that may provide further insight into the notion of *maximal opportunity*. It is the case of the painful death of an infant. The theist may handle such cases in either of two ways. He may argue that the infant is not a person, since he is not fully developed, in which case the question regarding opportunity for the development of moral maturity does not arise, or he may contend that in such cases maximal opportunity is available in the afterlife. Thus, whether in this life or the next, every person is assured of having a 'best shot' at imitating God. If the meaning of *maximal opportunity* has the meaning of 'having a "best shot" at imitating God,' then the phrase, 'the course of history' in (d) must be interpreted accordingly; i.e., it must include the eschaton or heaven, and the notion of *providence* must be extended to include both.

Yandell derives step

(e)   Logically necessary conditions of attaining moral maturity are: (α) free moral agency, where an agent A is free with respect to a choice x *or not-x* if and only if A can in fact choose x or choose *not-x*; (β) the existence of states of affairs which are evil (in the sense that it would be blame-worthy to allow them without morally sufficient reason) and which are logically necessary to states of affairs which are both good (in the sense of being virtues which comprise, or are logically necessary to, mature moral character) and at least counterbalancing

from the second main ethical thesis – a thesis which characterizes evil. He says:

It seems, then, a relevant (if perhaps partial) theistic characterization of evil to say that anything which frustrates (either prevents or diminishes) a man's attainment of his greatest good is evil. To the degree a man's own free actions and choices frustrate his self-attainment, he is evil. If God brings about, or allows, something to occur which frustrates such development, except insofar as permitting men to frustrate their own development is required for the existence of moral agency, or insofar as such frustration is just punishment, He is not all-good.[32]

The first part of step (e), which expresses the first logically necessary condition to attaining moral maturity, viz., a person must have free moral agency in the sense that moral agent A is free to choose x or *not-x*, goes beyond what has been made explicit in Part Two of an outline of theistic ethics. In the outline, he speaks of human agents as being able to choose actions which are evil in the sense that the actions are counter-productive to personal growth and achievement. Presumably, on the positive side, such agents could also choose actions which contribute positively to their growth and development. The point is that freedom of action is suggested but that the language is not as explicit and precise as we find it in (α) of (e). In (α) we have an IFF of *free moral agency*. Regarding choices x and *not-x*, we have a straightforward, categorical sense of 'could have done otherwise.' That is, *A can in fact* choose x or *not-x*.

The focus of (α) of (e) is also different in emphasis from the focus of Part Two of an outline of theistic ethics. The former looks at the sense in which a person is free, apart form contextual considerations, whereas the 'outline' relates human freedom to the whole matter of God's determining influence and power.

The second logically necessary condition to attaining moral maturity, viz., (β), is different in its focus from Part Two of his outline of theistic ethics. Whereas (β) talks about the existence of evil states of affairs necessary to attaining *moral maturity*, Part Two of the outline talks about evil states of affairs necessary to *free agency*. Several difficulties arise. It has already been observed that Yandell has only shown how the possibility of evil, not its actuality, is necessary to *free agency*. I have also argued that Yandell has not provided a good case for the thesis that evil states of affairs are necessary to mature moral character, since he has not shown that virtues (such as courage and pain-bearing fortitude) which logically require evil are necessary to mature moral character. Regarding the derivation of (β) from Part Two of his theistic ethic, it has not been made clear just how the existence of the evil states of affairs that he claims to be necessary to mature moral character (in (β)) is related to the existence of the evil states of affairs that he claims to be logically necessary to free moral agency (in Part Two of his theistic ethics). Thus the move from Part Two of his theistic ethics to (β) presents at least these three difficulties.

Step

(f) Some good overbalances the evil to which it is logically necessary

follows, according to Yandell, from the theistic belief *God's creation of men is a good state of affairs* (hereafter, I shall refer to this belief as S_1). This step in the argument clearly involves a greater-good notion. Whereas step (e) makes the point that some evils logically necessary to certain goods are *counterbalanced* by the goods in question, step (f) talks about the existence of evils logically necessary to certain goods which overbalance the evils in question. Does (f) follow from S_1? It all depends on how Yandell takes S_1. *Inter alia*, for Yandell it must mean that in God's creation of humans, some good is brought about which logically requires evil, and which *overbalances* the negative value of the evils that the good requires. If this is packed into S_1, then S_1 entails (f).

The conclusion to the argument is:

(g) (12) Every evil that God allows is logically necessary to some at least counterbalancing good state of affairs, and some evil is overbalanced by the good to which it is logically necessary, where one applicable criterion for a state of affairs being good is that it furthers the growth to moral maturity of some moral agent, and where the evils occurring to each agent are so arranged as to provide him maximal opportunity for moral maturity.[33]

Step (g) is a complex statement which may be broken down into the following components: The first is a categorical statement (I shall refer to it as (g_1)):

(g_1) Every evil that God allows is logically necessary to some at least counterbalancing good state of affairs . . . .

The second is the categorical statement (I shall refer to it as (g_2)),

(g_2) Some evil is overbalanced by the good to which it is logically necessary.

To these two is added the conjunctive statement (I shall refer to it as (g_3)),

(g_3) One applicable criterion for a state of affairs being good is that it furthers the growth to moral maturity of some agent, and where the evils occurring to each agent are so arranged as to provide him maximal opportunity for moral maturity.

Compound statement (g_3) consists of two statements (which I shall refer to as (g_{3a}) and (g_{3b}):

(g_{3a}) One applicable criterion for a state of affairs being good is that it furthers the growth to moral maturity of some agent.

(g_{3b}) The evils occurring to each agent are so arranged as to provide him maximal opportunity for moral maturity.

Statement (g_1) follows from step

(a)   (7) For every evil there is, God has a moral justification.

The argument for (a) – an argument reconstructed earlier in this chapter (pp. 84, 85, cf. p. 88) – has as its second premise

(b)   If God is omnibenevolent, then if he is able, every evil which he brings about or allows is an evil for which he has a moral justification.

In the discussion of (b), it was pointed out that the underlying assumption of the premise is that for every evil means God brings about or allows, he must have a morally just end. It was then observed that this is a qualified variation of the *ends justifies the means principle*, where a counterbalancing good end is viewed as justifying evil means. Thus statement (g_1) follows from (a).

Categorical statement (g_2) is but a verbal variation of

(f)   Some good overbalances the evil to which it is logically necessary.

Statement (g_{3a}),

> One applicable criterion for a state of affairs being good is that it furthers the growth to moral maturity of some agent

I take to be a criterion for a state of affairs' being *instrumentally good*, and so, to make this point explicit, I should like to suggest that (g_{3a}) be altered to read as

(g_{3c}) One applicable criterion for a state of affair's being instrumentally good is that it furthers the growth toward moral maturity of some agent.

In premise (e), free moral agency and evils logically necessary to mature moral character are listed as two conditions necessary to the attainment of moral maturity. We may speak of the latter as being *instrumentally good;* i.e., the evil in question is a means for growth to moral maturity. Thus (g_{3c}) is derivable from premise (e).

The move to (g_{3b}) may be simple or complex. It may be that Yandell sees it as following from (d) alone, i.e., if *the course of history* is taken to include evils. Thus we may read (d) as

(d')   God controls the course of history and evils that occur in that history so that each person has maximal opportunity to attain his greatest good.

In addition to this short derivation from (d'), a longer, more complex derivation may be constructed as follows (here I do not work with the revision of (d) to (d').

(d)   God controls the course of history so that each man has maximal opportunity to attain his greatest good.

(h)   Maximal opportunity to attain man's greatest good occurs in the realization of his capacities as one made in the *imago dei* and one who is to act always in *imitatio dei*. (Follows from (d) and (e) and the first of the two central ethical thesis, p. 83.)

(i)   To act always in *imitatio dei* is necessarily to exhibit moral maturity. (The latter is analytic of the former; hence (i) follows from (h).)

(j)   In order to provide maximal opportunity for moral matur-
        ity to occur, evil states of affairs must be created or allowed
        (or arranged). (Follows from (d) and (β) of (e).

Therefore,

(k)   God controls the course of history so that evil states of
        affairs are created or allowed (or *are so arranged*) *as to
        provide maximal opportunity for moral maturity*, since they
        are necessary to moral maturity. (Follows from (d), (h), (i),
        and (j) by a series of hypothetical syllogisms.)

The conclusion, (k) is roughly equivalent to (g_{3b}), if it is assumed
that the *evils occurring to each agent* in (g_{3b}) are *so arranged* 'by God.'
I take this addition to be implicit in (g_{3b}). As stated in (k), the
derivation can be regarded as a series of hypothetical syllogisms.

A number of questions are in order at this point. Do the premises
of the derivation follow from basic tenets of theism? Is the derivation
of the GGD from these premises correct? Is Yandell's formulation
of the GGD satisfactory, or is it in need of some revision? Finally,
there is a question somewhat related to the first one raised: Is
Yandell correct in his contention that the theist is committed to
some version of the GGD? How these questions are answered
have a direct bearing on the theist's formulation of the GGD as
a theistic defence and may significantly relate to the whole matter
of appraising Yandell's specification of the GGD in soul-growth
terms.

Do the premises follow from basic tenets of theism? We have seen
that the derivation of

(a)   For every evil there is, God has a moral justification

is, comparatively speaking, unproblematic, and that it follows from
propositions (1), and (2) and (4). (See p. 83)

But the derivation of

(b)   God wills that each person attain his greatest good

runs into difficulty, since (b) does not follow from (4) or from any
of the remaining members of the original set of essential tenets of
theism. (See p. 83.) If proposition

(13) Human beings are the most important focal point of God's omnibenevolence, and human well-being and personal achievement is the highest good in the created order

is added, then we *can* derive (b). The problem with this move is that tenet (13) on some accounts of theism might not be acceptable as an essential tenet of theism. Furthermore, if tenet (13) is not taken as an essential tenet of theism, then it is not clear that (d) is entailed by tenet

(11) God is providential.

If the derivation of (d) is held in question, then the shorter and longer derivations of (g_{3b}) are affected, since both assume the truth of (d), or an expanded reading of (d), viz., (d') (see p. 99).
    Yandell argues that

(c)   Man's greatest good is his realization of his capacities as one made in the *imago dei* and one who is to act always in *imitatio dei*

follows from the ethical tenet,

    man is created in the image of God and . . . his good is gained through (or comprised by) his imitation of God.

But Yandell has failed to spell out in clear terms the meaning and relation between the terms *image of God* and *likeness of God* which figure in both tenets. Hence it is incorrect to claim that (c) follows from the ethical tenet in question.
    Several difficulties regarding the derivation of (d) have already been suggested (see pp. 94, 95). Here I should like to add that he has not adequately defined the notion of *maximal opportunity* contained in the tenet. Furthermore, I seriously doubt that traditional theism has ever come near to holding anything like the idea the phrase in question even roughly suggests.
    The derivation of (α) and (β), which together make up (e) is also faced with difficulty. Statement (β) is especially problematic. Three difficulties were noted (see pp. 96, 97). The most serious may be the failure to show that virtues which require evil are necessary to mature moral character.

The last premise,

(f)   Some good overbalances the evil to which it is logically necessary

follows from (S_1), if the ideas discussed in connection with (S_1) are packed into (S_1) (see p. 97).

The conclusion of the argument

(g)   Every evil that God allows is logically necessary . . .

is made up of (g_1), (g_2), (g_{3b}), and (g_{3c}) and follows from premises (a) through (f) with little if any difficulty. Regarding the derivation of GGD, it is important to note that statement (12) not only contains Yandell's GGD (expressed in (g_1) and (g_2)) but also includes a criterion for a state of affairs' being good (expressed in (g_{3b}) and (g_{3c})). Concerning the latter, there might be some question as to whether the tenets used to derive the criterion of a state of affairs being good are essential to theism or are derivable from essential tenets of theism. That question aside, for the time being at least, the more pressing question is, Does the derivation of GGD rest on essential tenets of theism? Tenet (a) (from which (g_1) is derived) presents little if any difficulty, but there might be some question relative to (f) – in particular, regarding statement (S_1) from which (f) is derived. There might be difference of opinion as to whether (S_1) is essential to theism if one packs into (S_1) all that is necessary to derive (f).

By way of bringing our discussion of the derivation of the GGD to a close, I should like to make four points. First, (g), which is proposition (12), is not the GGD simpliciter, but it is Yandell's account of the GGD with a specification included, viz., the growth-to-moral-maturity specification, since the criterion referred to had as its focus growth to moral maturity. Needless to say, that complicates the derivation itself. Had the derivation been of GGD simpliciter, the procedure might have been much simpler and less controversial.

Second, the definition of the GGD given by Yandell in (g) (or (12)), is different from the definition that I offered in Chapter 3.[34] But this difference does not bear on the GGD derivation itself.

Third, for the theist committed to some form of the GGD, the task of deriving the defence from tenets of theism is perhaps easier than the ones thus far considered might be thought to suggest. What sort of meaning omnibenevolence has, and what sorts of defence mechanisms are logically compatible with that meaning, are two key issues that need to be addressed. If there is to be consistency of belief, and gratuitous evil is judged to be a fact of experience, then the theist will have to either unpack omnibenevolence and formulate a defence compatible with the attribute in question and the facts, or give up the attribute in question, or relinquish the task of offering a rational defence for evils of this sort altogether.

How might a simpler derivation go? Given beliefs (1)–(6), if there are not theological constraints to the contrary, one need only unpack *omnibenevolent* to fit the GGD in question so that the GGD follows. Thus one could go either way with the issue of gratuitous evil. Suppose the theist were to deny that such evils exist because they are justified and that he were persuaded of the truth of GGD_1. He could then unpack *omnibenevolent* as follows: 'God is omnibenevolent in the sense that he will not allow evil unless the evil in question, or some evil like it (in terms of amount of negative value) is logically necessary to some counterbalancing, or perhaps some overbalancing good.' Let this minimal sense of *omnibenevolent* be referred to as omnibenevolent$_1$. A simple Modus Ponens is all we need. The argument runs as follows.

(1)   God is omnibenevolent$_1$.
(2)   If God is omnibenevolent$_1$, then GGD_1 (is true).
(3)   Therefore, GGD_1 (is true).

Premise (2) is without controversy, since GGD_1 says that every evil (or some evil of at least equal negative value) is logically necessary to some either counterbalancing or overbalancing good. Thus if God exists and is omnibenevolent$_1$, then the antecedent of premise (2) is a sufficient condition for the truth of the consequent GGD_1. Thus the second premise is the controversial one. A number of theists have strongly objected to the claim that God has a justifying reason for every evil that exists, and so they would reject omnibenevolent$_1$. Michael Peterson, and more recently, Yandell, claim that there are gratuitous evils, and that these evils are among the options human free agents can actualize in their freedom. That is, maximal positive moral value can be an option for such agents only at the cost that maximal negative moral value be an option, i.e., gratuitous evil. On this view, a greater-good notion is at work, but particular evils are not matched in a one-to-one way with justifying goods. Given this picture, all the theist need do is redefine omnibenevolent to match the defence. Perhaps something like the following will do. God is omnibenevolent$_2$ if he will not allow gratuitous moral evils unless their possibility is required for the sort of freedom God values, where moral agents can freely choose to actualize gratuitous moral evils, or high moral goods. The logical moves are the same as with omnibenevolent$_1$. The theist could thus construct in rather simple fashion, working with either onmibenevolent$_1$ or omnibenevolent$_2$, a derivation of the corresponding GGD variant from tenets (1)-(6). A priori concerns and the experience of putative gratuitous evils are not the only factors relevant to formulating and deciding on a definition of omnibenevolent. Some theists in company with Peterson judge that the possibility of gratuitous evil is necessary to the sort and degree of freedom God wants for moral agents, and necessary if the world is to be a predictable and suitable environment for moral agents to live and grow.

Fourth, if some form of the GGD is derivable from tenets of theism, in particular from tenets which describe at least in part the nature of God, then the defence itself to some extent might reflect something of God's character, and maybe even his motive(s) for doing things. The same may be said, *mutatis mutandis* concerning specifications of more generally constructed defences.

In conclusion, two of Yandell's derivations have been examined carefully, and difficulties pointed out. However, none of the derivations were finally judged beyond repair. But if a simpler procedure is available, such as the one suggested, why complicate matters unnecessarily? Conceivably, the simpler procedure would work for different specifications of the GGD, the free will defence, the growth-to-moral-maturity defence, and the redemption defence discussed in Chapter 7. In the seventh chapter the three specifications are brought together under the umbrella of the GGD into a larger more comprehensive apologetic complex. I turn now to examine the first specification of the GGD, the free will defence, more particularly the modal version of it developed by Alvin Plantinga.

5

The Free Will Defence Specification[1]

One of the most significant defensive schemes offered by theists to resolve the problem of evil is the free will defence,[2] and of the varied accounts, Plantinga's modal version is the most talked about. Stripped of its modal sophistications and in simple dress, the defence claims that moral evil results from the misuse of human free agency.[3] A recent atheological counter to this defence claims that if God can make persons such that they *sometimes* freely choose to do the good, then conceivably he could make them such that they *always* freely choose to do the good.[4] Add possible-worlds talk to this counterargument, and it might take the following form. Consider a pair of possible worlds, say world W and W*, where W* is the 'counterpart' of W for every moral agent in W.[5] Suppose that there is at least one free moral agent who exists in W and W*. Since this person may be said to exist in W and W*, she enjoys a limited measure of transworld identity; hereafter she will be referred to as WIT.[6] One could easily imagine worlds W and W* having many such moral agents who like WIT enjoy this expansive sort of identity.[7] Assume that WIT freely does only good things in W*, but that she freely does both good and evil things in W. The atheologian could argue that, given the God of Christian theism, he could, since he is omnipotent, actualize world W* and WIT, and in so doing bring into existence a world which contains moral goods and where evil is entirely absent. Plantinga thinks that his possible-worlds-ontology version of the free will defence deals a decisive blow to an assault of this sort. Let us look at the defence of which he is so confident.

I shall consider a shortened version of the defence,[8] and fill in further details – where doing so might contribute to clarity of understanding – from the fuller accounts of it in *Profiles, Alvin Plantinga* and in *The Nature of Necessity*. As we begin to briefly sketch the conceptual landscape, it is important first to distinguish between the concepts *possible world* and *state of affairs*. The latter is the 'way things are.' A *state of affairs* is a possible world only if it is *complete* or *maximal*, i.e., it must be about 'everything that could have been.' In connection with the notion *everything that could have been*, the notions *inclusion* and *preclusion* are related to *states of affairs* thus. A possible world is a possible state of affairs S such that for every state of affairs S', S includes or precludes S', i.e., it is a complete state of affairs. There can be only *one* actual world because of its (the actual world's) completeness. If two worlds were actualized, say W and W^*, then there would have to be some state of affairs S' which W includes and W^* precludes. This would lead to the logically unacceptable conclusion that some state of affairs, viz. S', obtains and does not obtain.[9] Finally, the notion of free agency at work in the defence needs to be delineated. The libertarian notion that a choice is free IFF there are no antecedent causes or conditions that necessitate it is assumed.[10]

Understanding some of the key ideas of his possible worlds ontology and notion of freedom, we can seriously consider a central question at issue, that is, if as the theists say, God is omnipotent, can he not create or bring about any possible world he pleases? As was argued earlier, surely such a being could avoid bringing about world W, and instead create or bring about world W^*, where the good-'half' *WIT* does only the good. That is, there is something that God could have done, such that if he had, he could have avoided bringing about world W and the evil that results from the morally flawed choices of the good- and-bad-'half' *WIT*. So, even if, as the free will contenders claim, God were to want agents with significant moral freedom (that is, they are free at least in the minimal sense that they can choose freely to do good or evil), he could, since he can in his omnipotence bring about any possible world he pleases, create or bring about a world populated only with moral agents who freely choose to do only the good and which would thus be free of moral evil. This atheological counter rests on the mistaken assumption that God can actualize just any possible world he pleases. A critical distinction between *strong* and *weak* actualization helps show that this assumption is false.[11] In the case of the former, God is said to *strongly* actualize a state of affairs S if he causes S to be actual. But he cannot strongly actualize just any state of affairs. For example, God cannot strongly actualize S if S is, *Eve freely chooses to reject the apple*, because he cannot strongly actualize any state of affairs where creatures freely choose. Since God's strong actualization brings about the state of affairs in question, Eve's choosing to reject the apple cannot (logically cannot) be free if God strongly brings it about that *Eve freely chooses to reject the apple.* Consider Eve's free choice regarding the apple in the following way. Take two worlds, world W, where Eve freely eats the apple, and world W^* where Eve freely rejects the apple. So far as God's strong actualization is concerned, worlds W and W^* are identical. In the case of world W where Eve freely eats the apple, the largest state of affairs that God can strongly actualize without interfering with her freedom of choice is represented by $T(W)$, depicted in Figure 1.[12]

According to Figure 1, God strongly actualizes only that which is above the line. Included above the line, i.e., what is $T(W)$ or what is the case in W because of God's strong actualization, is the creation of Eve, and the making of Eve free, *inter alia.* Thus he strongly actualizes Eve's freedom (which is above the line), but *not* her freely choosing to eat the apple.

In Figure 2 the largest state of affairs that God *strongly actualizes* is what is $T(W^*)$, which is depicted by all that is above the line. He strongly actualizes Eve's freedom, as in Figure 1, but again this is above the line. But he does not strongly actualize her freely rejecting the apple. Hence, regarding God's strong actualization, worlds W and W^* are identical. God cannot strongly actualize what is below the line without cancelling the agent's freedom; so if he is to refrain from interfering with the freedom of the agent, he can do so only by strongly actualizing what is common to both worlds. Therefore, God by strong actualization could *not* have guaranteed in his act of creation that Eve would freely reject the apple.

The above shows that strong actualization is eliminated as a way whereby God can guarantee the truth of S, where S is, *Eve freely chooses to reject the apple,* because God's strong actualization of S is incompatible with S's being true. But the atheologian does not need strong actualization for his argument to go through, only weak actualization. Thus the atheologian might interject, 'Surely God can weakly actualize world W^* where Eve freely chooses to reject the apple' (which is similar to world W^* and the 'good-half' *WIT* mentioned earlier). But this move does not help the atheologian either. For God *cannot* (logically cannot) even *weakly* actualize just any possible world either. 'God *weakly* actualizes a world W if he

Figure 1

W

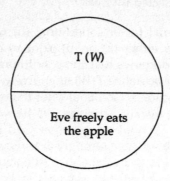

Figure 2

W*

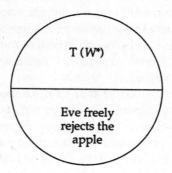

strongly actualizes some state of affairs S which counterfactually implies W, i.e., is such that if it were actual, W would be actual.'[13] Or, if God is G, and A is the state of affairs which counterfactually implies W, then

$G(A) \rightarrow W.$[14]

The argument for the claim that God cannot *weakly* actualize just any possible world can be set forth as follows. Let T(W) represent the largest state of affairs that God strongly actualizes in W.[15] Two conditionals are added.

(a)   If God were to strongly actualize $T(W)$, then the apple would be eaten by Eve.

(b)   If God were to strongly actualize $T(W)$, then the apple would be rejected by Eve.

Now either conditional (a) or conditional (b) will be true.[16] And so God would know either (a) or (b) prior to creating Eve.[17] Let us suppose, that God knows that the conditional (a) is true; i.e., if God were to strongly actualize $T(W)$, then Eve would eat the apple, as represented in Figure 3. God could not have weakly actualized world W^*, since to weakly actualize W^* he would have had to actualize $T(W^*)$, i.e., $T(W)$, because what God strongly actualizes in W is identical with what he strongly actualizes in W^*.

Now which world is W in the above, the actual world or some possible-non-actual world? Let us assume that W is the actual world. Then the argument runs something like the following. In W, Eve took the apple, but she did so freely. There is, however, another possible world, say W^*, where God does the same things, i.e., he strongly actualizes the same states of affairs as he does in the case of W, but in W^* Eve refrains from eating the apple. W and W^* are worlds where God strongly actualizes the same states of affairs, and in this respect $T(W)$ is identical with $T(W^*)$, or more formally, $T(W) = T(W^*)$.[18] But as conditional (a) says, Eve eats the apple, hence world W^* does not get actualized.

Suppose, on the other hand that God knows (b) is true, i.e., *if God were to strongly actualize $T(W^*)$, then the apple would be rejected by Eve.* This supposition is represented by Figure 4. God could not have weakly actualized world W. For if he had strongly actualized $T(W)$, i.e., $T(W^*)$, since $T(W) = T(W^*)$, then as conditional (b) says, Eve rejects the apple, hence it is not world W that gets actualized.

In either case there is a world that God could not have weakly actualized. In the case where God knows (a), he could not have weakly actualized world W^*, because to weakly actualize W^* he would have had to strongly actualize $T(W^*)$, that is $T(W)$, since $T(W^*) = T(W)$, and in this case, as (a) says, *Eve would eat the apple*, so that it is not W^* that gets actualized. In the case where God knows (b), he could not have weakly actualized world W, for then he would have had to strongly actualize $T(W)$, that is, $T(W^*)$, since $T(W) = T(W^*)$, in which case, as conditional (b) states, *Eve rejects the apple*, hence it is not W that gets actualized. Thus, there is a

Figure 3

W

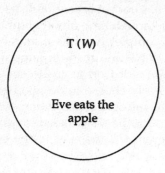

T (W)

Eve eats the
apple

Figure 4

W*

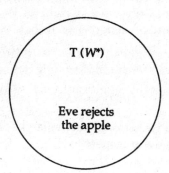

T (W*)

Eve rejects
the apple

possible world in either case which God could not have weakly actualized.[19]

At the end of stage one of the defence, we have seen that God cannot guarantee by strong actualization that an agent freely refrain from doing moral evil, since strongly actualizing the refraining interferes with the agent's being free. Thus with regard to bringing about any world populated with free moral agents, God cannot guarantee by strong actualization that the agents will freely refrain from all moral evil. The possibility of such a world has not been eliminated, only that he can guarantee such an outcome. But more importantly, the error of thinking that God can weakly actualize just any possible world that he pleases has also been shown. For in the case where God knows (a), he could not have weakly actualized world W^*, and in the case where God knows (b), he could not have weakly actualized world W. Thus we have been disabused of Leibniz's Lapse. It has not yet been established that it is 'possible' that God cannot even though he is omnipotent bring about a world with moral good but completely without moral evil.[20]

As a second step to his argument in support of the thesis that it might not be possible for God to create or bring about a world with creatures who freely choose to do good and freely choose to do no moral wrong, he introduces the notion of *transworld depravity*. In a preliminary account, he describes transworld depravity with regard to possible *persons* (I shall refer to this sense of the concept as TWD_1), and in his second revised account, transworld depravity is brought to bear upon possible *essences* of persons (this is referred to as TWD_2). Regarding the first he says,

TWD_1: A person P *suffers from transworld depravity* if and only if for every world W such that P is significantly free in W and P does only what is right in W, there is a state of affairs T and an action A such that

(1) God strongly actualizes T in W and W includes every state of affairs God strongly actualizes in W,

(2) A is morally significant for P in W, and

(3) if God had strongly actualized T, P would have gone wrong with respect to A.[21]

The main point is, if transworld depravity is a characteristic of a person P, then God cannot bring any world into existence in which P is both significantly free and does no wrong.[22]

But God could still create individuals who are without transworld depravity. Here, Plantinga draws upon the concept of the *essence of a person*, E, and applies the concept of *transworld depravity* to the E of person P. He argues that if we assume that it is *possible* that every creaturely essence E is infected with transworld depravity, then it is possible that God can create a world with moral good in it only by creating significantly free persons with essences infected with transworld depravity. Transworld depravity as it relates to essences is defined as

TWD$_2$:   An essence E *suffers from transworld depravity* if and only
              if for every world W such that E entails the properties *is
              significantly free in W* and *always does what is right in W*,
              there is a state of affairs T and an action A such that

    (1) T is the largest state of affairs God strongly actualizes
        in W,
    (2) A is morally significant for E's instantiation in W,
        and
    (3) if God had strongly actualized T, E's instantiation
        would have gone wrong with respect to A.[23]

The definition makes transworld depravity an 'accidental property'
of the essences it infects.[24] In the first place, 'it is possible' means
'there is a possible world' where the essences of all persons of
that world are transworld depraved.[25] Second, the *essences* in this
possible world are not necessarily thus depraved, since there might
be a possible world (or possible worlds) where they are *not* thus
depraved. Therefore, the property is not necessary, either with
regard to all possible worlds, or with regard to the essences of
persons in some possible world. So he is *not* claiming that the
essences of all persons in all possible worlds is transworld depraved,
and he is *not* saying that all persons who are transworld depraved
in some possible world, say world W^f, are thus depraved in every
possible world where they exist. Hence in bringing persons into
existence when bringing about a possible world, God is *not* of
necessity limited to transworld depraved persons. But though he
is not limited by necessity to such creaturely essences, since God
cannot guarantee which world will be actualized without interfering
with the freedom of the agents in question, it remains possible that
God could not have guaranteed that the world he creates populated
with free agents be a world without moral evil.

The two-staged argument is a clever piece of sophisticated logic.
The mass of critical material the defence has evoked and continues
to evidences something of its formidableness and the fascination it
holds, even for atheologians. Three central issues have been thought
to be causes for worry with regard to the defence's integrity:
the transworld depravity notion, middle knowledge, Plantinga's
possible-worlds ontology.

Mackie judges that the second stage of the modal free will defence
is flawed because Plantinga's account of the concept of transworld

depravity leads to nonsense. If the God of Christianity is omnipotent, Mackie queries, 'how could there be logically contingent states of affairs, prior to the creation and existence of any created beings with free will, which an omnipotent god would have to accept and put up with.[26] The interpretation above which sees transworld depravity as a *contingent property* means that it is not necessary that God is limited by transworld depravity. But Mackie's query cannot be so easily disposed of, because on Plantinga's account, (1) God *is* limited by transworld depravity, and (2) he has no control over the fact that he is. That is because he cannot make counterfactuals of freedom true or false. Furthermore, if God chooses to create free creatures, according to some he will be limited by *some* counterfactuals of freedom in *every* possible world, because some set of counterfactuals of freedom will be true in every possible world.[27] All of which suggests that there is a tension between these claims and the traditional understanding of omnipotence. Regarding the point that God cannot make counterfactuals of freedom true or false, that is a limitation God may choose to impose on himself, and in so doing, he sets a certain limit on his sovereignty, i.e., his sovereignty is not absolute after he brings into existence creatures who have libertarian free will. If however, he remains sovereign in those matters over which he wishes to retain sovereignty, then his sovereignty is not significantly diminished or impaired. I see no reason why God must, in order to be sovereign, retain control over all power. That notion has been rejected as incompatible with the idea that God brings into existence creatures who are genuine agents with power to act freely. That God could and so might bring into existence such creatures might be a greater attestation to his power and confidence in his sovereignty, than not doing so.

What about the claim that some set of counterfactuals of freedom will be true in every possible world? One could argue, as does Hasker, that counterfactuals of freedom are not true, or 'insofar as counterfactuals are true, they are not counterfactuals of freedom.'[28] Or, he could argue that counterfactuals of freedom are true, but only relative to certain possible worlds, and hence are not true in every possible world. The latter seems more plausible, but neither move cramps God's omnipotence. However, there is another potential worry, which is not internal to the argument's second stage, but rather arises when this stage is viewed in the context of certain religious beliefs essential to a traditional theistic stance. God is viewed as having incarnated himself in the world that he brought about, and further, one of the chief purposes of this incarnation, if not the central one, is to provide redemption for a humanity that is lost. The theist could contend that there is a possible world where all persons excepting the incarnate Son suffer from transworld depravity, since the concept formulated allows such a world is possible. The notion in question also allows that there are any number of possible worlds where free agents who enjoy an expanded sort of identity (are transworld) also do only the good, and so do not suffer from transworld depravity or any sort of depravity. These may be said to be transworld holy, that is, they enjoy a transworld identity and in more than one possible world where they may be said to exist and make morally free choices, none of their choices are morally flawed. Let us say that there is one such possible person who enjoys this sort of transworld holiness, say P^h, and that there is a possible world populated with P^h, but that the remaining agents in this possible world suffer from transworld depravity, let us call it world W^{hf}. This is precisely the sort of possible world the theist would see as compatible with the world picture his religious set of beliefs portray, since W^{hf} has a free human agent who does not sin, which corresponds to the theist's claims that the incarnational Son is without sin, but yet each remaining morally free agent makes choices, such that at least one of them is morally flawed, which reflects the theist's belief that humanity is in a morally fallen state.

The question is, can the theist hold that God can somehow guarantee that world W^{hf} come about rather than world W^f, given that the created agents of both possible worlds are *morally free*? Worlds W^f and W^{hf} bear some resemblance to our earlier worlds W and W^*, but the morally free agent in question adds a new dimension to the picture. That is, we have in mind the incarnate Son as existing in W^f, or as existing in W^{hf}. In the former, he suffers from transworld depravity, and in the latter he enjoys transworld holiness. For a moment, let us translate this into talk about essences, and follow Plantinga's preliminary account of essence, which though less than complete, is at least a start. No doubt it needs further tightening up. The essence E of the incarnate Son is such that only he has E, and 'everything distinct from him has $\bar{E}$ essentially.'[29] Now let us say, (1) essence E has TWD (transworld holiness) IFF (i) (if i is a free instantiation of E in W^f then i sins in W^f); (2) for any essence of a human there is a world in which it has no instantiation. Given (1), God cannot instantiate E in such a manner that the result acts always freely and rightly. Given (2), this is a contingent fact. Similarly, let us say, (1) essence E has TWH (transworld holiness) IFF (i) (if i is a free instantiation of E in W^{hf}, then i never sins in W^{hf}); (2) for any essence of a human there is a world in which it has no instantiation. Given (1), God can instantiate E in such a manner that the result acts always freely and rightly. Given (2), this is a contingent fact. In the above neither TWD nor TWH are necessary properties of the essence in question. Moreover, the essence of the incarnate Son is viewed as enjoying transworld identity in two possible worlds, W^f and W^{hf}, hence there is an endorsement of *Haecceitism* – the doctrine that an individual may be properly said to exist in more than one possible world, or enjoys a transworld identity. Like the rest of humanity, this special moral agent is morally free in both worlds.

Now the problem is, it is possible that in creating God could bring about a world that might be everlastingly lost, and what is even worse, there is a possible world (or possible worlds) where even an incarnate Son might also be everlastingly lost. That is, if world W^f were to occur, and an incarnation occur in order to effect redemption, that the incarnate Son would make a choice in W^f that is morally flawed, and so not be fit for a redemptive act. That is, in world W^f, all persons, including the incarnate Son are transworld depraved. This possibility points out that the creative option, given the modal free will defence, might be viewed as involving enormously significant risks for God *and* for possible agents and worlds – risks that might call into question the morality of the project of creating.[30] Whether this is a real risk for God hinges in part on what counterfactuals of freedom actually hold.

How can the theist at once hold to a modal free will defence, and resolve this difficulty? His answer might turn largely on the sort of Christology he adopts. Two central views prevail in the literature. According to the main-line Chalcedonian picture the incarnate Son of God has two natures, one truly divine and the other truly human, such that there is no confusion, no change, no division, and no separation of these two natures in the incarnate state.[31] According to Chalcedonian doctrine, as understood until quite recently, the Incarnate Word cannot sin because the Logos is the supposit of the human nature. Moreover, if the theist maintains that God possesses middle knowledge, then he can be sure that the incarnate Son will be flawless, and thus knows that if he assumes flesh, he won't sin. In more recent formulations of Chalcedonianism, philosophy of mind issues have been raised along with freedom of the will concerns. Those who want to defend some sort of Chalcedonian dualism and freedom of the will might say something like the following. There is a human mind somehow together with the divine mind, and so presumably the human nature is morally free in the way and sense that other human agents are morally free, that is, choices which are morally significant are made without antecedent causes and conditions necessitating them. Notice neither the divine nature nor the other persons of the Trinity could intervene in a free choice, that is, they could not go 'below the line' with regard to the free choices of the incarnate human nature. So in the case of the incarnate Son, as we saw with Eve earlier, God could not guarantee that the human nature of the incarnate Christ would be flawless. On this position, God could not guarantee that he not get world W^f, even with an incarnation, since he could not guarantee that his incarnate Son be flawless. If the theist were to argue that transworld holiness is a necessary property of the essence of the incarnate Son, this move would vitiate the freedom of the Son and so also the possibility of his doing morally good acts. The theist could argue, on this view, that morally flawed choices are extremely improbable for the incarnate Son if he is created in a state of innocence, and somehow 'joined' with the divine mind. Surely, if Adam and Eve's fall were in Hick's words a 'glaring improbability,' a morally evil choice springing from the incarnate Son is even more improbable. Still the Son may be viewed as free and able to make such a choice, but could be viewed as doing so only for the sheer 'hell' of it!

The alternative Christology – the kenotic view – might be viewed as eliminating the risk factor. This account of the incarnation holds that Jesus 'emptied himself'[32] in the sense that he set aside his distinctively divine attributes of omnipotence, omniscience, and omnipresence, and this pared-down version of divinity was fused with a human body or incarnated. In contrast to the revised Chalcedonian view which affirms two minds (the divine and human), this involves only a divine mind in reduced mode. Though the theist might hold that the divine mind is free in some significant way, perhaps free in a way similar to human agents, i.e. free from antecedent causes and conditions, God would not be viewed then as taking the same sort of risk as he might be thought to take as when he incarnates in the revised Chalcedonian way, since only the divine mind is making the choices, and so the risk factor relative to creation of a possible world might be viewed as mitigated. Though God might not be able to guarantee that the world he brings about with free moral agents be free from moral evil, he could personally guarantee that if a possible world with transworld depraved agents comes about, that he could provide a means for a redemption of that world through kenotic incarnation. Thus the theist might see this Christology as having an advantage over its rival. However, the theist might judge the proposal to be strongly disadvantaged on other grounds.[33] I am inclined to favor the former account, notwithstanding whatever risk factor that might remain. This I take to be a rather miniscule concern compared to the problems generated by the suggestion that God can somehow assume a mode which temporarily limits his power or knowledge. In any case, it does not appear that the notion of transworld depravity faces insurmountable difficulties philosophically or theologically.

A second set of problems concerns the issues of middle knowledge and Plantinga's possible-worlds ontology. It has been objected that the possible-worlds ontology in terms of which the argument is formulated is faulty and creates problems for the doctrine of middle knowledge, a doctrine that is assumed in the defence.[34] The concept of 'middle knowledge' dates back to Jesuit theologian Luis de Molina of the sixteenth century.[35] Molina held 'middle knowledge' (*scientia media*) to be divine knowledge that falls between God's knowledge 'of the merely possible and His knowledge of the actual, and between His knowledge of necessary truths and His knowledge of truth that He causes to be true.'[36]

The objects of this middle knowledge are counterfactual conditionals[37] that pertain to free choices of possible and actual beings.[38] According to Kenny, middle knowledge is an important part of Plantinga's defence, because if God is going to be able to bring about the world that has the greater good, he must know 'all true counterfactuals about the free actions of actual and possible creatures: for on this will depend which possible worlds he can and which he cannot actualize.'[39]

Numerous factors are listed as counting against the plausibility of the possible-worlds picture of 'divine foreknowledge and human freedom.'[40] But the main line of contention is that Plantinga's possible-worlds metaphysic cannot give account of 'divine foreknowledge of undetermined human actions in terms of divine omniscience in respect to counterfactuals.'[41]

The central points of Kenny's argument are as follows. First, even if God knew what free moral agents would do in an infinite number of possible worlds, this is not a sufficient condition for God's being able to predict anything about choices of actual beings. There is an 'incompleteness' regarding any possible world relative to its being able to afford or supply information as to the way things *are*. Secondly, it is not a sufficient condition that God know which counterfactuals are true in each of the possible worlds in order for him to be able to know how things are in the actual world. All that knowledge about possible worlds opens up to God or anyone is the way or ways possible worlds are.

Kenny acknowledges that neither Molina nor Plantinga claim that knowledge of all possible worlds is a sufficient condition for God to know the outcome of things in the real world in respect to action. Both see the need to add a piece of knowledge, viz., knowledge as to which possible world is actual. Here the critical question is raised, Can God, if and when he creates, really know which world out of the possible worlds he is creating?[42] The distinction made earlier between strong and weak actualization is brought to bear on the question. I shall confine my focus, as does Kenny, to weak actualization. It is argued that God can *weakly* actualize only those worlds where he has knowledge of the relevant counterfactual conditionals – those conditionals that pertain to the choices of free moral agents. Before God can weakly actualize such-and-such a world, say world W, and an agent in W, say A, he must know the relevant counterfactual conditionals relative to A's free choices. He must know that given certain conditions in W, A will act in such-and-such a way. The crucial issue is that prior to his actualization or bringing about of world W and A in W, God cannot know the relevant counterfactual conditionals regarding A's free choices because the conditionals are not true. Why? For the reason that on Plantinga's view their truth depends on 'which world is the actual world.'[43] It is concluded that since the truth conditions for the conditionals in question are not 'fulfilled,' the conditionals are not true, and if they are not true, then not even God can know them.[44]

Finally, there is a concern with the matter of individuation relative to possible-worlds ontology. The point made applies as well to the possible-worlds ontology of Leibniz as to the more recent Plantingian variety. Regarding the *concept* of an individual, say Adam, Leibniz is viewed as endorsing the following statement (I shall refer to it as S_2):

(S_2) The individual concept of Adam includes all that is ever true of him.

Statement (S_2) tells us that Leibniz held to a completeness regarding the individual concept of Adam. For Leibniz, the individual concept of Adam (I shall refer to it as *ICa*) is that concept of Adam which is conceived by God alone, since he alone knows the concept completely and analytically (Leibniz held that God possesses finite and infinite analytic knowledge of *ICa*). As a concept in the mind of God, *ICa* exists prior to Adam's being created, and it is to be distinguished from the individual Adam (I shall refer to it as *Ia*) who exists in the actual world. That we make an existence-in-the-actual-world claim about *Ia* and only an existence-in-the-mind-of-God claim about *ICa* might not be the only point of difference between *Ia* and *ICa*. Kenny questions whether we are talking about the same thing at all when we move from some possible world, say world W^*, and a concept of some possible thing in world W^*, say *ICa*, to the actual world. In fact, Kenny thinks that it is not even possible to individuate between *ICa* and another individual concept, say *ICb*. This is because Kenny seriously doubts that there can be individuation without actualization. So in our Leibnizian example, Kenny would contend that we cannot identify *ICa* with *Ia*, partly because we cannot individuate between possible individuals, and because the move from the concept to the actual may involve a change in respect to identity. Leibniz struggled with and did not know whether or not *existence* should be taken as a predicate and so counted as analytic of and necessary to *ICa*. He saw that an affirmative stance on the matter makes it difficult to make sense out of God's creative act, since on an affirmative reading the individual concept (say *ICa*) would already contain existence as a predicate. If, on the other hand, he denied that existence is a predicate, and denied that existence is analytic of the individual concept (say *ICa*), then if making *ICa* part of the actual world *B* is to be a significant act, how can he then maintain that *ICa* is identical with *Ia*? In order to give substance to God's creative act (in bringing the individual concept, say *ICa*, into existence in the actual world as *Ia*), the change from existence as a concept in the mind of God (as *ICa*) to existence in the actual world (as *Ia*) had to be significant. But how can Leibniz give substance to God's creative act without at the same time threatening a significant identity claim relative to *ICa* and *Ia*?

Though it appears that Leibniz did not have a ready answer to the above problem, he held that there is only one individual, viz., *Ia*, that answers to or satisfies *ICa*. Hence for Leibniz, there is a guarantee that because there is only one individual which exemplifies *ICa*, in bringing about *ICa* God is guaranteed that *Ia* will be actualized. Kenny, to the contrary, claims that since *ICa* cannot be individuated from other possible 'individuals,' God cannot be sure that in bringing about *ICa* that *Ia* will be actualized. Or to put it in Kenny's terms, if one works with Plantinga's possible-worlds ontology, states of affairs of possible worlds cannot be individuated, and that means that God could not know which possible world he can or cannot bring about.[45]

Kenny is not alone in his uneasiness with possible-worlds ontology. W. V. Quine's disdain for 'unactualized possibles' is well known. He suggests that 'Wyman's slum of possibles' be cleared altogether.[46] David Lewis, on the other hand, wants to talk about the 'realism' of possible worlds, but with guarded restraint. He is wary of 'unactualized possibles who lead double lives, lounging in the doorways of two worlds at once.'[47] For him there are 'unactualized possibles . . . confined each to his own world and united only by ties of resemblance to their counterparts elsewhere,' and in his judgment these 'do not pose any special problems of individuation.'[48]

As to the objection that Plantinga's middle knowledge thesis does not work with his possible-worlds metaphysic, there is no doubt that Plantinga holds to the former, and that in the shortened form of the defence we considered as well as the longer account in *The Nature of Necessity*, it is assumed that God knows at least some counterfactuals of freedom. But there is another reduced version of the defence which he offers in 'Self-Profile' (in response to Kenny's charge that he is a Molinist), where, though it is assumed that there are such counterfactuals, it is not assumed that God knows these counterfactuals, or that it is possible that God knows them.[49]

If Kenny and Quine are right regarding possible worlds talk, then this version of the defence collapses, since it assumes that one can talk meaningfully of the existence in some sense of possible worlds. Whether the skepticism is serious cause for concern remains a moot issue the resolution of which (if such were possible) would take us well beyond the limits of this inquiry. Though I will not take the space to say why here, reason and intuition incline me to side generally with Lewis and Plantinga.

Perhaps the modal free will defence is an answer to Mackie's contention that theism is inconsistent. But if the world that is brought about is populated with free moral agents who are transworld depraved, this does not disallow God's bringing about moral agents who are transworld holy in addition to the incarnate Son. Suppose for example, for any possible world, there are distinguishably many possible universes,[50] where a possible universe is a smaller set of possible states of affairs than any possible world of which they may be possible members. Like a possible world, a possible universe is maximally complete. Unlike a possible world, a possible universe when actualized is always less than 'all that is the case.' Possible universes in possible worlds are conceivably individuatable in different ways, depending upon various considerations. One possible universe U_1 might be distinguished from another possible universe U_2 in respect to some value or purpose that God might have relative to possible universes. Perhaps they are also distinguishable in terms of the possible location each might have, were they instantiated. Actual universes are distinguishable in terms of the actual properties they have corresponding to the possible properties they had in the possibility mode. Maybe our planet is part of a universe, which along with many other actual universes make up all that is the case. This planet is populated with free moral agents who appear to be depraved, and conceivably, in some other possible world might also be depraved. The actual world might then have moral agents who are transworld depraved. But there might be a universe (or universes) with one or more planets populated only with moral free agents who are transworld holy. Conceivably, there might be a universe (or universes) with a planet (or planets) where some of the moral agents are transworld depraved, and some are transworld holy. All of these are possible. But the free will defence shows that God could not guarantee that the world he brings about be free from moral evil. So conceivably, he could continue to bring about universes and fail to get one where the created moral agents are transworld holy, even should he desire to have one, for whatever purpose and value it might have for him. Perhaps there are many universes. The theist could argue that conceivably God could demonstrate his love in different ways given different universes. In a universe where free moral agents are transworld holy, he could show his love without a redemptive act, whereas in our universe he could show his love through an incarnative and redemptive act. And for a universe where there are both transworld depraved persons and persons who are transworld holy, perhaps redemptive *and* non-redemptive options are available. Actualizing universes with both sorts of free moral agents allows God to demonstrate his infinite love in more ways than one. Whether the universe where free moral agents are transworld holy, say universe U_1, has *more value* than some other universe where free moral agents suffer from transworld depravity and are offered redemption, say universe U_2, might not be necessary to determine, since if both are viewed as having positive value, conceivably God might desire to actualize both. In any case, God may judge that it is better to bring about a world with morally free agents, and risk the possibility of moral evil, rather than not create, or, bring about a world which because there are no free moral agents, there is no moral good. Were such agents to be forever lost as a result of the moral evils springing from their choices, the moral value of the first world might not be of sufficient worth to warrant bringing it about, unless some sort of redemption were made available. This opens up the prospect for the theist that the free will defence might be incomplete without some sort of redemptive concept. This proposal is discussed at some length in the final chapter, '*O Felix Culpa*, Redemption, and the Greater-Good Defence.'

6

Growth-to-Moral-Maturity/Soul-Growth Defence

1. INTRODUCTION

Two variants of what might be called the 'soul-growth defence' are discussed in this chapter: Keith Yandell's growth-to-moral-maturity defence, because he offers it as a specification of the GGD, and John Hick's soul-growth defence, because his account of it is the *locus classicus* of this defence. The focus of the former is narrower, at least the terminology suggests a more limiting domain, viz., moral growth or maturity, whereas Hick's defence includes the moral, spiritual, and intellectual dimensions.

2. KEITH YANDELL'S 'GROWTH-TO-MORAL-MATURITY DEFENCE'

Two fictive persons figure in Yandell's ethical picture as he develops it, Andrew and Alice. Andrew has experiences of fear which bring forth courage; and Alice has experiences of pain, and she exhibits pain-bearing fortitude. In each case we have evils logically necessary (though as Yandell observes, 'not *simpliciter*') to overbalancing goods. Yandell says that one way of taking the above description of Andrew and Alice is as follows:

(A)   Andrew's fears and Alice's pains are, considered by themselves, evil – at least in the sense that if an agent who could prevent or remove them did not, and had no morally suffi-

123

cient reason, he would thereby be morally blameworthy.[1]

(B)   Andrew's free response to his fears, and Alice's to her pains, was morally creative (virtuous) in such a manner that fears-plus responses and pains-plus responses were good states of affairs to which evils were necessary (though not simpliciter) but which overbalanced their respective evils (which are hence justified).[2]

The first point made in (A) is that the evils facing Andrew and Alice are intrinsic evils. If the evils in question are preventable and if they are not instruments to some good ends, then an agent who can prevent them but fails to do so would be on that account blameworthy. The point made in (B) is that free responses to evil states of affairs, where the evils in question are logically necessary to the free responses, and where the evils in question are overbalanced by the goods, are good states of affairs. The focus of (A) is upon natural evils and their justification; and the focus of (B) is upon evils which, Yandell holds, are necessary to free choice. Here, Yandell observes that the particular pains endured by Alice are not the only pains that can lead Alice to exhibit fortitude.[3] Other evils could serve as conditions to these virtues without conflicting with the truth of (A) and (B).

At this juncture, Yandell develops more fully his notion of freedom. He supposes that Andrew responds with fear instead of courage and that Alice shows an irritable and nagging disposition instead of fortitude. These negative responses raise questions concerning the relative merit of allowing the evils in question. Some people might judge that to allow evil in order to provide for only the possibility of virtue involves a course of action with less positive merit than not to allow the evil in question.

Yandell prefers to see the above option in more positive light. It is here that we see his strong free will thesis emerge in clear relief. He contends that the fears experienced by Andrew and the pain endured by Alice provide opportunity for 'free moral growth.'[4] If Andrew fails to grow, then the status of his 'moral failure' may be described in

(C)   It is better that Andrew be given opportunity to respond freely (and so creatively or destructively) to his fears than that he not have this opportunity – there is justificatory value in even the wrong exercise of moral agency.[5]

Here I should point out that an agent may become more moral in his desires and inclinations, as a result of a process other than through his freedom of choice. The agents in question might already have in place desires and inclinations which may, as a result of his choice, become 'part of the agents.' However, it is a good thing that agents themselves shall through their choice form such desires and inclinations. In the examples above, a necessary condition to actions having moral worth is that there be freedom of choice – that Andrew be free to respond negatively to fear, that Alice be free to act negatively to pain. If the condition of freedom is not satisfied in moral contexts, not only are Andrew and Alice not moral agents, they are not persons. Yandell allows that God could guarantee by intervention or providential control the outcome of a person's choice, but not without also destroying the possibility of that persons' having moral worth. This point was made earlier in connection with premise (e) (part (a)) in the derivation of the GGD (see pp. 96, 97). In the context of the present discussion, attention is directed to natural evils as providing an occasion for the free manifestation of virtue. Strictly speaking, the existence of natural evils is not logically necessary to there being free moral choices, but rather the existence of members of this class of evils – natural evils – is necessary for the virtues in question. So freedom is logically necessary to there being a moral response to the evils in question, and natural evils of this sort are necessary to the goods in question.

In this context a further refinement is introduced regarding the notion of freedom. The foregoing picture assumes that persons are moral agents just in case they are free and that agents are free just in case they are not determined. Yandell clarifies and reinforces this assumption by means of a distinction between 'free$_1$' and 'free$_2$,' and correspondingly between two kinds of agents.[6] Agents are free$_1$ just in case libertarianism and determinism cannot both be true regarding choices and actions. Agents are free$_2$ only if libertarianism and determinism can both be true. Yandell is of the opinion that free$_1$ agency is of far greater value than free$_2$ agency.

Three points regarding proposition (C) are in order. First, Yandell clearly and forcefully holds to an incompatibility thesis regarding *libertarianism* and *determinism*. Second, the meanings of libertarianism and determinism need to be more clearly understood to bring out their incompatibility as far as Yandell is concerned. On this point Yandell is in basic agreement with Plantinga's definition of freedom

given in *The Nature of Necessity*: 'If a person S is free with respect
to a given action, then he is free to perform that action and free to
refrain; no causal laws and antecedent conditions determine either
that he will perform the action, or that he will not.'[7] On this account,
freedom and determinism are clearly incompatible.

Third, two models can be distinguished regarding Andrew's
manifestation of courage when faced with danger. In the first
model Andrew might manifest fear – a 'fraidy-cats' feeling – or
he might show courage. In this case, when faced with something
or other that is a danger to Andrew, he might respond in either
of two ways, one (fear) is appraised negatively, the other (courage)
positively. On the second model, Andrew is faced with the same
danger, and he quite legitimately responds with fear. The fear is
in order – it is appropriate as a response to a really present threat
to Andrew. Regarding the fear, he could respond in either of two
ways: he could behave cowardly or he could behave bravely. The
second model best fits what Yandell has to say about Andrew
and his freedom. Andrew must be free to respond negatively to
fear. Presumably, then, fear itself need not be regarded negatively.
Rather in this context, negative and positive appraisals pertain to
how Andrew responds to fear, not to the fear itself.

Thus far, the main focus has been upon the condition of freedom
relative to 'attaining moral maturity.' Yandell says that the theist
may also hold to the following three theses:

(D)   For every moral agent A, A is given those circumstances
        of moral choice which maximize his opportunity to act in
        a morally creative way (though he may miserably bungle
        things anyway).[8]

(E)   There is no set S' of moral agents whose members, had they
        been created, would have chosen better than the members
        of the set S of actual persons have chosen.[9]

(F)   For any actual agent A, whatever the actual choices he
        makes, it is better that A exist (have been created) than
        otherwise.[10]

Yandell makes two points regarding (F). First, (F) seems *plausible* if
one assumes that the beings in question are created in the image of
God. Second, 'it is compatible with (F) that there be a (*possible* but
not actual) choice C such that an agent who made C would be such
that his non-existence was better than his existence.'[11] The second

observation calls attention to the compatibility of *possible* evil acts committed by C, not actual evil acts. Thus the following would be incompatible with (F). The *A* God brings about *actually* chooses evil acts, such that *A*'s non-existence is better in terms of positive value than his existence, even though he is created in the image of God.

Yandell is of the opinion, though he is not certain, that (D) is entailed by *God is providential*.[12] As a further point, he notes that salvation is a gift of free grace and that salvation includes the '"work" of a good moral character,'[13] or 'growth to moral maturity,' which is also a result of grace. Furthermore, he judges that if (D) is entailed by theism, the entailment will have to 'be understood in terms of a theologically-informed theistic ethic.'[14] He rejects what he calls 'popular versions of heaven' which operate with what he judges to be mistaken notions regarding *moral maturity* and *growth to moral maturity*. He contends that the heavenly state does not involve or require a sort of complete sanctification which would leave no room for further moral growth. Moreover, he suggests that the idea '"confirmed in righteousness"'[15] may be conceptually incompatible with being a person. Very little else is said regarding the theological meaning of *mature moral character* and *growth to mature moral character*, but he does enlarge upon certain philosophical understandings he has of these pivotal concepts in 'Theism and Evil: A Reply.' Before taking up his remarks about (E), I shall examine his philosophical account of these concepts.

'Theism and Evil: A Reply,' is a response to a critical essay by G. Stanley Kane, 'Theism and Evil.' As to the concepts, *mature moral character* and *growth to mature moral character*, I will refer to them as MMC and GMMC respectively. I should point out in this context that there is an important difference between MMC and GMMC. MMC is a dispositional state, whereas GMMC is a process leading to what might be considered various levels or degrees of approximation to MMC. The necessary and sufficient conditions of the former would likely differ from those of the latter. For example, the evil of fear is necessary to the virtue *courage*; and if the latter is judged to be necessary to MMC, then fear is necessary if one is to experience GMMC, but fear is not necessary to MMC as a disposition.

Yandell makes eight points in the development of his concept of MMC in response to Kane. I shall not discuss points (6), (7), and (8) since they address the 'dogma' issue raised in Chapter 3 (see p. 67). First, he is candid enough to admit that the concept itself is not yet fully developed and is not 'perfectly lucid.'[16] So his remarks are not intended as a thorough analysis.

In connection with the second point, he discusses the relation that may exist among character traits (or dispositional properties) and episodic properties. A person's character is largely a matter of character traits, which are 'dispositions to behave' in a certain way.[17] Character traits in turn are often associated with certain 'episodic properties,' such that, for example, Peter's being honest (a dispositional property) 'often presupposes that Peter has spoken the truth when under the duress to lie (has the episodic property of truth-speaking on relevant concrete occasions).'[18] Furthermore, certain character traits may be closely related to other character traits, so that if a person, say S, has character trait $T1$, S will also have character trait $T2$.[19] It may be, however, that a person S may have $T2$ and its associated episodic property $E2$ and $T1$ whether he has $T1$'s associated property $E1$ or not.[20] These considerations lead Yandell to reject the thesis that S's having $T1$ is a sufficient condition of S's having $E1$.

Third, in place of the above thesis (the one rejected), Yandell proposes statement

(α)   If S has trait $T1$, then either S has the corresponding episodic property $E1$ or S has some trait $T2$ such that if anyone has $T2$ then he also has $T1$.[21]

Statement (α) allows that S could have character traits without having any episodic properties. The following proposition excludes S from having character traits without episodic properties.

(β)   If S has a character trait T, then S has some episodic character-relevant property or other.[22]

He assumes the following: a necessary condition to a person's having a character trait T is that the person have some relevant episodic property E. Thus in order for a person to have character traits he must have had episodic properties. Given the above, one could infer the following with regard to prelapsarian Adam, viz. when he first appeared in the Garden as a result of God's fiat, he (Adam) was character-less since there were *no* episodic properties – properties necessary to his having character traits.

Fourth, Yandell takes propositions (α) and (β) above as 'abstract axioms of character-theory.'[23] If one assumes these two axioms, then according to Yandell there must be opportunities provided for the development of a person's character, and this means that there must be 'either opportunities for virtue or temptations to vice.'[24] The opportunities are the occasions of episodic properties which are necessary conditions relative to certain virtues. To the above outline he offers two reasons why there might not be a 'best temptation set' for any given moral agent:

(a)   for any character trait T, there may be a set $S1$ of episodic properties and another entirely distinct set $S2$ of such properties such that $S1$ and $S2$ are of equal value and such that possessing either $S1$ or $S2$ is sufficient for possessing T,

and

(b)   for any trait $T1$, there may be another trait $T2$ such that having $T2$ is sufficient for having $T1$ (and perhaps conversely), so that possessing $T1$ is possible either by possessing $T1$–relevant episodic properties or by possessing both $T2$–relevant episodic properties and $T2$.[25]

Fifth, given the conditions expressed in (a) and (b) above, it makes no difference, according to Yandell, whether an agent has $S1$ or $S2$, and it makes no difference whether he has relevant episodic properties relevant to $T1$ or $T2$. Furthermore, an agent will fare as well in developing his character with $S1$–relevant or $S2$–relevant properties, or with $T1$–relevant or $T2$–relevant properties.[26]

Yandell's concept of MMC is further enlarged upon in a response he offers to Kane's charge that Yandell's views are paradoxical. I shall look at only one of the supposed paradoxes, viz., the 'sinner paradox.'[27] Kane says that it is likely that the theist would want to include forgiveness as a necessary virtue to MMC if it is to be complete.[28]

In his response, Yandell considers two possible ways of taking Kane's charge. The first is,

(1)   If God is to have MMC, then he must create sinners and forgive them.[29]

The second reading is,

(2)   Only if a person sins can another forgive him, and if only
             Adam and Eve exist, each would have to sin at least once
             in order for each to exhibit the virtue of forgiveness.[30]

Yandell denies holding to either.

He gives a positive account of MMC as it relates to forgiveness in
terms of the following condition: if a person S has MMC, S possesses
the following character trait, say $T3$: if anyone sins against S, S
will forgive the offender.[31] He then observes that his trait does
not entail that in order to have people who possess MMC there
must be sinners. Instead we have the conditional, *if* sinners exist,
then one has MMC and so forgiveness as a disposition only if he
forgives the offender (providing certain other conditions obtain,
such as the offender apologizes, tries to put things right, etc.).[32]
As far as Yandell is concerned, this account is not paradoxical.

Before commenting on Yandell's account of MMC, and the larger
issue of the first specification of the GGD, I have yet to look at
Yandell's comments on proposition (E).[33] He has just three things
to say. First, the fact that S' in (E) is conceivable does not entail that
S' can be created.[34] Here, he makes the point (discussed earlier in
Chapter 2 (p. 36)) that although it is true that a world not created
by God could exist, it is not logically possible for God to create
a world not created by him.[35] Second, evidence concerning what
possible agents might do must be derived from what actual persons
have done.[36] We have access only to the activities of actual persons,
not possible persons. Third, he says that it would be a fallacy
'to infer that the members of the reference class (all actual and
possible persons) contains some subset of possible persons who
would (collectively or distributively) fare morally better (or worse)
than have members of the sample class (of all actual persons).'[37] To
argue thus is like inferring from the fact that all known elephants
(which is the sample class) fear mice that the reference class of all
elephants has a subset of elephants (which are unobserved) which
enjoy mice's company.[38] Thus he says, either we are familiar with
what possible persons would do if they were created, or we have no
idea as to what they might do. If it is the former, then this alternative
is evidence for (E); if the latter, then this alternative does not detract
from statement (E).[39]

It may be that Yandell's defence of (E) is not as ironclad as
he thinks. It might be argued that through the Biblical record
observations of some sort are possible regarding the human nature

of Christ. That is, according to the theist, though the historical Jesus is supposed to have had a supernatural origin, he is also supposed to have been complete in respect to his humanity. Furthermore, though the theist holds that the divine nature was somehow united with the human nature, he also holds that their natures were distinct. Thus he could hold that the human nature in question, being distinct, could experience moral growth and make moral choices independent of the divine nature. That is, the power and desire to do good or make good choices could conceivably come from Jesus's human nature, say a human nature that has the property of transworld holiness (TWH, as suggested earlier). It might then be argued that Jesus thus conceived is a one-member subset of the reference class. Furthermore, this one-membered subset could have a bearing on the subset of possible persons of the reference class. One might thereby give sense to a claim such as, *There are possible persons who, if created, would always choose freely and rightly.* But would we have any reason to think such a claim to be true? Clearly, there seems to be no difficulty with conceiving such a subset. As for reason to think that it might be true, maybe at least a beginning could be made. Conditions for an agent succeeding in the way described in (E) might include such aids as divine superintending, limitless access to divine power for enablement, etc. If one reasons thus, this could be viewed as evidence in support of the view that there could be (a) person(s) who might have chosen better than the set S of actual persons because the subset of possible persons might have chosen courses of action similar to those made by the person of the one-membered subset, viz., Jesus.

I should like to make three points regarding Yandell's discussion of the MMC concept and the paradox Kane sees in it. The first has to do with the distinction I made earlier regarding MMC and GMMC (cf. p. 127). In his discussion of the 'sinner paradox,' the argument Yandell attributes to Kane is as follows:

(1) Forgiving sins in this world is logically necessary to the development of a fully mature character.

(2) If sins are forgiven, there were sins to forgive.

So:

(3) A fully developed moral character (logically) requires that there be sins.[40]

If premise (1) is rewritten as a conditional,

(1')   If there is to be development of a fully mature character, then sins are forgiven.

and the conclusion is rewritten as a conditional,

(3')   If there is to be development of a fully mature character, then there were sins to forgive.

we have a pure hypothetical syllogism that does not significantly alter the distinction. The antecedent of premise (1') focuses on *growth* or *development* of fully mature moral character, and for that reason it may be symbolized as GMMC. The consequent may be symbolized as FS. Thus premise (1') may be symbolized as,

(1') $GMMC \rightarrow FS$.

The antecedent of the second conditional can be symbolized as FS because it is equivalent to the consequent of premise (1'), and the consequent can be symbolized as S, which gives us the following conditional,

(2) $FS \rightarrow S$.

In the conclusion the antecedent focuses again on the development of mature moral character; hence I shall translate the antecedent of the conclusion as GMMC and, finally, the consequent as S. The entire syllogism reads as,

(1') $GMMC \rightarrow FS$
(2) $FS \rightarrow S$
Therefore
(3') $GMMC \rightarrow S$.

The reconstruction makes explicit the validity of the original argument and helps call attention to the fact that the focus of the original argument is not upon MMC but GMMC.

Second, regarding the two axioms of character theory, viz., (α) and (β), Yandell admits to having said very little as to their scope. One might be tempted to ask, Might these axioms of character theory apply to angels, perhaps even to God, as well as to humans? Does

God experience GMMC or possess MMC? Or does he possess anything like MMC? Regarding MMC, a cluster of concerns arise. If the axioms apply to God as they do to humans, then God would have to endure or experience certain episodic properties *if* he is to possess certain character traits or dispositional properties. If courage and bearing-pain-with-fortitude are virtues necessary to MMC, then if God is to have the latter, he must experience fear and pain as episodic properties.

Traditional theism has tended to the view that God is above such things as experiencing pain or fear. That is, though God has been pictured as being very much aware of the sufferings of humanity, he has not been thought of as a being who *himself* has to endure evils in order to experience growth in character or in order to possess moral character. The concept of incarnation is a different matter. Here the picture is that of the God-man, not of God simpliciter.

Third, regarding MMC, Yandell acknowledges that he has only developed the concept in a preliminary fashion. I should like to explore here the possibility that there might be different sorts of MMC concepts. Yandell defends the view that there can be no growth to MMC unless there are evils – evils which are necessary if GMMC is to take place – and furthermore that a person cannot possess MMC unless he also possesses certain dispositional properties which in turn logically require episodic properties of a certain sort, some of which are evil. Beyond the pattern Yandell suggests, there is a range of alternatives which the theist might want to consider. Some theists, for example, might want to talk in Augustinian terms about pre-lapsarian humanity. They might take the fall as an historical occurrence and hold that pre-lapsarian humanity enjoyed a state of innocence and walked in obedience to the will of God. Given this pristine state, they might argue that growth to MMC without any evil is a possibility. Further, they might argue that pre-lapsarian humanity was capable of possessing some measure of MMC without having to first endure any evil episodic properties. I shall call this sort of MMC, MMC_1. Regarding MMC_1, the theist might make out a case similar to the line argued by G. Stanley Kane (even though the latter's sympathies are not in line with theism) when he says: 'the only necessary condition for the development of a fully mature moral character is the resistance of whatever temptation to evil may be present.'[41] But no actual evil is necessary, either for growth to moral maturity or for the possession of moral maturity.

If we continue with an Augustinian line, post-lapsarian humanity might be able to experience growth toward another sort of moral maturity, which I shall call MMC_2. MMC_2 might include as necessary ingredients the virtues of forgiveness, courage, pain-bearing-fortitude, etc. Such ingredients are necessary to mature moral character because moral evil has become a reality. Given these conditions, if person S' sins against person S'', S'' can be said to possess mature moral character only if S'' exhibits a willingness to forgive (under certain conditions). Thus the entrance of moral evil alters what is requisite to mature moral character.

One might extend the concepts of MMC and GMMC so as to make them applicable to some future blissful state. John Hick only hints at it.[42] Perhaps this is another sort of MMC, say, MMC_3, which cannot be experienced or possessed until after MMC_2 is possessed. Exactly why this might be so I need not say, since it is my purpose here only to suggest that there might be alternate MMC concepts which might hold some promise for the theist who is looking for plausible and suitable specifications of the GGD.

I have already called attention to certain limitations and deficiencies in Yandell's specification of MMC. One main objection raised is that the virtues requiring evils discussed in connection with MMC have not been shown to be necessary to MMC. I shall reserve further comment upon Yandell's specification of the GGD in terms of growth to moral maturity until after I have outlined John Hick's soul-growth theodicy. I turn now to that.

3. THE 'SOUL-GROWTH' THEODICY OF JOHN HICK

An alternative account of the growth-to-moral-maturity defence is John Hick's soul-growth theodicy. Central to the defence is a 'hybrid' free will defence that affirms the traditional doctrine of omnipotence, i.e., God is the actual or potential controller of all things, and he could have maintained absolute control, but of his own will he limited himself by bringing into existence free agents. It is a theodicy with a distinct Irenaean rather than Augustinian flavor as to the picture given of humans and creation. The Augustinian tradition views humans as created by God in a finished state, as finitely perfect beings[43] intended to fulfill God's will and purpose, and as falling away from this purpose. According to the Irenaean picture, persons are 'still in process of creation.'[44]

Irenaeus developed the idea of process in terms of a distinction between 'image' and 'likeness' which he thought was derivable from Genesis 1:26.[45] Humans were created in the image of God, he thought, and they were to grow into God's likeness, not by means of a divine gift, but through a process of 'hazardous adventure in individual freedom.'[46] God's reason for making this world then, is to 'bring many sons to glory,'[47] and this reason has a determining effect on the sort of world he creates.

At the very heart of the problem of evil is sin. And the central question is, Why has God allowed sin to enter creation? At this point Hick offers a free will defence formulated in three stages. The first, as he sees it, 'establishes a conception of divine omnipotence,'[48] which recognizes limitations of a logical sort, pointed out earlier in Chapter 2.[49] The second stage of the argument contends that persons who are free, must be able to choose good or evil. As to the third phase, Hick grants the points of stages one and two, but now the question is, Could God not have so made persons that they would have freely done only that which is right or good? In response to the question, Hick agrees with J. L. Mackie's contention that he (God) had such an option.[50] But there is another question which Hick thinks that Mackie has not considered, viz., 'Is it logically possible for God so to make men that they will freely respond to Himself in love and trust and faith?'[51] To this question Hick offers a 'no' on the 'ground' that if love, trust, and faith are to be authentic, they cannot be forced. They must be offered freely, and the only sort of freedom that will do the job for Hick is an epistemic sort, since this is the only sort of freedom that allows humans to be autonomous. It is epistemic in the sense that God distances himself from humans cognitively. As Hick says,

In other words, the reality and presence of God must not be borne in upon men in the coercive way in which their natural environment forces itself upon their attention. The world must be to man, to some extent at least, *etsi deus non daretur*, 'as if there were no God.' God must be a hidden deity, veiled by His creation. He must be knowable, but only by a mode of knowledge that involves a free personal response on man's part, this response consisting in an uncompelled interpretative activity whereby we experience the world as mediating the divine presence. Such a need for human faith-response will secure for man the only kind of freedom that is possible for him in relation to God, namely cognitive freedom, carrying with it the momentous possibility of being aware or unaware of his Maker.[52]

This epistemic distance is not something that enters as a result of some historic fall. Rather, humans from the very beginning were distant from God and lived more closely to the world than to God.[53] In fact, an 'inevitable' outgrowth of this epistemic distance, is that humans will direct their efforts to organize life 'apart from God,' and in 'self-centered competitiveness' with their fellows.[54] Epistemic distance from God and allegiance to the world 'constitutes fallenness' right from the beginning, so that for Hick there is no historic fall.[55]

Only God can save humans from the 'fallenness' or 'self-centered alienation' from himself (God). The way to God and heaven is by way of divine redemption, a redemption offered freely in the Gospel. The '*O felix culpa*' insight of the medievals, thus constitutes a principle central to his theodicy. Human fallenness, not an historic fall, provides opportunity for God to manifest his love through redemption, which provides a way whereby humans, created in the image of God, may grow into his likeness, enabled and enobled by divine grace. This enablement and enoblement takes place in a world created as an environment for soul-growth. That is, the world is a vale for soul-growth – evils such as pain and suffering are allowed by God in order to provide opportunities for persons to experience soul-stretching and growth. Even so-called gratuitous evil provides an opportunity for the testing and growth of faith.

I shall confine critical discussion to several points of rather pivotal concern. The waters through which Hick (or any theodicist for that matter) has to chart a course for his theodicy may be treacherous. The situation facing him is not unlike the one faced by the ancient mariners who were imagined to pass through the mythological Straits of Messina.[56] If in formulating a defence, there is no depravity thesis (which thesis might make at least moral evil likely, because a depraved nature of some sort is *likely* to result in evil choices sooner or later), then does the defence in question account for *actual* evil or only for its possibility?[57] Or, if in order to account for actual evil, a depravity thesis of some sort *is* affirmed, then how can such a thesis be formulated without making evil a necessity? Either course may threaten the very lifeblood of a theodicy. Let us speak of the former danger as the 'Charybdis' and the latter as the 'Scylla.' How might the theist avoid the Charybdis of accounting for only the *possibility* of evil?

Among the many options, five are discussed in this study.[58] The first, the transworld depravity notion of Alvin Plantinga, has already been examined at some length in Chapter 5, and the difficulties with this option have been flagged. The second may be developed along lines similar to those found in Aristotle's discussion of practical reason in his *Nichomachean Ethics*. More particularly, in the context of his discussion of the *incontinent man* (ακρατες, *akrates*), he distinguishes between two kinds of desire: desire (ορεξις, *orexis*) which works in accordance with practical reason, and the motive of passion or desire (επιθυμια *epithumia*, which is closely connected to bodily or psychological states), which works against the desire that cooperates with reason and against practical reason. Prima facie, it might be thought one could account for actual evil choices on such a view quite handily by affirming that persons, like Aristotle's incontinent person, have been created with both kinds of desires – i.e., with desire which is in accordance with practical reason and with desire which is not. Evil choices come about, then, when persons allow themselves to be motivated by desire which goes against practical reason. But at least two difficulties stand in the way of taking the view seriously as a way out of the above difficulty. First, the idea that God creates creatures with a desire which acts contrary to practical reason goes against the belief held by mainstream theists that God originally made creatures good. Second, Aristotle's view cannot account for the *origin* of evil choices made by the incontinent man; for the person who yields to passion which runs contrary to practical reason possesses a knowledge of the wrongness of the particular action *prior* to his coming under any kind of negative influence of negative passion. Any view which is developed along Aristotelian lines is going to have to deal with the question, Why does the incontinent person, who originally possesses knowledge of the wrongness of a given action, then allow himself to come under the influence of negative passion?

The third way suggested by Richard Swinburne, on some points has some similarity to Aristotle's proposal, but there are important differences as well. Swinburne's analysis of the doctrine of proneness to sin is found in 'Original Sinfulness.'[59] First he points out with regard to the theological doctrine of Original Sin, that there are three main parts to a full account of the doctrine:[60] a doctrine of 'an initial proneness to sin'; second, a doctrine that this original tendency is brought about by an original sin of the first person, i.e., Adam; third, there is also a doctrine of Original Guilt.[61] Second, a person is morally praiseworthy or blameworthy with regard to an action, dependent upon his beliefs. He is blameworthy for doing something he believes to be wrong, and praiseworthy for doing something he believes to be right.

From his two philosophical assumptions, he says it follows that there are two kinds of wrongdoing, objective and subjective.[62] The former involves those things which are 'obligatory not to do,'[63] and the latter involves those things which the *agent* believes he is under obligation not to do.[64]

Persons are a complex of beliefs and desires,[65] and the latter in particular are understood as 'natural inclinations to do certain sort of actions.'[66] The spectrum of desires is wide enough to include desires for friendship, power, food, drink, comforts, etc. The desires natural to us, 'lead' us into situations of conflict, i.e., conflicts with the desires of others. When our desires lead us to seek after more than our 'fair share' in a world of limited goods, those desires are objectively sinful. He says, 'Since seeking for ourselves more than our fair share of the available food, friendship, power, and such like, is sinful, there is in man a proneness to objective sin, whether or not man realizes this.'[67] On the subjective side, when God conferred upon humans the 'capacity and inclination' to act contrary to his conscience, they were given the 'capacity for subjective sin.'[68]

There are two elements involved in the propensity to sin: 'moral belief and self-centered desire.'[69] There is no moral culpability in the *fact* of the first, and regarding the second, Swinburne says that the propensity to sin or 'self-centered desire' is biological – we inherit it 'through our genes.'[70] But for Swinburne such desires do not necessitate sin, they only influence our wills which are free.

Accordingly, original sin or the fall came about as a result of the movement of the will in response to a desire which is 'self-centered.' This desire is something that is inherited genetically. Following Swinburne, one could argue that the genetically determined desires which are a precondition of sin are biologically useful and hence are not bad on the whole.[71]

However attractive the proposal might initially appear, there might be a feature about it repugnant to the traditional theist. While the proposal does not cast any doubt on the first man being innocent initially of actual sin, it does suggest that he was not initially well endowed with moral propensities or intellectual capacities.[72]

A fourth way is a proposal by Hick. According to Hick God wants the free response of moral agents to himself in a process of soul-growth. A necessary condition to this process is that a person be free – free in the sense that he have a limited creativity. For Hick this freedom is cognitive, a freedom that exists because of an epistemic distance that exists between God and humans – a condition that can itself obtain because God is hidden from humanity. Humans are placed in an environment where God is not directly present; an environment where humans are free to believe or not believe in God. On this account Hick believes he can justify both natural and moral evil. Sin, or moral evil, is justified on the ground that it is the 'virtually inevitable' result of man's being epistemically distant from God. Natural evil is justified on the ground that it is an aspect of 'an appropriate environment in which morally and spiritually immature creatures may develop morally and spiritually.'[73]

The account presents the following difficulty. On the one hand, Hick maintains that in order for a person to do something that has moral worth, he must be free – free to believe or not believe in God. On the other hand, Hick speaks of 'the inevitability of sin as a corollary of man's epistemic distance.'[74] Still another place he talks about the 'virtual inevitability of sin.'[75] It appears that while trying to avoid the 'Charybdis' of accounting for only the *possibility* of sin Hick comes close to being consumed by the 'Scylla' – evil is a necessity. Hick wants to affirm both the inevitability of sin and the freedom of moral agents who sin. One or both of two important reasons may account for his wanting both theses. The first is that if some moral evil were not an inevitable result of freedom, then his theodicy would only account for natural evil (for Hick, natural evil accentuates the hiddenness of God, and it is necessary to an environment that will be suitable for soul-growth), because on this account (where sin is not inevitable) full maturity of the soul could be attained without sin. The second point is that calling into question as he does the Augustinian concept of the fall (that humans were created in a state of innocence and lost it in the fall), if he did not hold to the inevitability of sin in some sense, then his view regarding freedom would hold open the possibility that some, or possibly all, humans might be able to live lives of sinless perfection and therefore might be able to achieve soul-growth without the help of God – a doctrine that conflicts with Hick's belief that divine redemption is a necessary part of the soul-growth process.

The preceding discussion suggests that Hick faces a dilemma. Either he must deny the doctrine of the inevitability of sin and therefore allow that humans could achieve soul-growth without God's help (a move already shown to be unsatisfactory for Hick), or he must affirm the doctrine of the inevitability of sin, which might, depending on how the *inevitability of sin* phrase is interpreted, have rather curious implications. For example, though no particular sin or fall might be necessary, some sin or other *is*, if sin is inevitable. Though a person might be free as to *when* sin is chosen, that is, an agent may elect to commit a sinful act at time t_1 as opposed to t_2, if some sin or other is inevitable, then it is necessary that it occur, and if it is necessary that it occur at some time or other, in what sense can a moral agent be said to be morally responsible for the sin in question?

The fifth proposal is discussed at some length in Chapter 7 in connection with the Redemption Specification of the GGD, so I will not enlarge upon it here.[76] I should like to make two further points – one by way of observation, and the second as an objection to the growth-to-mature-moral-character specification of the GGD. In developing both, I shall draw upon two objections that G. Stanley Kane raises against the soul-making theodicy of John Hick.[77] I shall give account first of the objections as Kane directs them at Hick,[78] and then show how I wish to apply them to Yandell's growth-to-moral-maturity specification of the GGD.

The first of the objections, Kane believes, devastates Hick's theodicy. It is the charge that Hick's view of the world as a 'vale of soul-making' where persons can develop moral character only through a 'fierce struggle against evils,' is pointlessly absurd.[79] Regarding qualities of character contemplated in soul-growth, Kane distinguishes three elements: (1) the process or acquisition of the dispositional properties (which is roughly equivalent to the GMMC concept); (2) possessing the dispositional property (which is roughly equivalent to MMC); (3) the use of the dispositional property, or that property in action.[80] Kane says that on Hick's view, the most important of the above elements is the *possession* of the qualities, since his focus is eschatological, i.e., his attention is upon the final goal where persons achieve or reach 'likeness' to God. Persons struggle through evils in order to achieve soul-growth, but once they reach that long awaited final state, there is 'neither need nor opportunity to put them [virtues] to use.'[81] Kane asks, Is this not a 'cruel joke'? Once in heaven, where virtues are perfected, there is no longer need to exercise them. Hick's answer to Kane is that there can be growth in the final state. That is, there is another order of virtues which belong to the afterlife.[82]

Yandell holds that in all likelihood there will be growth toward moral maturity and the acting out of virtue in the final state. Some theists allow that this process will include evils as necessary conditions to the virtues in question. But if one holds that there are evils in the eschaton, how does this square with the claims of certain New Testament writers (notably John – especially in Revelation 21:4) who describe the final state as without *any* negative elements such as fear, pain, death, etc.? One way to go would be to suggest that morally free agents can continue to grow in the absence of such conditions. This of course raises the question, Why then did God not set things up this way originally, if soul growth can occur without evil?

Hick considers several possible scenarios, one of which is that the virtues which are possessed and exhibited in the final state will transcend those of earth, and the former will be achievable only after the latter have been acquired. Thus Hick may at once avoid the difficulty facing Yandell's position and at the same time provide a partial answer to the difficulty posed by Kane; i.e., after all the struggle and heartache which persons go through in this life in order to reach moral maturity, the virtues they work for in this life are *possessed* in the life to come, and though there is no occasion for their further manifestation or acting out, the possession of virtues necessary to mature moral character in this life is a necessary stage to another sort of soul-growth appropriate to the heavenly state. However, he has no ready answer to the question, Why is the first sort of MMC necessary to the sort that will be sought after in the life to come?

The second point I wish to make is formulated in terms of an objection to the growth-to-mature-moral-character specification of the GGD.[83] Kane, as we have seen, argues that mature moral character is attainable without actual evils. He contends, for example, that such virtues as courage and fortitude may be manifest without evil episodic properties. A person might be said to exhibit courage and fortitude in terms of persistence, steadfastness, and perseverance when called upon to accomplish some long-range goal, such as writing a doctoral dissertation.[84] He adds, a person could also manifest the dispositional property *compassion* toward the person engaged in such a long-term project. Kane is claiming that though these virtues may be different from the sort of courage and fortitude manifest when a person faces certain evils, the latter set of virtue traits have a lot in common with those Kane describes. This leaves the theist with a 'formidable problem.' For in order to give an adequate justification for his soul-making defence, the theist has to show that the difference between the two sets of virtues is such, that those which require evil are of such positive worth that in spite of the 'disvalue' of the evils they require, their existence (of the goods in question) is of greater positive value than the existence of those virtues which require no evil.[85]

Hick's response is roughly that whenever there is real character growth, a close examination of the situations which give rise to the growth involves in one way or another, experiences which are negative (evil episodic properties). 'It . . . does not seem to me,' he says, 'that there is a viable possibility of a "soul-making" world from which we exclude all risk of severe hardship and injury, with desperate and even suicidal misery as the extreme point of the one continuum, and death as the extreme point of the other.'[86] To this it may be added that the world does not have to contain the particular evils that it does in order to be a soul-making environment, but it does have to have some evils which are real.[87] On his account evils are not required for certain virtues that are necessary to a mature soul; rather, if evil were to be completely eliminated, the laws of nature would have to be so altered that the resultant environment would not be suited to soul-growth.[88] Thus Hick holds that evil is logically necessary for soul-growth. If the theist chooses to follow Hick on this matter, his defence would count as a specification of the GGD since in order to be a specification of the GGD, the evil in question or some evil like it has to be *logically* necessary to the good contemplated. Whether Hick is right in his contention that a world without evil could not be an environment for soul-growth is still open to debate.

The moral-maturity sort of defence and the soul-growth theodicy have been given due consideration as possible specifications of the GGD. Significant objections to both formulations were found, but it is argued in Chapter 7 that these objections might be handled by a variant of the moral-maturity defence, and on the condition that it is incorporated into a larger complex defence. And second, some of

Hick's principles in the soul-growth theodicy are incorporable in a specification of the GGD yet to be presented in Chapter 7.

Four disparate accounts of the 'proneness to sin' doctrine were subjected to scrutiny, none were found to be especially satisfactory. A fifth, to be offered in Chapter 7 in conjunction with the Redemption Specification, though not necessary to the specification, is judged to be more attractive. I turn now to that third specification of the GGD, and our final account of the 'proneness to sin' doctrine.

7

O *Felix Culpa*, Redemption, and the Greater-Good Defence

Common to Alvin Plantinga's Free Will Defence, John Hick's Soul-Growth Theodicy, and Keith Yandell's Growth-to-Moral-Maturity Specification of his Greater-Good Defence, is a concept that almost gets lost in laberynthian discussions of possible-worlds ontology, epistemic distance, and justification patterns. The concept is redemption, and in the following I argue that the concept in question should be given a more central role in the formulation of a Christian theistic response to the problem of evil than the above defences might be thought to suggest. An effort is made to furnish a preliminary account of how this concept might be used to formulate a specification of the Greater-Good Defence. The defence runs roughly as follows.[1]

GGD   For every evil that God permits, there is a good state of affairs which counterbalances and which logically requires the evil in question (or some other evil of at least equal negative value), and some evil is overbalanced by a good state of affairs (or good states of affairs) which logically require the evil in question (or some other evil of at least equal negative value).[2]

In order to meet the above criterion, a specification must be of a good or kind of goods which, when separately considered, logically require an evil of some sort, and the good or kind of goods when separately considered, must either counterbalance or overbalance the evils they require. But the GGD does not require that a specification be comprehensive – that it cover all the goods thus justified

144

because it is a specification. It only requires that a GGD specification meet the conditions of both conjuncts. If a proposal satisfies only one of the conjuncts, then the proposal counts as a 'partial' GGD specification. If the good in question only counterbalances some evil or other that it requires, then it falls within the scope of goods which are contemplated in the first conjunct; but if the good overbalances some evil or other that it requires, then it falls within the scope of those goods which are contemplated in the second conjunct.

The specification of the GGD I wish to propose meets the conditions of both conjuncts. Simply stated, the good which logically requires the *existence* of evil is *redemption*. And the sort of evil that must exist in order for there to be redemption in any meaningful way is moral evil – evil that is brought about by moral agents who abuse their freedom of choice. Pre-lapsarian humanity does not need redemption, but post-lapsarian humanity does. It is precisely this point that led some of the early church fathers to view the fall as a 'happy' event. Influence of this early perception can be detected in the mainstream of theodicy literature down to the present. According to Hick, some form of the 'happy fall' concept is thematic to both the Augustinian and Irenaean theodicies.[3]

The notion in early thought was part of the fuller paradoxical locution, "'*O certe necessarium Adae peccatum, quod Christi morte deletum est! O felix culpa, quae talem ac tantum meruit habere redemporem!* (O fortunate crime (or, happy fault), which merited [to have] such and so great a redeemer!)."'[4] Known down through the centuries as the '*felix culpa*' principle, the above utterance occurs in the Roman Missal as part of the '*Exultet*,' a hymn of praise offered to God, after the paschal candle is lit and placed on its stand,[5] which is celebrated on Holy Saturday – the Saturday before Easter. The utterance became part of the Easter liturgy perhaps as early as the fifth, but no later than the seventh century.[6]

As to the author of the 'felix culpa' utterance, Arthur Lovejoy lists several possible candidates. St. Ambrose of the fourth century A.D. is mentioned because of his remark that Adam's sin brought 'more benefit than harm.'[7] Another has suggested St. Ennodius of Pavia (d. 521).[8] Most noteworthy among them is Augustine. Lovejoy conjectures that this is because of a reference which Augustine made to his having written a hymn in his discussion of the 'fall of the sons of God.' But as Lovejoy correctly points out, the context shows clearly that the hymn is not the '*O felix culpa*.'[9]

The authorship question aside, Lovejoy and Walker make two

points important to the proposed specification of the GGD. In the Latin locution the fall of the human race is reckoned as a 'happy fault' (*felix culpa*) *and* as 'certainly necessary' (*certe necessarium*).[10] The 'fault' or 'fall' is happy because it provides occasion for something good to take place, viz., redemption. At the same time the reality of the fault confronts us when we see its intrinsic negative value – inherently it (the fall) is an evil thing. Its positive value is instrumental only. Moreover, this 'happy fault' is 'certainly necessary' not because it follows necessarily from some flaw residing in the moral agents who precipitate it. It is a necessity that attaches to the evil in question because without it or something like it, redemption would be gratuitous. Redemption is meaningful and possible only against the backdrop of some sort of fall. As Lovejoy says, 'Adam's sin was . . . necessary to the very possibility of the redemptive act, which, it may be supposed, was by the author of the hymn, conceived as itself a necessary, and the central event in the divine plan of the terrestrial history.'[11]

John Hick sees in the *'felix culpa'* principle a whole theodicy ready to be unpacked, and he unpacks it with an emphasis on soul-making. He does so not along Augustinian lines, in which humans, the chief actors, are regarded as having been created by God in a 'finished state' of 'finite perfection,' but along Irenaean lines, in which humans are 'in process of creation.'[12] It is a process through which God desires to bring many persons to glory.[13] In this process persons are 'drawn by God' from a lower life of biological existence to a higher-quality life involving personal fellowship with God through Christ as redeemer.[14]

The 'starting-point' for Hick is the fact that humans are created in the image of God *and* that they are called to a soul-making process whereby they reach out to become *like* God.[15] Redemption has a place in the overall theodicy, since the only way whereby a fallen humanity can be rescued from its self-centered alienation from God is by a divinely initiated redemptive act.[16]

Working with some of Hick's ideas, I want to argue on an Augustinian base (because it appears to have fewer liabilities, a point which I hope to make shortly) that some sort of fall is necessary to the meaningfulness of redemption as a *theological concept*, and to the possibility of redemption as a *restorative act*.[17] On the conceptual side, some sort of the evil-of-the-fall notion is built into the concept of *redemption*. On the *restorative act* side, on a priori grounds, an act such as redemption is gratuitous unless some sort of fall has occurred. If the preceding point is basically correct, then it looks as if we have a good which in order to exist requires a prior existence of evil. We have not yet looked at the question, Does the good of redemption overbalance or even counterbalance the evil it requires? Let us assume for the moment a point that is argued later, viz., that the way divine love can be manifest in a fall-redemption world has a special merit or value that a world without a fall of some sort cannot have because it cannot provide the conditions needed for a disclosure of love in this special way. On this assumption we might have a specification where the good which logically requires an evil counterbalances, perhaps even overbalances, the evil required. Assuming that the good in question overbalances the evil it logically requires, let us call this the 'R-specification.' The task now before us is to look more closely at some of the ideas and issues important to the suggestion, in order to obtain a fuller picture of the R-specification. Then we shall take up the matter of whether the good specified might be viewed legitimately as overbalancing the evil it requires.

It might be helpful to sketch something of a theological prolegomena to serve as a handy reference point for the proposal. Let us look first at the concepts of *redemption* and *necessity*, principally as they figure in the belief-system of traditional Christianity as conceived, for example, by Augustine, Anselm, and Aquinas. In a rough and ready way, the source or cause of redemption according to the aforementioned medieval thinkers is the love of God. In very general terms the concept of redemption involves the idea that God's purpose and plan for post-lapsarian humanity is salvation, which includes forgiveness and a new life extending forever into the future, vouchsafed by Christ's atonement, but conditioned on a repentance/faith response on the part of the creature.

The term *necessity* has come to have a very important role in distinctions made relating to the doctrine of the atonement, a kindred notion to the notion of redemption. Two central views regarding the necessity of the atonement have been distinguished in theological discourse: hypothetical necessity and consequent absolute necessity. The former view, held by Augustine and Aquinas,[18] is the idea that God could have forgiven sin and brought about salvation without an atonement, but the atonement is the route whereby the greatest number of blessings can be made available, and by this means God's grace is most gloriously demonstrated. So on this account, given the circumstances of post-lapsarian humanity, atonement is the way God redeems, but there is nothing in his nature that requires he take this route. Strictly speaking, there is no necessity to the atonement, but it is merely the most *fitting way* for God to provide redemption. *Consequent absolute necessity*, on the other hand, is the view that, 'Necessarily, if God redeems, he does so through an atonement.' While God was not bound to save, since salvation was his purpose, 'it was necessary to secure this salvation through a satisfaction that could be rendered only through substitutionary sacrifice and blood-bought redemption.'[19] The consequent-absolute-necessity view, where something in the nature of God requires that he redeem, is especially compatible with supralapsarianism – the doctrine that God creates the universe in order to redeem it. Furthermore, a doctrinal synthesis of this sort would strongly support the *'felix culpa'* principle. And presumably, on such a view, the good of redemption would likely count at least as a counterbalancing good, since the good of redemption is something required for some reason or other by God's nature. Just how plausible and desirable the synthesis is remains to be seen.

I should like to make three points regarding evil as actual. First, the evil putatively justified, is not merely possible evil (some possible evil or other) or the 'possibility of evil' (an occasion or environment which allows evil to occur). An evil necessary to the good of redemption has to be real – it has to exist in the world with which we are familiar. Second, the evil paired with the good that justifies it also has to be real in the sense that it is genuinely antithetic to God's goodness and what we know to be goodness. Thus, if the evil in question were not a means to some good, it would have no positive value, and so agents who did not (try to) eliminate or avoid it (God included) would be blameworthy for failing to do so if they could (eliminate it or avoid it).[20] Third, a fall of some sort or other is logically necessary to redemption, but no one particular moral evil as opposed to some other is necessary.[21] According to one interpretation of the Biblical narrative of the fall, the prohibition that was issued in the Garden required that Adam and Eve not eat of the fruit of a certain tree. Here two points are in order. The doctrine of the fall need not be tied to such a literal reading of the Biblical data. Second, a fall could have come about any one of a number of ways and any one of the moral failures would have given meaning to the redemptive act.

On the creaturely side, in some way or other the agents who precipitate the fall are blameworthy for having done so. On the basis of some sort of libertarian thesis the agents would be thought to enjoy some measure of freedom of choice, and thus to be responsible for their actions.

In the above, I argue that in order for redemption to be meaningful, some sort of fall or moral failure is necessary. In our discussion the doctrine of the necessity of the atonement came into view. Little if anything was said as to the nature of the atonement. The following is in small measure designed to take care of that hiatus.

More generally construed, atonement may be viewed as including at least two components: repentance and reparation or payment.[22] Repentance involves first an acknowledgement on the part of the person who did the wrong that he is responsible for the offense. In addition, there needs to be some change of mind regarding the act. There must be evidence of a desire to turn away from the wrong, or avoid similar sorts of behavior in the future. By contrast, reparation or payment involves an attempt if possible to make things right, to make payment or restore what was taken away, or what was rightfully the possession of another person. In the following, I will argue that repentance is not constitutive of the divine Atonement, but is rather a condition to accepting God's gift of atonement, and that Christ's atonement is mainly reparation, or as some would say, ransom in the sense of 'payment.'

Given the Christian understanding that the human condition suffers from the consequences of sin, there is strong indication that help for rescue must come from outside – from God. How has the Church viewed that rescue effort? As a matter of fact, there is little in the way of a definitive statement of the nature of the Atonement, when compared with the clear and definitive formulation of the doctrine of the Trinity in the credal statement of the Council of Nycea and the doctrine of the Incarnation in the pronouncement of the Council of Chalcedon. The only thing that the literature strongly indicates is that theologians have been at odds as to how the Atonement is to be understood. Views range from the 'example' theory of Socinus, to Augustine's and Origen's 'ransom' view. There is Biblical evidence for taking God's redemptive act as a ransom, since that is stated as a central purpose of the Atonement in both Matthew's and Mark's gospels.[23] The idea of ransom appears to be indicated by these passages, but there is controversy as to how central the notion of ransom is, since those who hold a satisfaction view of the atonement reject the atonement as ransom. But even if a ransom view is held, theologians have puzzled over the agent to whom payment is made. Origen held that ransom is paid by Christ to Satan. But why should one think Satan needed payment? If one argues that Christ 'made payment' to God, the suggestion might be thought reducible to, 'God makes payment to God,' if one takes seriously the claim that Christ is God. If payment is made by Christ to the Father, then that might be taken to suggest that somehow the Father is offended by sin, but Christ the Son is not, since the former requires payment, whereas the Son does not. There is yet another way to go with the ransom view. The theist could contend that on a Chalcedonian view, the human nature – Jesus of Nazareth – made payment to God. The ransom view aside, there is a satisfaction or reparation view offered by Swinburne. He suggests that Christ's offering on the cross could be construed as a gift such that, those seeing that they need redemption could freely choose to accept God's offer in faith. He comments, 'On this model Christ's death has no efficacy until men choose to plead it in atonement for their sins.'[24] It is thus taken as an offering of payment for sin available to the sinner, and the sinner can take this gift and present it to God in faith. Payment then is something that God offers so that the sinner can make payment to God. Until he perceives this gift and offers it in faith, it does not count as 'penance and reparation.' Acceptance of this gift involves an act of faith, which may be taken as the positive side of a believer's turning to God for help. Swinburne includes apology and repentance as part of the atonement notion. Strictly speaking, those of the Augustinian and Calvinian tradition might disagree, since repentance and apology have been construed as human actions. If the atonement is something that God alone does, in order for it to be a matter of grace, then repentance and apology cannot be constitutive of atonement.[25] Moreover, if salvation is to be a matter of grace, theologians of the Reformed tradition have argued, among others, that repentance and faith itself must somehow issue from grace. Whatever the case, the Atonement can be viewed then as satisfaction in the sense that payment is made for sin by the sinner by accepting God's free gift.

God is also an actor in the whole drama, because he is the one who decrees redemption and who assumes the role of redeemer. During the Reformation era, two positions regarding his decrees[26] were distinguished, supralapsarianism and infralapsarianism.[27] L. Berkhof comments that supralapsarianism 'proceeds on the assumption that in planning the rational mind passes from the end to the means in a retrograde movement, so that what is first in design is last in accomplishment.'[28] The order of the decrees according to this view is:

(a)   The decree of God to glorify Himself, and particularly to magnify His grace and justice in the salvation of some of the perdition of other rational creatures, which exist in the divine mind as yet only as possibilities.

(b)   The decree to create those who were thus elected and probated.

(c)   The decree to permit them to fall.

(d)   The decree to justify the elect and to condemn the nonelect.[29]

The order of the decrees according to the infralapsarian position reflects a 'more historical' arrangement:

(a)   The decree to create man in holiness and blessedness.

(b)   The decree to permit man to fall by the self-determination of his own will.

(c)   The decree to save a certain number out of this guilty aggregate.

(d)   The decree to leave the remainder in their self-determination in sin, and to subject them to the righteous punishment which their sin deserves.[30]

Historically, Augustine, Anselm, and Aquinas held views which are fairly well in line with the infralapsarian position, and those in the mainstream of orthodox theism who were not part of the Counter Reformation have tended to support infralapsarianism rather than supralapsarianism. Supralapsarianism was introduced by a 'certain class of Augustinians'[31] and was affirmed later by John Calvin in his early theological career, and reaffirmed by Beza, Calvin's successor in Geneva.[32] One of the more weighty objections to the supralapsarian view has been the contention that given this scheme of things, it might be a greater good for God not to create. Whether one opts for the view that God creates in order to redeem (supralapsarianism) or whether one holds the doctrine that God first decrees to create, then to allow the fall, and then to effect redemption (infralapsarianism) may depend on how strong a reading one gives to the *'felix culpa'* principle. For example, the theist who sees redemption rather than creation as the principal value might on this account be more comfortable with supralapsarianism than infralapsarianism. Of course, if the theist argues that God created in order to redeem, then if redemption is something God wills, and in order to bring it about, He has to allow the fall, then the theist might face at least two major difficulties. First, such a view might attribute to God an ethical stance that is both deontological and teleological if the prohibition has a deontological base, and the allowance to sin is teleological. On this account the fall is blameworthy (on deontological grounds), and praiseworthy (on teleological grounds). If the theist allows that the fall is justified, as in the account I have given of Adam's fall, then the fall though still an evil is not so bad after all, since on the teleological scheme, the ends are all that count (there are intrinsically evil ends, but not intrinsically evil acts). Is there any way out of either or both difficulties? One possible route might be to affirm that God desired to create, and that created free moral agents are obligated to God according to some sort of deontological ethic. Such an account is not incompatible with his allowing some sort of fall and his making good use of that fall. On such a view, the free moral agent's fall would be an evil, but it is something God can use to a good end. The proposed construction is consonant with infralapsarianism but incompatible with supralapsarianism as it is generally conceived, since the latter view holds that God created in order to redeem. According to the proposal, God created the world not in order to bring about redemption, but ultimately to manifest His love. The choice of the free moral agent to disobey God is wrong, but God can make good use of it in providing redemption. Thus for God, the fall in question becomes a means to a good end, but His ethical modus operandi was and continues to be deontological.[33]

As to whether the fall is likely or even possible, Hick has drawn attention to what may be a major flaw in the Augustinian description of pre-lapsarian humanity. Pre-lapsarian humans, according to Augustine, have unspoiled wills; and, as Hick argues, the prospect of Adam and Eve's turning away from the good purpose of God and choosing a 'lesser reality' is a 'glaring improbability.'

I should like to propose the following resolution to the difficulty (of accounting for the likelihood of the fall). Suppose that pre-lapsarian Adam and Eve, on the basis of information given to them by God, know that a violation of a certain prohibition regarding the fruit of a certain tree – the tree of the knowledge of good and evil

– would bring about disastrous consequences. Suppose further that they come by another piece of information (either as a result of some rational process or other that is reliable, or because God discloses it to them), such that they know that if they fall, a counterbalancing, perhaps even overbalancing good would result. We have then the following scenario. Adam and Eve are both morally obligated to refrain from taking the forbidden fruit. But they also know that the evil of taking the fruit will become a means to some counterbalancing, perhaps even overbalancing good.[34] They might even know that the good would be redemption. They would thus be obligated to refrain from an evil that they know to be justified, i.e., God is just in allowing it. We have before us an instance of an evil which is both justified and someone has an obligation to try to remove it.

In the above, that which is right, viz., *refraining from eating the forbidden fruit*, arguably might not result in the greater amount of good over evil when compared with the result of *eating the fruit*, because the latter act brings about circumstances which make redemption meaningful and possible, which result might be at least as great a good as the good resulting from obedience. Most theists perhaps would hold that innocence and perfect obedience is the greater good, since redemption's role involves restoring a fallen humanity to a state of 'innocence' by means of justification. That is, the person who believes is constituted and declared righteous by reason of the imputed righteousness of Christ. But a theist might argue that redemption is at least as great a good (envisioned as an end motivationally by Adam and Eve), on the grounds that it (redemption) not only involves a restoration to righteousness, but redemption allows God to demonstrate his love in a way that otherwise he could not. There is a hint in this direction in the words of Peter, when he wrote about the redemptive sufferings of Christ in the context of a brief discourse about anticipatory revelations given to the prophets of old, 'It was revealed to them [the prophets] that they were serving not themselves but you, in the things which have not been announced to you by those who preached the good news to you through the Holy Spirit sent from heaven, things into which angels long to look.'[35] The language suggests that angels who had not fallen were curious to inquire into redemptive revelation, presumably because there was something there about which they were ignorant. The next verse, directs the reader's attention to another revelation, viz., Jesus

Christ, and to the grace that was to 'be brought' to believers. Then, interestingly, there is an exhortation to holiness. The fuller picture is that redemption brings about a restoration to holiness, so that the fall/redemption motif, includes a *restoration* to what was lost in the fall, and beyond that, an unfolding of God's love in a special way. Thus redemption includes the good things that obtained before the fall, with the added values of grace and love that come through the unique channel of God's redemptive revelation, Jesus Christ. I do not wish to contend here that a fall/redemption universe clearly brings about a greater good than a universe where no fall occurs, but only want to argue that there is some plausibility in the suggestion that the former might bring about as much good as one where no fall occurs, and possibly more.

A number of objections to the 'fortunate fall motif' have been raised by Bruce Reichenbach.[36] The first objection is, this sort of justification has weight only if it is reasonable to take the fall as historical. This, Reichenbach avers, is not a viable option since modern science has shown that there was 'no earlier golden era of ideal moral life,' and so he claims that the view that there was a fall is mythological. He cites Hick to back up his claim. The reference to Hick involves a passage, where Hick himself fails to provide a detailed account of why a fall cannot be taken seriously. All one has to do is go over the 'biological, anthropological, geological, and paleontological work of the past century and half,'[37] and one would conclude the position is untenable. It is not my purpose here to show how Hick's claim is mistaken, but rather to call it into question on the ground that it rests on insufficient evidence. However, a theist who might wish to defend an historical fall, admittedly has precious little evidence to go on, except perhaps the Biblical data. There are able Biblical scholars who take an historical reading of the early chapters of Genesis seriously, who also have awareness of the findings of contemporary science.[38] Surely a pre-fallen state is conceivable. That there is little if any evidence for such a state, if there ever was one, should come as no surprise since its time of existence is so far removed from our own. That contemporary scientists have difficulty imagining such a state and its implications for nature, might be evidence of imagination's impoverishment, rather than evidence that such a world never existed.

The second objection is, if this justificatory pattern works, it justifies only moral evil not natural evil. First, this study was not designed to be a theodicy, though the discussion has at times taken on the appearance of a theodicy. Not a lot of attention has been given to natural evil. But a fall/redemption motif could be expanded to handle at least some natural evils. One such strategy is the soul-growth line of Hick and Yandell. That is, if there are to be certain virtues, given the fall, then natural evils are required. Since this has been discussed at some length earlier, I will not expand on it further here.

A number of variables would have to be considered and appraised before any judgment can be made as to which option – obedience or disobedience – holds the greater positive value, if such a judgment can be made at all. Some of those variables are roughly expressed in the following. What is good for God? What is good for humankind? What is good for creation, humankind aside? What is good for some species that might be of greater worth to God than the human family (allowing that there might be such a species)? The rather complex and difficult issue of which option – obedience or disobedience – is a greater good aside, if we assume that redemption, which requires the moral evil of a fall, *is* a greater good than the evil it requires, and further that this good is at least as great a good as (or a greater good than) the positive result accompanying obedience to the original prohibition, can God be moral and require of Adam and Eve obedience? How one answers the question might depend on what sort of ethical principles are entertained, or might be thought 'authorized' or 'warranted' by some sort of theistic ethic (thus far, much of the discussion of the greater-good defence has been in teleological ethical categories, since the focus has been largely on consequences). Working with a deontological approach, one might argue that obedience to God is right no matter what the circumstances. Or one might reach a similar conclusion working with the utilitarian line that obedience to God in general results in the greatest amount of good over evil. (It is only this one act of disobedience [to the prohibition of the probation] that allows a greater good to become a reality, viz., redemption.)[39]

The preceding account is only one possible way to draw the distinction between *right* and *duty*. At best it is only a preliminary and tentative theological and ethical conceptual-scheme for the R-specification. No doubt it raises more questions than it answers. But, then, any more elaborate attempt would take us beyond the limits and concerns of this chapter.

With the basic R-specification in place, I should like to consider two further, perhaps more weighty objections against it. The first is a variation on an objection raised by G. Stanley Kane against Yandell's concept of mature moral character (hereafter, MMC). Kane sees Yandell as holding that forgiveness is logically necessary to MMC. He contends that this means that if there is to be forgiveness, then sin must exist. So the possession of MMC requires the existence of sin. The objection to the view is that the MMC of one person is 'parasitic' on the fall of another. In a somewhat similar fashion the atheist might argue against the R-specification that God's redemption – including his forgiveness, which comes through his redemptive decree and act – is parasitic on the fall of humanity. God cannot be forgiving – i.e., he cannot be disposed to forgive – without the occurrence of the episodic property of man's fall. Another way of putting the difficulty runs as follows: traditionally at least, theologians have argued that the fall provides an opportunity for God to show the redemptive side of his nature. But what sense does it make to speak of the redemptive side of his nature if the 'side' or disposition in question cannot exist apart from the occurrence of an episodic property – the fall?

One possible way of answering the objection involves drawing a distinction between an eternal disposition, on the one hand, and a disposition toward the creature, on the other. The theist could speak of the eternal loving disposition of the divine nature (assuming God has a nature) as not depending on the occurrence of episodic properties for its existence. Then redemption (mercy/grace/forgiveness/salvation) might be viewed as a manifestation of this loving disposition to the creature. The manifestation of the latter, in contrast to the former, is conditioned by the occurrence of episodic properties. On this view redemption is a particularization and concretization of love in behalf of the creature. But God does not need the creature or the occurrence of episodic properties relative to the creature in order for him to love, since according to traditional theism at least, love is extant among the persons of the Trinity.

A variant of the objection, with a slightly different twist, occurs in the Biblical writings of Paul when he asks the Romans, 'What shall we say then? Are we to continue in sin that grace may abound?'[40] This question reflects somewhat the thought of an earlier one he raises – one that might come closer in substance to the issue presently being discussed: 'And why not do evil that good may come.'[41] One of his responses to the issue occurs in the context that includes the earlier of the two questions, and it (the response) may be constructed as an argument as follows:

(1)   If Christians are to live as though they were 'dead' to sin, then they ought not still live in sin.

(2)   Christians are to live as though they were 'dead' to sin, therefore,

(3)   They ought not still live in sin.[42]

Several points are in order here. First, Paul does not offer a carefully couched argument to counter the inference, but a question instead. If the Christian is 'dead' to sin, then, how shall such a person 'live in it [sin]?' Just as death and life cannot be predicated of a person, the believer cannot live in sin if she is supposed to be dead to it. Second, there is a counter in Paul's rejoinder that comes to the reader indirectly. That is, since the believer is to be 'dead' to sin, she is to be 'alive' to righteousness. More precisely, the believer's first and highest obligation is unqualified obedience to God. This is 'living' in righteousness. Doing evil that good may come, clearly, on Paul's account, does not involve compliance with that highest obligation, but rather, in fact, goes counter to it. Paul answers the mistaken inference, indirectly, but decisively. The question more to the point at hand is, Does God's redemptive act not depend on some sort of fall or transgression? Paul's response to this question – a response only roughly sketched below – might be taken as also suggesting support for the R-specification. He does say in the fifth chapter of the same epistle that sin, or moral evil, entered by Adam (by the fall) and that the remedy for this moral failure is the 'one righteous act' (redemption) of the 'Second Adam' (Christ).[43] Thus a very plausible reading of Paul's reasoning here is that the fall, precipitated by the sin of the first Adam, provides an occasion (the occurrence of an appropriate episodic property) and a context for the meaningfulness and possibility of the second Adam's redemptive act.[44]

Whatever one's verdict regarding the Biblical data cited and their relevance to the question before us, there does not appear to be any good reason for not answering the question originally posed (Does God's redemptive act require the fall?) in the affirmative. Doing so need not carry the implication that God's omnipotence is thereby diminished. Redemption is not logically possible without some sort of fall (if our earlier reasoning is correct); hence not even God can redeem without a fall. The justification contemplated then is of God allowing persons freely to choose evil, because this makes possible (not necessary) God's freely redeeming those who have fallen.

If in order for an agent to possess MMC he must possess the dispositional property of forgiveness, and if in order to possess the property in question the agent must endure or pass through episodic properties relevant to the dispositional property in question (such episodic properties as being offended or injured in some way by another), then obviously the agent cannot be said to possess MMC without certain episodic properties or something like them. But the condition obtains only in a world where created moral agents offend each other or God, say world W^*. By contrast in world W, where no evil occurs, forgiveness would be unnecessary, and persons could be said to have MMC without forgiveness. Forgiveness is thus only hypothetically necessary to MMC. Similarly, God cannot be forgiving or redemptive without a fall or move away from innocence (assuming with Augustine that created moral agents were initially innocent) on the part of the creature. For this reason a redemptive act on his part would be parasitic on humanity's fall or move away from innocence. But then the fall or something like it is logically necessary to redemption's being meaningful for the creature – that the one (the dispositional property) is parasitic on the other (some episodic property of the sort in question) – does not detract from divinity. As with the creature, so also for God, forgiveness is only hypothetically necessary to MMC. That is, forgiveness is necessary to MMC just in case there is a need for forgiveness. So God does not need a fall, and he does not need to be forgiving, unless there is something to be forgiven.

The second objection can be expressed as a question: Could God not have created a world, say W, containing moral worth, without redemption, and so without the evil necessary to redemption? Such a world was a possibility for God, but the free will defence points out that God could not, in creating, guarantee that he get such a world. The R-specification theorist might argue by way of response, that perhaps God has brought about numerous universes, which make up the world or all that is the case. Perhaps there is a universe, say U_1, where there is no evil, and so no redemption. Clearly there is a universe where evil has occurred. Perhaps the latter universe, call it U_2, has as much positive value as U_1, because U_2 is a universe where some sort of fall occurs or where free moral agents are morally flawed, and so God can offer redemption, and hence the mercy-grace side of God can be disclosed to the creature with greater depth and to a greater degree than in U_1. The viability of this claim, viz., that U_2 might have at least as much positive worth as U_1, might turn on whether the theist can *show* that redemption is a positive value, *not* independent of its being a remedy for the fall, and that this positive value arises from the consideration that a fall-redemption universe perhaps provides a better context or environment for the manifestation of certain dispositional properties of divinity than its rival. Here, I should only like to suggest that this might be so. The theist might want to argue that love is or can be more fully manifest to the creature in fall-redemption sort of universe U_2 than in U_1. Numerous theologians have held that it is through the act of redemption that God manifests his love more clearly and fully to the creature. The Biblical parable of the prodigal son helps illustrate the point.[45] As the story goes, the father had two sons, one who was obedient to the father's directives, the other took his inheritance and left home, and followed a life of moral bankruptcy. When he ran out of money, he came to have a change of mind, and returned home. The father is pictured as seeing the son from a great distance, and when the two met, he forgave, accepted and embraced the son. Here is a story of a father's love, and so a heavenly Father's love. As an embellishment to the story, we might say that the obedient son knows the special favor of the father through a closeness that comes because of obedience, and from being with the father daily. But there is a special insight into the father's love on the occasion of the return of the profligate son. There is another dimension of love unknown by the obedient son, because there was no occasion for its manifestation in a meaningful way. Moreover, we should not be surprised that the father loved the obedient son. But love comes in a special way to the profligate son. The theist might then contend, similarly, the door of heaven is ajar, and the universe is shown heavenly love in a tender and compassionate way through redemption. Love comes through this event with clarity and distinctness. Through forgiving mercy, there is no mistaking God's intent to reach down to the creature. One might be hard pressed if asked to rank the loves or weigh them. Arguably, love for the profligate is as profound a manifestation of love as love for the obedient son. Similarly, God's love for fallen humanity evidences divine love as uniquely and profoundly as love for prelapsarian agents.

If the R-specification can be formulated to handle the really significant objections, as our preliminary exploration is intended to show, and if furthermore it satisfies the conditions discussed earlier in connection with the GGD, the theist may be on his way toward providing substance to his claim that faith in a loving God exercised in a world which contains evil is rational.

Maybe the theist can develop other specifications which do not answer the GGD description, but which justify evils, given the fall. This suggestion might require more complex and involved greater-good notions than the GGD. Such revised notions would have to allow that there might be goods, which, on the condition that the fall occurred, might justify certain evils. Here, we have goods which require evils, but the logical necessity is conditional on there being a fall.

In conclusion, the theist might be a long way from providing anything in the way of a complete justification for the different sorts of evil that there are in the world. The preliminary and tentative account of the R-specification we have considered does not justify those natural evils which are so prolific and so (apparently) unmitigated. And then there is the question, Might it not be a greater good had God not created at all, rather than bring about a world where in order for redemption to meaningfully occur, a fall must take place, which will inevitably result in everlasting condemnation for part of humanity and part of the angelic host? One way whereby the theist might be able to affirm that creation is the greater good, might involve some sort of 'second-chance' thesis, which might lead to some sort of universalism. The mainstream of theism has tended to reject such a proposal. As incomplete as the defence is, the theist is not left with the plight of having no pattern of justification at all. We have considered only one possible specification of the GGD in a positive light, viz., the R-specification. No doubt it stands in need of further clarification and development than can be given in this preliminary study.

If the theist utterly fails to supply a plausible specification of the GGD, then there might be good reason to doubt whether the GGD pattern for which certain specifications are sought and explored is very useful as a defence. Furthermore, if the theist is not able to come up with a pattern which proves itself useful in this way, then when confronted with the reality of evil in the world he might rightly question the rationality of his belief that God is good. In this Chapter and the two preceding it which focused on other justification patterns, I have tried to show that the theist's cupboard is not all that bare – that there is a pattern that is worth exploring, viz. the GGD pattern, or some variant of it, and that there are specifications (the free will defence, the soul-making defence, and the R-specification) that might be places where the theodicist (in the non-technical sense of that term) can begin to stake off the terrain of rationality.

In chapters 5, 6, and 7, three different specifications of the greater-good defence have been examined. The first two, the free will defence and the soul-growth defence, Peterson extends so as to allow for and cover surd$_2$ evils. Each specification, including the expanded versions, assumes some sort of ends-justifies-the-means principle. Notwithstanding the differences of the respective specifications, there is a sense in which they bear a 'family resemblance,' because they operate with a common pattern of reasoning, viz. evils in some way or other are justified by some greater good. Perhaps it is in order to say that the greater-good defence is in some way 'parent' to its specificational 'offspring,' even though theorists rarely, if ever, piece together some particular specification after having first consciously thought out a general greater-good defensive scheme.

Genealogically, the GGD pattern has itself a 'parent,' viz. the EJM Principle. The latter is more general yet than the GGD pattern. The former says that some state of affairs is a means to some other state of affairs, and that the former justifies in some way or other the latter. There is no claim that the justifying state of affairs *outweighs* the other state of affairs, as in the case of the greater-good defence. Moreover, the greater-good defence, at least the GGD$_1$ version, explicitly states that *every* evil is thus justified.

If there is a certain priority of the EJM Principle over the GGD because the former is more logically primitive, and in turn the GGD also has a priority over its 'offspring insofar as they count as offspring,' what sort of connections are there, or might there be with regard to the 'offspring' themselves? For starters, perhaps the theist might see it to his advantage to work with some sort of redemption specification in tandem with a version of the free will defence. We have seen that Plantinga's version of the modal free will defence answers Mackie's challenge (if our analysis is correct), that God could not guarantee that a world that he creates populated with morally free creatures be a world without moral evil. But conceivably, the free will defence would be strengthened, if the theist were to add the redemption specification, since if the possible world God brings about ends up being the one populated with morally free agents who are transworld depraved, then though the good of freedom of choice is preserved, and though moral goods are possible in the world in question, if the creatures inflicted with this depravity end up forever lost because of it, that would likely make bringing about such a world clearly objectionable because the negative consequences might be viewed as outweighing the above mentioned goods. But if the moral free agents turn out to be transworld depraved, then the moral failure or 'fall' of these agents makes something like a divine redemptive act meaningful, and further, God can perhaps thereby show his love in a special way that would not otherwise be possible. The free will defence completes the apologetic story, since there can be no genuine fall unless persons are genuinely free. So there is a sense in which the redemption specification needs the free will defence, and the latter needs the redemption specification. Regarding the order of the two defences, there is obviously a priority of free will defence over the redemption specification, since in order to have redemption as a meaningful act, there must be some sort of fall, and there cannot be a genuine moral fall unless persons have a freedom to choose between good and evil.

Finally, according to most traditional theists, the good of redemption is necessary if persons are to experience soul growth (given, that some sort of fall has occurred). Hence there might be a priority of the redemption specification over the soul-growth specification (given a fall of some sort). If there is a priority, it is conditional, since it obtains only if some sort of fall has taken place. Conceivably, then if there is no fall, soul growth is possible without redemption, since redemption would be unnecessary. This is compatible with regard to the incarnate Son and the property of TWH. That is, the Son may be spoken of as experiencing soul growth without redemption, since at every stage of his life, conceivably there was perfect obedience to the revelation he had at that stage, as well as the moral requirements laid upon him. The Scriptures speak of his having learned obedience. But this learning need not have involved anything in the way of failure. Rather, at each stage, as revelation came, he exhibited obedience – full complicity with the Father's will. Hence he was not in need of redemption himself, since his every act and motive was in conformity to divine righteousness and holiness. Thus on this account, the Son may be properly spoken of as experiencing soul growth, without his having experienced a fall or moral failure, and without his having need in any way of redemption.

In this study of the GGD, we have not been so bold as to think or suggest that the GGD and its 'offspring' comprise a comprehensive justification for all the evils that there are. This would be to assume a theodicy posture. The theist might wish to argue that there are surd$_2$ evils, so long as he can subsume them under one of the specifications outlined. Even if only one of the justification patterns works, the inconsistency strategy is defused. I have argued that the redemption specification works, and that the parent GGD does as well. Further, it has been contended that Plantinga's free will defence also works and is compatible with the redemption specification. The theist could also incorporate the soul-growth defence into a larger apologetic complex, since they are not only compatible, but they complement each other in significant ways. All defences together, weaken the probabilistic argument, since if these defensive schemes work, they reduce the kinds of evil unaccounted for, thereby diminishing the probability that God does not exist.

It has been contended that the GGD and its 'offspring' can be formulated as viable defences. If this effort does not represent ill-gotten apologetic gains, then in the final round of this study of the rationality of theism the theist has secured a place to stand. In doing so, the defender has not staked off a wholly new terrain of rationality in respect to the issue of evil. He clearly falls within the tradition of Augustine, who said, "'God judged it better to bring good out of evil than not to permit any evil to exist,"'[46] and of Aquinas, who similarly remarked, "'God allows evils to happen in order to bring a greater good therefrom,"'[47] both of which comments arise in conjunction with the *'felix culpa'* principle, and the third and final specification of the GGD.

More apt concluding lines perhaps cannot be found than those in John Milton's *Paradise Lost.* After being given a glimpse of the Incarnation, Redemption, and Second Coming by the angel Michael, Adam expresses both the paradoxical *'felix culpa'* principle *and* a greater-good notion:

> O goodness infinite, goodness immense!
> That all this good of evil shall produce,
> And evil turn to good; more wonderful
> Than that which by creation first brought forth
> Light out of darkness! Full of doubt I stand

Whether I should repent me now of sin
By me done and occasioned, or rejoice
Much more, that much more good thereof shall spring,
To God more glory, more good will to men
From God, and over wrath grace shall abound.[48]

Notes

CHAPTER 1: INTRODUCTION

1. This study is an examination of a limited set of problems as they relate to Christian theism in particular. There are two principal reasons for this restriction. A large measure of the material written on the subject deals with it in relation to Christian theism. Second, this focus is of greatest interest and concern to me.

2. Two lines of argument continue to occupy the center stage: the free will defence (see Alvin Plantinga's, *The Nature of Necessity*, The Clarendon Press, 1974, or the simpler account in *God, Freedom, and Evil*, Harper Torchbooks, 1974), the soul-making defence (see John Hick's, *Evil and the God of Love*, revised edition, Harper & Row, 1978).

3. In recent literature, one of the few other philosophers who discusses it directly at any length is William Wainwright in *Philosophy of Religion* (Belmont: Wadsworth Publishing Company, 1988), pp. 72–79. He calls it the 'Greater Goods Defence.' The plural reference *goods* rightly suggests that there is or might be a number of greater goods. However, I shall continue to refer to the defence as the greater-good defence.

4. For a helpful discussion of ways of constructing the problem of evil see Chapter IV, 'The Problem of Evil,' in *Belief in God*, by George Mavrodes (Random House, 1970).

5. Lactantius, *The Wrath of God, Lactantius, The Minor Works*, Vol. 54, The Fathers of the Church, trans. Mary Francis McDonald (Washington: The Catholic University of America Press, 1965), pp. 92, 193.

6. In *Mind*, LXIV, No. 254 (April, 1955).

7. Ibid., p. 200.

8. George Mavrodes, *Belief in God*, p. 98.

9. Ibid., p. 40.

10. Ibid., p. 40.

11. Ibid., p. 41.

12. Ibid., pp. 102, 103.

13. The ISI and ISE are both rightly called *ad hominem*. That is, an *ad hominem* argument is understood to mean any attempt to discredit the system of beliefs S of a person P by showing that S is inconsistent, or by showing that P *must* hold other beliefs which are logically incompatible with S. According to the first disjunct we have an ISI which is directed against the theist qua theist. The other strategy, i.e. the ISE, tries to show that in addition to his Christian beliefs the theist must hold other beliefs because they are obvious truths, again with the result that the final set is inconsistent.

14. William James and Peter Bertocci fall into this camp. Interestingly,

165

Alvin Plantinga has also been included, most likely because of his strong free will thesis; cf. 'The Problem of Evil,' unpublished paper delivered at the Wheaton Philosophy Conference, October, 1980, p. 5.

15. See Yandell's discussion of the finitist position in 'The Problem of Evil' (1980), pp. 1–4. His conclusion is, finitism does not provide an answer to the challenge, 'but an end to theology.'

16. In *Mind*, LXIV, No. 254 (April, 1955), p. 200.

17. Alvin Plantinga points out that this answer is provided by a theorem of modal logic, viz., $\{\Diamond(P\&R)\&[(P\&R)\rightarrow Q]\}\rightarrow \Diamond(P\&Q)$, 'Self Profile,' *Profiles, Alvin Plantinga* (Boston: D. Reidel Publishing Company), p. 42. One of the parenthesis (the eighth), missing in the text, has been supplied. The formula translates as, 'if there is an R such that P is consistent with R, and the conjunction of P & R entail Q, then P is consistent with Q.'

18. Michael Peterson has a helpful introductory discussion of the evidentialist argument in *The Christian God*, Chapter 3 (Grand Rapids: Baker Book House, 1982). See Keith Yandell, *Basic Issues in Philosophy of Religion* (Boston: Allyn and Bacon, Inc., 1971), p. 52 for a similar argument. For a lengthy discussion see Alvin Plantinga's 'The Probabilistic Argument from Evil,' *Philosophical Studies*, Vol. 35, No. 1 (January, 1979), 1–51.

19. John Hick, Michael Peterson, Keith Yandell and Bruce Reichenbach are exceptions. Hick, for example, argues that some measure of 'pointless' evils is allowed as a condition for soul-making, but for this reason, such evils, strictly speaking, would not be gratuitous, since they serve to promote soul growth, pp. 334f, *Evil and the God of Love*, rev. ed., (New York: Harper & Row, Publishers, 1978).

20. Robert M. Adams, 'Plantinga on the Problem of Evil,' *Profiles: Alvin Plantinga* (Boston: D. Reidel Publishing Company, 1985), p. 238.

21. Ibid., p. 238.

22. Rudolf Carnap, 'On Inductive Logic,' *Probability, Confirmation, and Simplicity*, Marguerite Foster and Michael Martin (editors). New York: The Odyssey Press, Inc., 1966), p. 35.

23. Brian Skyrms, *Choice and Chance*, p. 206.

24. Ibid., p. 206.

25. Ibid., p. 206.

26. Ibid., p. 206.

27. Ibid., p. 15.

28. John Hick, *Faith and Knowledge* (Ithaca: Cornell University Press, 1966), p. 136.

29. Hans Reichenbach, 'The Frequency Interpretation,' *Probability, Confirmation, and Simplicity*, Marguerite H. Foster, and Michael Martin (editors), (New York: The Odyssey Press, 1966), p. 80.

30. Alvin Plantinga, 'The Probabilistic Argument from Evil,' *Philosophical Studies*, Vol. 35, No. 1 (January, 1979), pp. 33f.

31. The difference between the modes can be formally expressed using the following notational devices. If we let a and b be variables ranging over statements, and '∇' be introduced as a one-place

probability functor, then for any statement *a*, we may say, ∇a, 'prob-ably *a*,' or 'it is probable that *a*.' The probability mode indicates an epistemic probability since it applies only to propositions. However, if the probability mode applies to the inference itself, we would need a two-place probability functor. Working with variables *a*, and *b*, we may formulate a general notion of a conditional statement thus: 'if *a* then *b*.' No specification has been given as to the precise nature of the conditionality involved. If the probability mode applies to the inference itself, then the inference reads something like the following: 'if *a*, then probably *b*.' If we let '$\rightsquigarrow$' be the two-place probability functor, then for any two statements *a* and *b*, we may say, '*a* $\rightsquigarrow b$,' 'if *a*, then-probably *b*.' Since the probability affects the inference itself, we have an inductive probability. Some of the difference in meaning of the two probability modes can be seen in the following. In the case of '*a* $\rightsquigarrow b$,' the negation of the consequent makes *not-a* only probable, and the truth of *a* only allows us to say *then-probably b*. Note further, that *then-probably b* is not the same in meaning as *it is probable that b*. The negation of the former would make it only probable that *not-a*, whereas the negation of the latter would entail *not-a*. A fuller discussion of the many patterns of Modus Ponens which are possible when the one-place and two-place probability functors are employed would take us too far afield. It is sufficient for our purposes to note here some of the differences, and how important the place of the probability functor is to formalizing the argument in the probability mode.

32.   Max Black, 'Probability,' *The Encyclopedia of Philosophy*, Vol. 6, Paul Edwards, editor (New York: The Macmillan Company, 1967), p. 468.

33.   Ibid., p. 468.

34.   Howard Kahane, *Logic and Philosophy* (Belmont, Wadsworth Publish-ing Company, 6th ed., 1990), p. 372.

35.   For a helpful discussion of Bayes' Theorem see Richard Swinburne's, *An Introduction to Confirmation Theory* (London: Metheun, 1973), Chapter 3. Cf. Chapter 2 of Bruce Reichenbach's *Evil and a Good God* (New York: Fordham University Press, 1982) and p. 237 *Profiles Alvin Plantinga*. For a general form of the theorem see Howard Kahane, *Logic and Philosophy A Modern Introduction* (Belmont: Wadsworth 6th ed, 1990), p. 371, note*.

36.   See Wesley Salmon, 'Religion and Science: A New Look at Hume's Dialogues,' *Philosophical Studies*, Vol. 33, No. 2 (February, 1978), p. 147. See also Bruce Reichenbach, *Evil and A Good God*, pp. 26, 27.

37.   Wesley Salmon judges that the design argument, and the other arguments should be abandoned since 'all such considerations are irrelevant to the existence or non-existence of God.' 'Religion and Science,' p. 166. See Nancy Cartwright's 'Comments On Wesley Salmon's "Science and Religion . . . "' for a careful response to Salmon's contention, in *Philosophical Studies*, Vol. 33, No. 2 (February, 1978), pp. 177–183.

38. Robert Prevost, 'Swinburne, Mackie and Bayes' Theorem,' *International Journal for Philosophy of Religion*, Vol. 17 (1985), p. 176.
39. Ibid., p. 180.
40. Mackie says that the boundary between natural and moral evils is not 'simple or clearcut.' *The Miracle of Theism* (Oxford: The Clarendon Press, 1982), p. 163.
41. Alvin Plantinga extends the free will defence to explain the occurrence of natural evils in terms of the misuse of free agency by fallen angelic beings, pp. 192, 193, *The Nature of Necessity* (Oxford: The Clarendon Press, 1974). Cf. Mackie's, *The Miracle of Theism*, p. 155. Bruce Reichenbach uses the defence to cover natural evils too in *Evil and a Good God*, Chapter 5.
42. J. L. Mackie, 'Evil and Omnipotence,' *Mind*, Vol. LXIV, No. 254 (April, 1955), p. 206. See also the *Miracle of Theism*, pp. 154, 155.
43. Ibid., p. 206.
44. Ibid., p. 207.
45. 'IFF' is interpreted as, 'if and only if.'
46. M. B. Ahern, *The Problem of Evil* (New York: Schocken Books, 1971) pp. 56–57. Cf. George Mavrodes, *Belief in God*, p. 93.
47. John Hick, *Evil and the God of Love*, rev. ed., p. 334.

CHAPTER 2: OMNIPOTENCE, OMNISCIENCE, AND OMNIBENEVOLENCE

1. William Lane Craig, *The Only Wise God: The Compatibility of Divine Foreknowledge and Human Freedom* (Grand Rapids: Baker, 1987), p. 11.
2. Admittedly, many of the divine attributes are philosophically interesting in their own right. Problems and puzzles of one sort or another have been viewed as standing in the way of coherent and meaningful definitions.
3. See M. B. Ahern, *The Problem of Evil* (London: Routledge & Kegan Paul, Ltd., 1971), p. ix.
4. See Alvin Plantinga's, *Does God Have a Nature?* (Milwaukee: Marquette University Press, 1980).
5. For a discussion of the inconsistency strategy, see pp. 5–7 of Chapter 1.
6. Such a view need not entail God has a nature. It may be developed along nominalist lines or it may follow a Cartesian possibilism, see Plantinga's *Does God Have a Nature?* pp. 95–110.
7. Ibid., p. 95.
8. Ibid., p. 116.
9. Suppose that God does choose to bring about free moral agents, after which he purposes to limit his influence and control over these agents (assuming that it makes sense for God to do this), then before the actualization of a creation thus pictured he could be viewed as unconditionally omnipotent (so far as his power over

logically possible states of affairs is concerned), but after the fact of bringing such beings into existence, one might conceive of him as then having a self-imposed sort of limited omnipotence (limited in the sense that there might be times when he would not interfere with or control the free choices of those agents), which might be judged a variant limited-God thesis. However, what continues to distinguish even this sort of 'limited' or attenuated omnipotence from the garden-variety limited-God view is the latter's affirmation that God is *not* omnipotent, but is quite definitely limited in power and control, and this limitation is neither self-imposed nor does it come about as a result of a divine decision to limit divine power and control over states of affairs he might wish to allow.

10. For a helpful discussion of this doctrine see Plantinga's *Does God Have a Nature?* pp. 95–110. Cf. P. T. Geach, *Providence and Evil* (Cambridge University Press, 1977), p. 8f, and Anthony Kenny, *The God of the Philosophers* (Oxford: Clarendon Press, 1979), pp. 91f.

11. Alvin Plantinga, *Does God Have a Nature?*, p. 100.

12. Ibid., p. 103.

13. P. T. Geach, *Providence and Evil*, p. 9. Cf. Plantinga, *Does God Have a Nature*, p. 103.

14. Alvin Plantinga, *Does God Have a Nature*, p. 106.

15. Ibid., p. 110. See Descartes' letters to Mersenne, *Descartes Philosophical Writings*, trans. Elizabeth Anscombe (London: Thomas Nelson and Sons Ltd, 1969), pp. 259–263. In the third letter, Descartes says that God is the 'efficient and the total cause' of these truths, ibid., p. 261.

16. Descartes writes in his third letter to Mersenne, 'God is a cause whose power surpasses the limits of human understanding, whereas the necessity of these truths does not go beyond our knowledge, therefore they are something inferior and subordinate to that incomprehensible Power . . . . ' *Descartes: Philosophical Writings*, p. 261. In the fourth letter he says, 'not only would there be no space, but not even the so-called eternal truths, like a whole is greater than its parts, would be truths, if God had not established things so . . . . ' Ibid., p. 263.

17. Alvin Plantinga, *Does God Have a Nature?*, p. 122.

18. Ibid., p. 122.

19. Ibid., p. 123.

20. Ibid., pp. 124, 125.

21. W. V. Quine, *Methods of Logic* (New York: Holt, Rinehart and Winston, Inc., 1950), p. 3.

22. Ibid., p. 3.

23. Here I am following the advice of George Mavrodes that we should quantify over propositions or over 'sets of possible states of affairs' (or sets of possible actions) rather than over 'states of affairs,' since quantifying over the latter creates problems that the former does not, 'Defining Omnipotence,' *Philosophical Studies*, Vol. 32 (1977), p. 192.

24. Since, according to universal possibilism, there are no logically

necessary truths, even if a proposition is contradictory (i.e., its description is not coherent), God can make it true by bringing about a non-compossible state of affairs (or non-compossible states of affairs) which satisfies(y) the proposition in question. Thus it does not matter whether a proposition has a coherent description or not, God can make it true.

25.   Roughly, *de dicto* certainty is certainty that pertains to propositions, and *de re* certainty to existence. All bodies are extended is an example of the former. There can be *de re* necessity that a property belongs to some individual, as well as *de re* necessity that some individual exists. *God exists necessarily* is an example of the latter, and Socrates is male would be an example of a necessary property of an individual.

26.   There is still disagreement as to whether existence is a predicate. A. J. Ayer, John Wisdom, C. D. Broad, and Jerome Shaffer are in general agreement with Kant that it is not. For an interesting account of this matter as it relates to the ontological argument and Kant's criticism, see Plantinga's *God and Other Minds*, pp. 26–63.

27.   The definition considered is a reconstruction of what Descartes might be viewed as having held, given that he held to universal possibilism as opposed to limited possibilism.

28.   Alvin Plantinga, *God and Other Minds* (Ithaca: Cornell University Press, 1967), p. 171. In this context, Plantinga addresses the 'omnipotence paradox' introduced by J. L. Mackie in 'Evil and Omnipotence,' p. 210. The paradox is started by the question, Can God make things he cannot then control? If we say 'Yes,' then once he has made them he is not omnipotent. If we say 'No,' then we are admitting that there are things that God cannot do.

Richard La Croix argues that it is a concept that is impossible to define, in 'The Impossibility of Defining Omnipotence,' *Philosophical Studies*, Vol. 32 (1977), pp. 181–190.

29.   My account of *omnipotent* is a slightly different construction from Swinburne's. He quantifies over actions, whereas omnipotent$_2$ quantifies over sets of actions. See footnote 23. I have also used 'logically possible' in place of, 'of which the description is coherent.'

30.   Richard Swinburne, *The Coherence of Theism*, p. 149.

31.   This example was supplied by an anonymous reader.

32.   Richard Swinburne, *The Coherence of Theism*, p. 152.

33.   Ibid., p. 152.

34.   Ibid., pp. 152–158.

35.   Richard Swinburne, *The Coherence of Theism*, p. 143.

36.   See S. Morris Engel, *With Good Reason* (New York: St. Martin's Press, 1976), p. 145.

37.   Richard Swinburne, *The Coherence of Theism*, p. 159.

38.   Ibid., p. 159.

39.   Alvin Plantinga, *God and Other Minds*, p. 170.

40.   Richard La Croix, 'The Impossibility of Defining Omnipotence,' *Philosophical Studies*, Vol. 32 (1977), p. 183.

41.   Bruce Reichenbach, *Evil and A Good God*, p. 161.

42. See Chapter 5 for a discussion of God's strong and weak actualization.
43. See P. T. Geach, *Providence and Evil*, p. 24. Richard La Croix thinks that the term cannot be satisfactorily defined, see 'The Impossibility of Defining Omnipotence,' cf. n28. J. L. Mackie questions whether omnipotence entails omnificence (the doctrine that God does everything), *The Miracle of Theism*, p. 161.
44. P. T. Geach, *Providence and Evil*, p. 24.
45. Richard Swinburne, *The Coherence of Theism* (Oxford: Clarendon Press, 1977), p. 162.
46. In an earlier version of the paper read at the Midwestern Regional Meetings of the Society of Christian Philosophers, I used the proposition, 'It is 4 P.M.' George Mavrodes has pointed out an ambiguity of the locution. Proposition *P* eliminates some of that ambiguity, but there are still worries that further specification does not resolve. For the moment I will work with *P*, and address some of the problems Mavrodes raises shortly.
47. Here, I am assuming that the omniscient being is within time even though he might be eternal. A very different rendering would be required if the theist were to hold that God is omniscient and atemporally eternal. See Eleanore Stump's and Norman Kretzmann's article, 'Eternity,' *The Journal of Philosophy*, Vol. 78, No. 8 (August, 1981), pp. 429–458.
48. This particular locution is attributed to Elizabeth Anscombe by Anthony Kenny, *The God of the Philosophers* (Oxford: Clarendon Press, 1979), p. 48, n. 1. The counterexample is supplied by Norman Kretzmann.
49. J. R. Lucas, *The Freedom of the Will* (Oxford: The Clarendon Press, 1970), p. 71.
50. R. W. K. Paterson thinks that the theist is going to have to 'scale-down' one or more of the attributes to resolve the problem of evil, or reduce the number of different sorts of evil that he sees in the world, in 'Evil, Omniscience and Omnipotence,' *Religious Studies*, Vol. 15, No. 1 (March, 1979), p. 1.
51. Reformed theologians, John Murray and Ned B. Stonehouse, and apologist Cornelius Van Til argued that there is such a radical difference, challenging Gordon H. Clark on the matter of God's incomprehensibility at his ordination examination. See Fred H. Klooster, *The Incomprehensibility of God in the Orthodox Presbyterian Conflict* (Franeker: T. Wever, 1951). Cf., John H. Frame, *The Doctrine of the Knowledge of God* (Grand Rapids: Baker Book House, 1987), pp. 21–40.
52. George Mavrodes, 'How Does God Know the Things He Knows,' *Divine and Human Action*, Thomas Morris (ed.), Notre Dame: University of Notre Dame Press, 1989.
53. René Descartes held to an absolute omnipotence doctrine such that God is somehow supralogical and hence can, 'if he wants,' nullify or set aside the canons of logic and make true a contradictory proposition or do something that would be contradictory for him

to do. Actually, his position was ambiguous. His writings may be interpreted as supporting either universal or limited possibilism. The former is the view that Descartes' 'eternal truths,' e.g., the truths of logic, mathematics, etc., are not necessary truths. The latter position by contrast affirms that eternal truths are necessary, but they owe their necessity to divine decree. See Alvin Plantinga's, *Does God Have a Nature?* (Milwaukee: Marquette University Press, 1980), pp. 95–110.

54. Nelson Pike, 'Divine Foreknowledge, Human Freedom and Possible Worlds,' *The Philosophical Review*, Vol. 86, No. 2 (April, 1977), p. 209. In *Divine Nature and Human Language* (Ithaca: Cornell University Press, 1989), William Alston argues that God does not have beliefs, pp. 178–193

55. Assuming of course that Tokyo would continue into the future to be the capital of Japan. Alfred J. Stenner says God believes *p* only when *p* is true, in 'A Paradox of Omniscience and Some Attempts at a Solution,' *Faith and Philosophy*, Vol. 6, No. 3 (July, 1989), p. 304.

56. Linda Trinhaus Zagzebski, *The Dilemma of Freedom and Foreknowledge* (New York: Oxford University Press, 1991), p. 142.

57. Ibid., p. 141.

58. William Lycan, 'The Trouble with Possible Worlds,' *The Possible and the Actual*, ed., Michael J. Loux (Ithaca: Cornell University Press, 1979), p. 287.

59. See Peter van Inwagen's *Material Beings* (Ithaca: Cornell University Press, 1991), for an interesting account of such things as trees, clouds, and puppy dogs' tails.

60. Here, I am employing a rather simple account of the correspondence theory of truth. There are of course not only different accounts of this theory (Russell, for example, worked out six different accounts of the correspondence theory), but there are other theories such as the coherence, pragmatic, redundancy, and semantic theories of truth.

61. See Linda Trinhaus Zagzebski, *The Dilemma of Freedom and Foreknowledge*, for a helpful discussion of the 'No-grounds Objections,' pp. 141f, as well as other objections.

62. Nelson Pike, *God and Timelessness* (New York: Schocken, 1970), pp. 121–129, cf., Zagzebski's *The Dilemma of Freedom and Foreknowledge*, pp. 43f., for other criticisms of this view of God's eternity.

63. William Hasker, 'Response to Thomas Flint,' *Philosophical Studies*, 60, (1990), p. 120. See this article for an elegant argument against middle knowledge.

64. Linda Trinhaus Zagzebski, *The Dilemma of Freedom and Foreknowledge*, p. 125.

65. J. R. Lucas, *The Future* (Oxford: Basil Blackwell, 1989), p. 226.

66. William Hasker, 'Response to Thomas Flint,' p. 123.

67. Ibid., p. 124.

68. Mavrodes suggested this example in a communication, January 20, 1990.

69. Richard Swinburne, *The Coherence of Theism*, p. 165. Swinburne has taken the principle from Hector-Neri Castenada's 'Omniscience and

Indexical Reference,' *Journal of Philosophy*, No. 64 (1967), pp. 203–210. Swinburne appealed to this principle in *The Coherence of Theism* (cf. n. 12) but he has since come to reject this proposal (communication from Swinburne), see 'Tensed Facts,' *American Philosophical Quarterly* (1990).

70. Ibid., p. 165.
71. R. W. K. Paterson, 'Evil, Omniscience and Omnipotence,' p. 1.
72. See Charles Hartshorne, *The Divine Relativity* (New Haven: Yale University Press, 1948), pp. vii, 43, 83, 94. The theist, of course, can benefit from some of Hartshorne's insights, without buying into process theology.
73. John 14:2,3. In 14:2, Jesus says, 'I go to prepare a *place* for you . . . . ' The term is τοπον, and means, 'place,' 'position,' 'region.'
74. See Thomas Aquinas, *Summa Theologiiae*, Blackfriars (New York: McGraw-Hill Book Company) I:8.
75. J. R. Lucas, *The Freedom of the Will*, p. 71. See Chapter 14 for a defence of an attenuated omniscience thesis.
76. George Mavrodes brought it to my attention that this statement is misleading. There is a sense in which it is true. In fact, its consequent, 'everything that God foreknows must happen,' (though misleading in the same way) is true independently of the antecedent. That consequent is a necessary truth and therefore follows from every proposition. And the consequent would remain true if we removed 'God' and replaced it with any other name – with say, 'Mikhail Gorbachev.' For that consequent is just what we have called elsewhere the truth condition for knowledge.

We can usefully re-phrase that consequent in the style of standard quantification logic. A first stab at that would be 'For any *e*, if God foreknows that *e* will happen, then *e* will happen.' What we have is not quite complete, because the original contains 'must,' which presumably represents a modality, some sort of necessity. That modality is not yet represented in the transcription. Where is the modal operator to be inserted? That depends on its proper scope.

The proper transcription, including the modality, would be '□(for any *e*, if God foreknows that *e* will happen, then *e* will happen).' This is quite different from 'For any *e*, if God foreknows that *e* will happen, then □(*e* will happen).' The former is true, and represents part of the stock analysis of the concept of knowing. There is no reason to think that the second is true, and in fact appears to be false. Our original locution is misleading on this point, because of the placement of the word 'must.' English characteristically expresses the modalization of an hypothetical by inserting a modal word into the grammatical consequent. But this idiom tends to mislead us into thinking that the real scope of the modal operator is the consequent, rather than the hypothetical as a whole.
77. Bruce Reichenbach, 'Evil and a Reformed View of God,' *International Journal for Philosophy of Religion*, Vol. 24 (1988), pp. 67–85, particularly pp. 70–74.
78. Martin Luther, *The Bondage of the Will*, trans. J. I. Packer and O.

R. Johnston (Westwood, N. J.: Fleming H. Revell Company, 1957), p. 80.

79. David Ray Griffin contends that Augustine and Thomas Aquinas 'ascribe' free will 'verbally,' 'while denying it in effect,' *God, Power, and Evil* (Philadelphia: The Westminster Press, 1976), p. 105.

80. Augustine, *The City of God*, Introduction by Etienne Gilson and edited by Vernon J. Bourke (New York: Image Books, 1958), Book 5, Chapter 10 (p. 110).

81. John Calvin, *Institutes of the Christian Religion* (Grand Rapids: Wm. B. Eerdmans Publishing Company, 1957), I, 15, 8.

82. Augustine, *The City of God*, Book 5, Chapter 10, (p. 107).

83. Ibid., Book 5, Chapter 10, (p. 110).

84. Alvin Plantinga, *The Nature of Necessity*, p. 166. Cf. pp. 14f., Peter van Inwagen, *An Essay on Freewill* (Oxford: Clarendon Press, 1983).

85. George Botterill, 'Falsification and the Existence of God: A Discussion of Plantinga's Free Will Defence,' *The Philosophical Quarterly* (April, 1977), Vol. 27, No. 107, pp. 114–134.

86. For Biblical examples supportive of this thesis see p. 177, Richard Swinburne, *The Coherence of Theism*.

87. Richard Swinburne, *The Coherence of Theism*, p. 176.

88. Representing the Western tradition, Henry Mansel and Emil Brunner fall into this camp. Both held to the unknowability of God and so also its corollary the unknowability of his goodness. See Emil Brunner's *God and Man* (London: SCM Press, 1936), pp. 59, 60, 76–84. Cf. G. Stanley Kane, 'The Concept of Divine Goodness and the Problem of Evil,' *Religious Studies*, Vol. II, No. 1 (March, 1975), 49–71. Kane includes Karl Barth, see Barth's *Church Dogmatics*, II. 1, pp. 188, 189; II. 2, pp. 631–636 (Edinburgh, T. & T. Clark, 1936). Barth *also* clearly affirms God's knowability, see *Church Dogmatics* II. 2, pp 4f., 147ff., 156f., 158ff.

89. Keith Yandell, 'The Greater Good Defense,' p. 2.

90. Richard Swinburne, *The Coherence of Theism*, p. 71.

91. Yandell admits in a footnote that it is not clear that a good father would not lie under any circumstances, or allow his children to suffer under any conceivable conditions, *Basic Issues in the Problems of Philosophy*, n. 5, p. 63.

92. Keith Yandell, *Basic Issues in the Problems of Philosophy*.

93. Ibid., p. 45.

94. Richard Swinburne, *The Coherence of Theism*, p. 71.

95. For example, remarks Yandell makes in his discussion of God and positive properties in 'The Greater Good Defense' strongly suggest the view that there must be a univocal element in 'just' as it is used in divine and creaturely predication, p. 2.

96. James F. Ross, *Introduction to the Philosophy of Religion* (London: The Macmillan Company, 1969), p. 167. For a more detailed discussion of the concept of analogy see, James F. Ross, 'Analogy as a Rule of Meaning for Religious Language,' *Inquiries into Medieval Philosophy*, James F. Ross (editor), (Westport: Greenwood Publishing Company, 1971), pp. 35–74.

97. Ibid., p. 167.
98. Ibid., p. 168.
99. Frederick Ferré, *Language, Logic and God* (New York: Harper and Row, 1961), p. 75. The terms *neo-orthodox* and *reformed* do not designate two clearly distinct groups, since some neo-orthodox theologians would be comfortable with the designation, 'reformed.'
100. Karl Barth does not wholly reject the idea of analogy. He says, 'We . . . do not oppose the . . . doctrine of the *analogia entis* by a denial of the concept of analogy. But we say that the analogy in question is not *analogia entis*, but according to Romans 12:6 the *analogia fidea* [analogy of faith], the correspondence of the thing known with the knowing, of the object with the thought, of the Word of God with the word of man in thought and in speech, even as it distinguishes true Christian prophecy taking place in faith from all that is untrue,' *Church Dogmatics*, I.1, p. 279. Words in brackets are added.

    Richard Swinburne says that though Aquinas' view on theological language historically puts him between Scotus and Ockham (who tend toward a univocal meaning view) and those who stress that there is a chasm between God and humans, he (Swinburne) tends to take Aquinas as leaning toward a univocal view. See pp. 78, 79, *The Coherence of Theism*.
101. Frederick Ferré, *Language, Logic and God*, p. 76.
102. Keith Yandell, 'The Greater Good Defense,' p. 1.
103. Ibid., p. 2.
104. This point is made by Anthony Kenny in *The God of the Philosophers*, p. 110.

CHAPTER 3: THE GREATER-GOOD DEFENCE

1. Keith Yandell argues that the theist is 'committed to some version of the greater good defence,' because he (the theist) appeals to God's goodness and providence in giving account of evil, 'The Greater Good Defense,' p. 6. He later points out that the free will defence falls 'under the rubric' of the greater-good defence as he construes it (the latter defence), p. 7. In *The Miracle of Theism* J. L. Mackie says that the free will defence works with a greater-good notion, pp. 154, 155, 165. In 'Evil and Omnipotence,' the same defence is viewed as working with the greater-good defence on a higher level, p. 208. In accounting for natural evils, Bruce Reichenbach argues in *Evil and a Good God* that 'God in creating had to create a world which operated according to natural laws to achieve this higher good [i.e., the good of persons who could freely choose good or evil],' p. 101, words in parenthesis added (New York: Fordham University Press, 1982). Richard Swinburne with a slightly different turn argues that natural evils make higher-order goods possible, and so his defence is a variation on the greater-good defence idea, see *The Existence of God* (Oxford: The Clarendon Press, 1979), pp. 214ff.

2. See 'The Greater Good Defense,' *Sophia*, Vol. XIII, No. 3 (October, 1974), 1–16. See also William J. Wainwright, *Philosophy of Religion*, pp. 72–79 (Belmont, CA: Wadsworth Publishing Company, 1988).
3. Melville Stewart, 'O Felix Culpa, Redemption, and the Greater Good Defense,' *Sophia*, Vol. 25, No. 3 (October, 1986), p. 18. See 'The Greater Good Defense,' p. 4 for Yandell's definition.
4. For a fuller discussion of these attributes, see Chapter 2.
5. See the discussion of Leibniz's Lapse, Chapter 5.
6. See Chapter 5.
7. Thomas Aquinas, *Summa Theologica*, Ia, 25, 6, Vol. I, trans. by the Fathers of the English Dominican Province, rev. by Daniel Sullivan, in *Great Books of the Western World* (Chicago: Encyclopedia Britannica, 1952).
8. Ibid., Ia, 25, 6.
9. Ibid., Ia, 25, 6.
10. Frederick Copleston ascribes to Aquinas the view that 'there can always be a better universe than the one God actually produces . . . ,' because 'God's power is infinite . . . .', *A History of Philosophy, Medieval Philosophy*, Vol. 2, Part II (New York: Doubleday & Company, 1962), p. 89.
11. Keith Yandell, 'The Problem of Evil,' Cp. 2 in *Basic Issues in the Philosophy of Religion* (Boston: Allyn and Bacon, 1971), p. 50.
12. Alvin Plantinga uses the term 'turp' in talking about units of evil. See Alvin Plantinga's, *The Nature of Necessity*, p. 193. I have simply introduced 'ben' as a term to designate units of goods. It has no connection in sense with the Scottish word 'ben' which means 'within.'
13. Winslow Shea in 'God, Evil and Professor Schlesinger,' *The Journal of Value Inquiry*,' Vol. IV, No. 3 (Fall, 1970), p. 226, contends that one may make a similar point regarding the concept 'God,' if by 'God' we mean 'the best of all possible beings,' or 'the greatest conceivable being.' One might respond to Shea with the Plantingian line that God is 'maximally excellent,' cf. pp. 106–108, *God, Freedom, and Evil*, Alvin Plantinga (Grand Rapids: William B. Eerdmans Publishing Company, 1974).
14. Keith Yandell, 'The Problem of Evil,' p. 50.
15. Ludwig Wittgenstein, *Tractatus Logico-Philosphicus*, trans. D. F. Pears & B. F. McGuinness (London: Routledge & Kegan Paul, 1961), 1.
16. Alvin Plantinga, *The Nature of Necessity*, p. 45.
17. See J. L. Mackie, *The Miracle of Theism*, p. 173, for a similar point.
18. For this reason, only one possible world can be actualized. See Alvin Plantinga, *The Nature of Necessity*, p. 45.
19. I am assuming that God might have no particular reason for creating or bringing about a possible world at one particular time rather than at another, and that time is not a creation of God.
20. See p. 152, Richard Swinburne, *The Coherence of Theism*, and Alvin Plantinga, *The Nature of Necessity*, pp. 44ff., for a discussion of possible worlds and possible states of affairs.
21. Cf. Richard Swinburne, *The Coherence of Theism*, pp. 129ff.

22. The motive for selecting the weaker sense has to do with the proposal that follows. A world containing evil could not be properly described as 'flawless' or 'without defect,' in the strict sense of those terms, because the world in question contains evils. One might argue that such a world in a very narrow sense is 'without defect,' since the evil is important to what God wants for some possible universe contained in that world.

23. John Wisdom, 'God and Evil,' *Mind*, Vol. XLIV, No. 173 (January, 1935), pp. 1–20.

24. Ibid., p. 5.

25. Ibid., p. 6.

26. Ibid., p. 19.

27. Ibid., p. 6. Words in brackets are added.

28. Richard Swinburne holds that God is 'perfectly free' and omnipotent, and that with regard to evil choices, he could not bring about any contingent state of affairs if he had an overriding reason for refraining from bringing about the state of affairs in question. See pp. 158–161, *The Coherence of Theism*.

29. J. L. Mackie, *The Miracle of Theism*, p. 164.

30. Ibid., p. 164.

31. Keith Yandell, 'The Greater Good Defense,' p. 4. Letters in brackets are added. The definition of *overbalance* is obviously incorrect in the text. It reads, 'A good G overbalances an evil E IFF G *exists* entails E *exists* and an agent who creates or permits G for the sake of E is thereby morally praiseworthy.' It cannot be that an agent would be praiseworthy if he created or allowed a good G for the sake of an evil E, since that would mean the agent in question would be using a good for an evil end. If anything, such an action would increase or aggravate his moral culpability. If the letters in brackets are exchanged for the letters outside the brackets, the error is corrected.

32. J. L. Mackie discusses Hick's soul-making theodicy, the modal free will defence, and variations of the greater-good defence as instances of a 'means-end' principle, where 'evil is often necessary as a means to good.' *The Miracle of Theism*, pp. 152–156.

33. J. L. Mackie, *The Miracle of Theism*, p. 153. William Wainwright briefly discusses the maxim, 'Permit evil that good may come,' in *Philosophy of Religion* (Belmont: Wadsworth Publishing Company, 1988), p. 72. He mentions Jonathan Edwards as holding that only God can make use of the utilitarian idea because his 'wisdom is infinite and his goodness is perfect,' Ibid., p. 72, taken from Jonathan Edwards, *Freedom of the Will* (New Haven: Yale University Press, 1957), p. 411. Merold Westphall in *God, Guilt, and Death*, devotes an entire chapter to a more general consideration of the topic in 'Religion as Means and as End' (Bloomington: Indiana University Press, 1984), pp. 122–137.

34. Ibid., p. 153.

35. Ren Descartes held that God is *absolutely* omnipotent in the sense that he is somehow supra-logical and hence can, 'if he wants' nullify

or set aside the canons of logic and make true a contradictory proposition or do something that would be contradictory for him to do. Two readings of Descartes' *possibilism* have been given by Alvin Plantinga in *Does God Have a Nature?* (Milwaukee: Marquette University Press, 1980). The first, 'universal possibilism,' is the view that Descartes' 'eternal truths,' e.g., the truths of logic, mathematics, etc., are not necessary truths. 'Limited possibilism' by contrast affirms that eternal truths are necessary, but they are necessary by divine decree. P. T. Geach thinks Descartes held the latter view, while Plantinga thinks Descartes was unclear on the matter. Whichever of the two positions he held, both allow that God is not bound by 'logical necessities.' If Cartesian possibilism is affirmed, a teleological justification for evil would be ruled out, since God could then bring about any end without an evil means, even if the end logically required the existence of evil.

36. See pp. 16, 64–65.
37. Bruce Reichenbach proposed this definition in response to an early draft of this manuscript.
38. See p. 68.
39. See J. L. Mackie, 'Evil and Omnipotence,' p. 208, *The Miracle of Theism*, p. 154.
40. Bruce Reichenbach, *Evil and a Good God* (New York: Fordham University Press, 1982), p. 39. Words in brackets added.
41. See p. 98.
42. For a fuller discussion of God as scrupulously provident, see p. 74f, 77f.
43. For a fuller discussion of surd or gratuitous evil, see pp. 79ff.
44. Keith Yandell, 'The Problem of Evil and the Content of Morality,' *International Journal for Philosophy of Religion*, Vol. 17 (1985), p. 140.
45. Ibid., p. 140b.
46. Ibid., p. 141.
47. Ibid., p. 141.
48. Ibid., p. 141.
49. Ibid., p. 142.
50. George Mavrodes, 'Keith Yandell and the Problem of Evil,' *International Journal for Philosophy of Religion*, Vol. 20 (1986), pp. 45–48.
51. Ibid., p. 45.
52. Ibid., p. 45.
53. Ibid., p. 45.
54. Ibid., p. 46.
55. Ibid., p. 46.
56. Ibid., p. 46.
57. I am inclined to think that while Yandell's response to the critic might need further clarification, Yandell's response is basically on track.
58. This construction of the argument was suggested to me by an anonymous reader.
59. Michael Peterson discusses the doctrine at length in *Evil and the Christian God* (Grand Rapids: Baker Book House, 1982), and refers to it as 'meticulous providence,' pp. 92–96. For a fuller theological

discussion of providence in general, see Benjamin Wirt Farley's *The Providence of God* (Grand Rapids: Baker Book House, 1988).

60. Peterson lists Augustine, Aquinas and Leibniz as among those who take this line in *Evil and a Christian God*, p. 93, n. 9.

61. Among those who argue thus are Edgar Sheffield Brightman, Karl Barth, and Alfred North Whitehead, *Evil and the Christian God*, p. 93, n. 10.

62. The teleological and deontological distinction drawn here is somewhat different from how these terms are understood in current ethical theory, where the teleological orientation denotes ethical egoism and ethical universalism or utilitarianism, and the deontological approach includes such theories as intuitionism, natural law theory, etc.

63. This is my revision of Keith Yandell's greater-good defence as I have stated it in 'O Felix Culpa, Redemption, and the Greater Good Defense,' *Sophia*, Vol. 25, No. 3 (October, 1986). For Yandell's version see 'The Greater Good Defense,' *Sophia*, Vol. 13, No. 3 (October, 1974).

64. Keith Yandell, 'The Greater Good Defense,' p. 96. Yandell more recently has sided with Peterson on the issue of gratuitous evil, see, 'The Problem of Evil and the Content of Morality.'

65. Michael Peterson, *Evil and the Christian God*, p. 97.

66. Ibid., p. 97.

67. For an account of Alvin Plantinga's free will defence see, *God, Freedom, and Evil* (Grand Rapids: Eerdmans Publishing Company, 1974), or *The Nature of Necessity*. See also Chapter 5 of this Study.

68. Michael Peterson, *Evil and the Christian God*, p. 103.

69. Ibid., pp. 57–58, 73–99. Cf. Bruce Reichenbach, *Evil and a Good God*, p. 39. He defines gratuitous evils as 'evils which are not logically or causally necessary for there being a greater good, p. 39.

70. John Hick, in *Evil and the God of Love* (rev. ed.) suggests that there might be surd evil in the world. Its existence creates *mystery*, and this in turn makes more real an 'epistemic distance' between God and the creature, and this provides opportunity for soul growth, pp. 333ff.

71. Michael Peterson, *Evil and the Christian God*, pp. 107–117. Cf. Bruce Reichenbach, *Evil and a Good God*, pp. 108f.

72. Ibid., p. 87.

73. John Hick, *Evil and the God of Love* (rev. ed.), p. 378.

74. Ibid., p. 378.

75. Ibid., p. 378.

76. Ibid., p. 335.

77. Ibid., p. 335.

78. Ibid., p. 324.

79. Michael Peterson, *Evil and the Christian God*, pp. 102–107, 111–117, 117–122.

80. Keith Chrzan, 'When is a Gratuitous Evil Really Gratuitous? *International Journal for Philosophy of Religion*, Vol. 24 (1988), p. 90.

81. Ibid., p. 90.

82. Ibid., p. 90.
83. Ibid., p. 90.
84. Michael Peterson, *Evil and the Christian God*, p. 121. Cf. Frederick Sontag, The God of Evil: An Argument from the Existence of the Devil (New York: Harper and Row, 1970), p. 4.

CHAPTER 4:   DERIVATIONS OF THE GREATER-GOOD DEFENCE

1. Keith Yandell, 'The Greater Good Defense,' pp. 1–16.
2. Ibid., pp. 2–12.
3. See p. 1 of Chapter 3 for a general picture of how tenets (1)–(6) are to be interpreted.
4. Keith Yandell, 'The Greater Good Defense,' *Sophia*, Vol. XIII, No. 3 (October, 1974), 1–16.
5. Ibid., p. 2. Underlining is added.
6. Ibid., p. 2.
7. John Hick, *Evil and the God of Love*, rev. ed., 1966 (New York: Harper & Row), p. 211.
8. Hick, as S. Paul Schilling remarks, 'recognizes the exegetical dubiousness of Irenaeus' distinction between the 'image' and the 'likeness' of God in Genesis 1:26,' pp. 161, 162, *God and Human Anguish* (Nashville, Abingdon), 1977, cf Hicks *Evil and the God of Love*, rev. ed., p. 254. Hick's uncertainty regarding the distinction is not surprising. The Genesis 1:26–27 pericope referred to may not support the distinction. The term translated 'image' in the RSV is בְּצַלְמֵנוּ (*betzalemenu*), and is from the root צֶלֶם (*tzelem*), and may be translated 'image' or 'likeness.' The second term translated 'likeness' in the RSV is כִּדְמוּתֵנוּ (*kidemutenu*), and is from דְּמוּת (*demuth*), and may be translated 'similitude,' 'likeness,' or 'image.' In the passage in question there appear to be two parallelisms in Hebrew verse, the first in verse 26 ('Let us make man in our image, in our likeness') and the second in verse 27 ('Let us make man in our image, in our likeness') and the second in verse 27 ('So God created man in his own image, in the image of God he created him . . . .') (NIV). It appears then that one might have to look elsewhere to support the 'image'/'likeness' duality claim.
9. Keith Yandell, 'The Greater Good Defense,' p. 2.
10. I should add that Yandell has more recently argued that there are gratuitous evils (see 'The Problem of Evil and the Content of Morality,' *International Journal for Philosophy of Religion*, Vol. 17 (1985), which goes against his earlier contention that every evil has at least a counterbalancing, and maybe an overbalancing good. This shift in position would obviously require a different approach to the derivational task, since though the original set of beliefs ((1) through (6)) might not have changed, interpretation of one or more of them likely has.

11. See pp. 65–69 of Chapter 3 for a fuller discussion of the ends-justifies-the-means principle.
12. Keith Yandell, 'The Greater Good Defense,' p. 3.
13. There is an obvious slip in Yandell's argument, see p. 3 of 'The Greater Good Defense'. What he wishes to ascribe to the atheist critic is the denial of (3) *Every evil is such that God has a morally sufficient reason for creating or allowing it*: instead, he gives the denial of the denial, which is of course equivalent to (3) itself. There is a similar slip in the conclusion. Again he wishes to ascribe the denial of (27) *God exists and is omnipotent, omniscient, omnibenevolent, and he is the Creator and Providential Sovereign of the universe* to the critic, but instead he gives the denial of the denial, which is equivalent to (27). Since there is no question as to his intention I have reconstructed the above argument made up of premises (a)–(c) and conclusion (d) so as to avoid this difficulty.
14. Keith Yandell, 'The Greater Good Defense,' p. 3.
15. Ibid., p. 4.
16. Ibid., p. 4.
17. Ibid., p. 4.
18. Ibid., p. 4.
19. Ibid., p. 4.
20. Ibid., p. 4.
21. Ibid., p. 4.
22. William Hanson called my attention to this ambiguity. See p. 69 for two possible readings.
23. Keith Yandell, 'The Greater Good Defense,' p. 5.
24. Ibid., p. 5.
25. Ibid., p. 5.
26. Ibid., pp. 5–6.
27. Ibid., p. 6.
28. Cf. pp. 92–93 of this chapter.
29. Keith Yandell, 'The Greater Good Defense, p. 2. Cf. p. 91 of this chapter.
30. Ibid., p. 2.
31. Ibid., p. 2.
32. Ibid., pp. 5–6.
33. Ibid., pp. 5–6.
34. See p. 56.

CHAPTER 5: THE FREE WILL DEFENCE SPECIFICATION

1. Alvin Plantinga first encountered the name 'free will defence' in the writings of J. L. Mackie and Antony Flew, and he says in 'Self-Profile,' *Profiles, Alvin Plantinga*, p. 41, that the latter is the first to use the expression.
2. J. L. Mackie opines that this defence is the most significant proposal offered to resolve the problem of evil, 'Evil and Omnipotence,' *Mind*,

Vol. LXIV, No. 254 (April, 1955), p. 208. He sees it as working with the greater-good defence on a higher level, ibid., p. 208.

3. Traditional theists have contended that natural evil results from the misuse of freedom by fallen angels, p. 149, *God and Other Minds* (Ithaca, NY: Cornell University Press, 1967). In *The Nature of Necessity*, Augustine is listed as a staunch defender of this view, pp. 191, 192 (Oxford: The Clarendon Press, 1974). In the former work, Plantinga offers a revised free will defence for natural evils that have 'free non-human spirits' as 'counterparts' to human spirits in the argument dealing with moral evil.

4. This is roughly J. L. Mackie's strategy in 'Evil and Omnipotence,' p. 209.

5. Plantinga discusses counterpart theory at some length in *The Nature of Necessity*, pp. 102–120. See also David Lewis, 'Counterpart Theory and Quantified Modal Logic,' *Journal of Philosophy*, 65 (1968), pp. 114, 115. For Lewis, 'world bound individuals' typically have counterparts in other possible worlds.

6. No doubt there are many differences between WIT as she exists in W and as she exists in W* – differences which create difficulties for a transworld identity claim regarding WIT. David Lewis is uncomfortable about talking about possible individuals that have identities in different possible worlds, see *Counterfactuals* (Cambridge: Harvard University Press, 1973), p. 88. I should note that Mackie's line doesn't trade on an identity claim of this sort.

7. Here, only two possible worlds are considered. Conceivably, there might be any number of possible worlds where WIT might be said to exist.

8. The basic outline of the shortened version was presented in lecture form by Plantinga at Bethel College, March 11, 1982. I appreciate his allowing me to make use of it in this study.

9. Alvin Plantinga, *The Nature of Necessity*, p. 45.

10. See Alvin Plantinga, *The Nature of Necessity*, p. 166. Obviously, this thesis involves the denial of compatibilism. For a careful critique of compatibilism see, Peter Van Inwagen, *An Essay on Free Will* (Oxford: The Clarendon Press, 1983).

11. Plantinga judges that Mackie's fatal mistake in his criticism of the free will defence is his failure to take this very distinction into account. In *The Miracle of Theism*, Mackie says that the distinction 'disposes' of Leibniz's lapse, p. 173, and so he appears to agree that God could not either strongly or weakly bring about just any possible world.

12. The largest state of affairs that God strongly actualizes in a world is the conjunction of all the states of affairs he actualizes or brings about in that world. So the largest state of affairs that God strongly actualizes in W are all the states of affairs which are such that if W had been actual, then God would have strongly actualized them.

13. This is a definition of 'weak actualization' Plantinga offered in a communication, June 30, 1987. Cf. p. 49, 'Self-Profile,' *Profiles, Alvin Plantinga*, and p. 173, *The Nature of Necessity*.

14. Alvin Plantinga, 'Self-Profile,' *Profiles, Alvin Plantinga*, p. 51.
15. See n. 12 for an explanation of the largest state of affairs God strongly actualizes in a world.
16. According to a Russellian analysis, every counterfactual is true since each has a false antecedent (if the antecedent is true, then the consequent must also be true, but then, strictly speaking, we would not have a counterfactual). On another more tempting analysis, a true counterfactual is the one that 'is true in the closest possible world.' See p. 33, 'Introduction,' in *The Possible and the Actual*, edited by Michael J. Loux (Ithaca: Cornell University Press, 1979). If one is working with a libertarian account of free will, as Plantinga is, it is not clear that any counterfactual of freedom is true in this sense. A more promising route would be to say that all counterfactuals of freedom are false. This line also leads to a denial of middle knowledge. See William Hasker, *God, Time, and Knowledge* (Ithaca: Cornell University Press, 1989), pp. 28, 29ff. I am inclined to think that Hasker is right in his contention regarding counterfactuals of freedom, and further that God does not have middle knowledge.
17. In this account of the defence, Plantinga employs the doctrine of middle knowledge. In another shortened version appearing in 'Self-Profile,' this doctrine is not assumed, see pp. 51, 52. Middle knowledge is God's knowledge of 'conditionals of freedom,' such as (a) and (b).
18. The conjunction of the largest state of affairs that God strongly actualizes in W is identical with the conjunction of the largest state of affairs that God strongly actualizes in W^*.
19. In 'Self-Profile,' Plantinga works with Lewis' Lemma, which is, 'For every world W in which God exists, God could have weakly actualized W only if $G(T(W)) \rightarrow W$,' p. 50. He offers a proof for the Lemma, and then argues, that God can weakly actualize W and W^* just in case it is true that $G(T(W)) \rightarrow W$ and $G(T(W^*)) \rightarrow W^*$. Since it is the case that W and W^* are logically incompatible, the counterfactuals in question can be true just in case it is impossible that $G(T(W))$, i.e., if $G(T(W))$ is necessarily false. But since $G(T(W))$ is possible, then it cannot be that it is necessarily false. Therefore it is not within God's power to weakly actualize either W or W^*.
20. Alvin Plantinga, *The Nature of Necessity*, pp. 184, 185.
21. Ibid., p. 186.
22. Ibid., p. 186.
23. Ibid., p. 188.
24. J. L. Mackie makes a similar point, contending that 'the range of possible persons is therefore logically contingent,' p. 174, *The Miracle of Theism* (Oxford: Clarendon Press, 1982).
25. I am indebted to James Sennett and George Mavrodes for making this point clear to me in a discussion at the Society of Christian Philosophers conference at Pittsburg State University, October 14, 1989.
26. J. L. Mackie, *The Miracle of Theism*, p. 174.

27. See William Hasker's, *God, Time, and Knowledge* (Ithaca: Cornell University Press, 1989), p. 38. This is a view that Hasker rejects.

28. See William Hasker's, *God, Time, and Knowledge*, p. 52.

29. Alvin Plantinga, *The Nature of Necessity*, p. 70.

30. William Hasker talks about God as a 'risk-taker' in *God, Time, and Knowledge* (Ithaca: Cornell University Press, 1989), pp. 197ff.

31. See Thomas V. Morris, *The Logic of God Incarnate* (Ithaca: Cornell University Press, 1986). The Council of Chalcedon of 451 A.D. affirmed that Christ had two natures, one truly divine and the other truly human, and that regarding these two natures there was no confusion, no change, no division, and no separation. Henry Bettenson, *Documents of the Christian Church* (New York: Oxford University Press, 1947), p. 73.

32. Philippians 2:7.

33. See Thomas V. Morris, *The Logic of God Incarnate*, pp. 89–102.

34. Anthony Kenny, *The God of the Philosophers*, pp. 65ff.

35. Robert Merrihew Adams, 'Plantinga on the Problem of Evil,' in *Profiles Alvin Plantinga*, p. 230.

36. Ibid., p. 230.

37. Robert Merrihew Adams suggests that they should be called 'deliberative conditionals' rather than 'counterfactual conditionals' because some do end up getting actualized, 'Middle Knowledge and the Problem of Evil,' *American Philosophical Quarterly* 14 (1977) p. 112.

38. Ibid., p. 230. C. Anthony Kenny, *The God of the Philosophers*, pp. 62–63.

39. Anthony Kenny, *The God of the Philosophers*, p. 66.

40. Ibid., see p. 67 for the list.

41. Ibid., p. 67. Cf. George Botterhill's 'Falsification and the Existence of God: A Discussion of Plantinga's Free Will Defense,' *The Philosophical Quarterly* (April, 1977), Vol. 27, No. 107, pp. 114–134, for a similar attack.

42. Ibid., p. 69.

43. Ibid., p. 70.

44. Ibid., p. 70.

45. Ibid., p. 66.

46. W. V. Quine, *From a Logical Point of View* (New York: Harper Torchbooks, 2nd ed., 1961, p. 4.

47. David Lewis, *Counterfactuals* (Cambridge: Harvard University Press, 1973), p. 88.

48. Ibid., p. 87.

49. Alvin Plantinga, 'Self-Profile,' p. 50.

50. For an interesting discussion of worlds and universes see John Leslie's *Physical Cosmology and Philosophy* (New York: Macmillan Publishing Company, 1990), pp. 1–28, and the collection of readings in Michael J. Loux's, *The Possible and the Actual*.

CHAPTER 6:   GROWTH-TO-MORAL-MATURITY/
SOUL-GROWTH

1.   Keith Yandell, 'The Greater Good Defense,' p. 10.
2.   Ibid., p. 10.
3.   Ibid., p. 10.
4.   Ibid., p. 10.
5.   Ibid., p. 10.
6.   Ibid., p. 11.
7.   Alvin Plantinga, *The Nature of Necessity* (Oxford: The Clarendon Press, 1974), pp. 165–166. It is important to note that this is for Plantinga a sufficient condition of what it is for an agent to be free.
8.   Keith Yandell, 'The Greater Good Defense,' p. 11.
9.   Ibid., p. 11.
10.   Ibid., p. 11.
11.   Ibid., p. 11. Underlining is added.
12.   Ibid., p. 11.
13.   Ibid., p. 11.
14.   Ibid., p. 11.
15.   Ibid., p. 11.
16.   Keith Yandell, 'Theism and Evil: A Reply,' p. 3.
17.   Ibid., p. 3.
18.   Ibid., p. 3.
19.   Ibid., pp. 3–4.
20.   Ibid., p. 4.
21.   Ibid., p. 4, the letter (A) has been changed to (a).
22.   Ibid., p. 4, the letter (B) has been changed to (b).
23.   Ibid., p. 4.
24.   Ibid., p. 4. Cf. John Hick, *Evil and the God of Love*, pp. 253–261, for a discussion of the sort of world needed for character or soul-growth.
25.   Ibid., p. 4.
26.   Ibid., pp. 4–5.
27.   G. Stanley Kane, 'Theism and Evil,' p. 19.
28.   Ibid., p. 19. See Chapter 7 of this study, pp. 155–157 for further discussion of Kane's point.
29.   Keith Yandell, 'Theism and Evil: A Reply,' p. 6.
30.   Ibid., p. 6.
31.   Ibid., p. 6.
32.   Ibid., p. 6.
33.   (E) There is no set S' of moral agents whose members, had they been created, would have chosen better than the members of the set S of actual persons have chosen.
34.   Keith Yandell, 'The Greater Good Defense,' p. 12.
35.   Ibid., p. 12, n. 7. Cf. p. 25 of Chapter 1 of this Study.
36.   Ibid., p. 12.
37.   Ibid., p. 12.
38.   Ibid., p. 12.
39.   Ibid., p. 12.

40.   Keith Yandell, 'Theism and Evil: A Reply,' pp. 5–6.
41.   G. Stanley Kane, 'Theism and Evil,' p. 18.
42.   John Hick, *Evil and the God of Love*, rev. ed., p. 351.
43.   Ibid., p. 351.
44.   Ibid., p. 254.
45.   See p. 84, Chapter 4.
46.   John Hick, *Evil and the God of Love*, rev. ed., p. 256.
47.   Ibid., p. 256, Hebrews 2:10.
48.   Ibid., p. 265.
49.   See p. 25.
50.   John Hick, *Evil and the God of Love*, rev. ed., p. 271.
51.   Ibid., p. 272.
52.   Ibid., p. 281.
53.   Ibid., p. 286.
54.   Ibid., p. 286.
55.   Ibid., p. 287.
56.   In the Straits one faced either being sucked into Charybdis on one side, which meant almost certain destruction, or being consumed by Scylla, the sea monster with six heads who made her lair opposite the threatening whirlpool.
57.   Alvin Plantinga's defence is a noteworthy exception, since it is not his intention in his defence to account for *actual* evil.
58.   For a good historical treatment of the ideas of the fall and original sin, see N. P. Williams, *The Ideas of the Fall and of the Original Sin* (London: Longmans, Green and Company, 1927).
59.   The article appears in *Neue Zeitschrift Für Systematische Theologie Und Religionsphilosophie*, Vol. 27, No. 3 (1985), pp. 235–250.
60.   Ibid., p. 235.
61.   Ibid., p. 236.
62.   Ibid., p. 237.
63.   Ibid., p. 237.
64.   Ibid., p. 237.
65.   Ibid., p. 240.
66.   Ibid., p. 240.
67.   Ibid., p. 244.
68.   Ibid., p. 245.
69.   Ibid., p. 245.
70.   Ibid., p. 245. Cf. Richard Swinburne's, 'Comment on 'Original Sin in Anselm and Kant' by Philip Quinn,' (unpublished paper), p. 5. In this paper he talks about 'bad desires,' and in this respect sounds like Aristotle when the latter talks about desires that are not in accordance with reason.
71.   Reinhold Neibuhr, in *The Nature and Destiny of Man*, Vol. 1, pp. 181, 182f (New York: Charles Scribner's Sons, 1941), makes a similar point.
72.   Richard Swinburne argues that the doctrine of Adam's 'original righteousness' was a late-comer in Christian thought. See pp. 141, 144, *Responsibility and Atonement* (Oxford, Clarendon Press, 1989).
73.   Communication from John Hick.

74. John Hick, *Evil and the God of Love*, rev. ed., p. 324.
75. Ibid., p. 322.
76. See pp. 213–214 of Chapter 7.
77. G. Stanley Kane, 'The Failure of Soul-Making Theodicy,' *International Journal for Philosophy of Religion*, Vol. VI, No. 1 (Spring, 1975), pp. 1–22.
78. These two objections are part of a five-pronged attack against Hick's soul-making theodicy. The three points not applied to Yandell, deal with Hick's concept of 'epistemic distance.' Cf., John Hick's *Evil and the God of Love*, rev. ed., pp. 376–379.
79. G. Stanley Kane, 'The Failure of Soul-Making Theodicy,' (1975), p. 8.
80. Ibid., p. 8.
81. Ibid., p. 10. The word in brackets is added.
82. John Hick, *Evil and the God of Love*, rev. ed., p. 383.
83. G. Stanley Kane presents it as the first objection of five that he raises against Hick's theodicy in 'The Failure of Soul-Making Theodicy,' pp. 2–22.
84. G. Stanley Kane, 'The Failure of Soul-Making Theodicy,' p. 2.
85. Ibid., p. 4.
86. John Hick, *Evil and the God of Love*, rev. ed., p. 378.
87. Ibid., p. 378.
88. Ibid., p. 378.

CHAPTER 7: *O FELIX CULPA*, REDEMPTION, AND THE GREATER-GOOD DEFENCE

1. Cf. p. 56 of Chapter 3.
2. In the discussion that follows there will be no need to observe the distinction made in the second conjunct between *a good state of affairs* and *good states of affairs* which logically require some evil, cf. p. 69 of Chapter 3. I am not going to discuss different greater-good defences either, hence I shall simply refer to the greater-good defence as GGD.
3. John Hick, *Evil and the God of Love*, rev. ed., p. 239.
4. Ibid., p. 244, n. 1. See S.T., pt. III, Q. i, article 3, where Aquinas cites the same locution as part of the liturgy of the Pascal candle. Cf. Anthony O'Hear, *Experience, Explanation and Faith* (London: Routledge & Kegan Paul Ltd., 1984), p. 220. (The same statement appears in Aquinas' S.T., pt. III, Q. i, article 3.) Gottfried Leibniz makes a direct reference to the *Felix Culpa* locution in his *Theodicy*, p. 129, Austin Farrer (ed.), E. M. Huggard (Trans.), (London: Routledge and Kegan Paul Ltd., 1952).
5. According to Lovejoy, in the early church it was the practice of the deacon to write his own hymn of praise to the Easter candle, a custom which is traceable back to Augustine, p. 286, n. 23, *Essays in the History of Ideas* (Baltimore: The Johns Hopkins Press, 1948).

6. Charlton Walker, 'Exultet,' *The Catholic Encyclopedia*, Vol. V (New York: The Encyclopedia Press, 1909), p. 730. Cf., John Hick, *Evil and the God of Love*, rev. ed., p. 244, and Arthur Lovejoy, Essays in the History of Ideas, p. 286.

7. Arthur Lovejoy, *Essays in the History of Ideas*, p. 286, n. 23.

8. Ibid., p. 286, n. 23.

9. Ibid., p. 286, Cf., *Augustine's City of God*, 15, 22, p. 416, *Great Books of the Western World*, Vol. 18 (ed. Raymond Hutchins) (Chicago: Encyclopedia Britannica, Inc., 1952). Dennis R. Danielson in *Milton's Good God* (Cambridge: Cambridge University Press, 1982), p. 209, translates a passage from Francis Roberts' *Mysterium et Medulla Bibliorum (The Mysterie and the Marrow of the Bible*, London, 1657) that in the original contains the '*O felix culpa*' locution. According to Danielson, Roberts attributes the passage to Augustine: '"August. in meditat. lib. cap. 6. Tom. 9,"' p. 264, n. 20, but Danielson admits that it was probably not written by Augustine, p. 264, n. 20.

10. Ibid., pp. 285–286. Cf., Charlton Walker, '*Exultet*,' p. 731.

11. Ibid., p. 286.

12. John Hick, *Evil and the God of Love*, rev. ed., p. 254.

13. Ibid., p. 254.

14. Ibid., p. 257.

15. Ibid., p. 259.

16. Ibid., p. 287.

17. Here, in agreement with Augustine, I am assuming that the human family began in a state of innocence. An Irenaean account might not require a fall, since it is allowed that the human family might not have been untainted by sin from the very beginning. I should also note that by the term *fall* here, all is meant is some sort of lapse from innocence or goodness, that is, some sin or other is necessary. If the Augustinian account is taken, then some sort of fall is necessary, and if the Irenaean picture is assumed, then some sort of sin is necessary. Fall is not taken thus as equivalent in meaning to sin, though there might be a sense of the former that is coterminus with a standard sense of sin, viz., some sort of violation of God's law by an actual transgression or neglect.

18. Augustine, *On the Trinity*, Bk. XIII, Chapter 10, and Thomas Aquinas, *Summa Theologica*, Part III, Q. 46, Arts, 2, 3.

19. John Murray, *Redemption Accomplished and Applied* (Grand Rapids: William B. Eerdmans Publishing Company, 1955), p. 16. Murray refrains from expatiating on just what there is in the nature of God that requires satisfaction for sin in just this way, but only draws attention to the fact that some things are necessary for God. In this case, there is, according to his view, a clear Biblical teaching that 'without the shedding of blood, there is no remission,' but he resists going any further on the grounds that the Scriptures do not say 'what is *de jure* indispensable for God,' p. 16.

20. In drawing attention to the point that the Redemption Specification of the Greater-Good Defence works with and justifies actual evil – evil associated with some sort of fall, I should hasten to add that

the possibility of evil might still (in part or whole) be justified by the Free Will Defence.

21. Actually a fall is not necessary to redemption, but some sort of state other than innocence in respect to sin is necessary. As I have already observed, if an Irenaean line is taken, then a fall isn't necessary, since humanity is already in some way spoiled by sin, and so is in need of redemption. A fall isn't necessary then, but something roughly akin to what is involved in the lapsarian condition is necessary, i.e., some sort of transgression of some divine prohibition or requirement is necessary.

22. Richard Swinburne lists four, repentance, apology, penance and reparation, but I think that apology may be subsumed under repentance, and penance and reparation could be lumped together under payment or ransom. See p. 81, of Swinburne's, *Responsibility and Atonement* (Oxford: Clarendon Press, 1989).

23. Matthew 20:28 and Mark 10:45 use the same term, λοτρον which translates as, 'ransom,' or 'price of release.'

24. Richard Swinburne, *Responsibility and Atonement*, p. 153.

25. John Murray, in *Redemption Accomplished and Applied*, for example, sees repentance as part of the order of the application of redemption (the *ordo salutis*). See pp. 140–143. For a discussion of the nature of the atonement, see pp. 25–56. Moreover, if salvation is to be a matter of grace, theologians of the Reformed tradition, among others, have argued that repentance and faith itself must somehow issue from grace. Whatever the case, the Atonement is clearly a ransom in the sense that payment is made for sin by the sinner by accepting God's free gift.

26. Some theologians prefer to speak of the decree rather than decrees of God.

27. Those representative of the Counter Reformation strongly objected to the Reformed doctrine of predestination. Predestination unto reprobation was explicitly anathematized in the Council of Trent's 'Canons of Justification,' see John Clarkson, John Edwards, William Kelly, John Welch, *The Church Teaches* (St. Louis: B. Herder Book Co., 1955), p. 244.

28. L. Berkhof, *Systematic Theology* (Grand Rapids: Wm. B. Eerdmans Publishing Company, 1959), p. 119.

29. Ibid., pp. 119–120.

30. Ibid., p. 120.

31. Charles Hodge, *Systematic Theology* (Grand Rapids: Wm. B. Eerdmans Publishing Company, 1952), Vol. II, p. 316.

32. L. Berkhof, *Systematic Theology*, p. 118.

33. See Chapter 3 for a fuller discussion of God as operating with both frameworks, the deontological and teleological.

34. Here I should note that from the point of view of Augustine, Anselm, and Aquinas that Adam's having been confirmed in uprightness prior to the fall – had he not sinned – would have been a greater good than his redemption, involving as it does the perdition of many of his descendents.

35.   I Peter 1:12, Revised Standard Version.
36.   Bruce Reichenbach, 'Evil and a Reformed View of God,' *International Journal for Philosophy of Religion*, Vol. 24 (1988), 67–85.
37.   John Hick, *Evil and the God of Love*, p. 175.
38.   The list includes Meredith Kline and the late Edward J. Young. The former takes a framework hypothesis reading of Genesis 1, but holds to a pristine state before a fall, and the latter takes the fall as historical.
39.   The view that Adam and Eve's fall provided opportunity for a greater good than if they had remained innocent has never characterized the mainstream of Christianity. According to Arthur Lovejoy in 'Milton and the Paradox of the Fortunate Fall,' the number of theological writers and religious poets who gave clear expression to the *'felix culpa'* principle itself has never been very large, p. 279. But it is noteworthy that some who endorsed the principle also held that the fall provided an opportunity for God to bring about a greater good than if Adam and Eve had not fallen. John Milton (17th c.), for example, held that three greater goods spring from the fall: (1) greater glory to God; (2) greater benefits to man from God; (3) manifestation of God's grace as predominant over his wrath, ibid., p. 285 (Cf. the passage taken from Milton's *Paradise Lost*, p. 329). The list of those who agreed with Milton that a greater good results from the fall includes: St. Ambrose (4th c.), Pope Leo I (5th c.), Gregory the Great (6th c.), Thomas Aquinas (13 c.), John Wyclif (14th c.), Du Bartas (17th c.), Francis de Sales (17th c.). Jonathon Edwards espoused such a view in *Freedom of the Will*, pp. 410, 411, Yale University Press, 1957.
40.   Romans 6:1.
41.   Romans 3:8.
42.   Romans 6:2, my own paraphrase.
43.   Romans 5.
44.   Romans 5:21, 'So that, as sin reigned in death, grace also might reign through righteousness to eternal life through Jesus Christ our Lord,' (RSV) might be viewed as suggesting that the fall provides an occasion for redemption.
45.   Luke 15:11–32
46.   John Hick, *Evil and the God of Love*, rev. ed., p. 239, taken from Ench. viii. 27.
47.   Ibid., p. 239, taken from *S. T.*, pt. III, Q.i, art. 3.
48.   Dennis Richard Danielson, *Milton's Good God*, p. 204, taken from *Paradise Lost*, [12.469–78].

Bibliography

Adams, Robert Merrihew. 'Middle Knowledge and the Problem of Evil,' *American Philosophical Quarterly*, Vol. 14, No. 2 (April, 1977), 109–117.

Ahern, M. B. *The Problem of Evil*. New York: Schocken Books, 1971.

Aiken, Henry. 'God and Evil: A Study of Some Relations Between Faith and Morals,' *Ethics*, Vol. XLVIII, No. 2 (January, 1958), 77–97.

Alston, William P. *Divine Nature and Human Language*. Ithaca: Cornell University Press, 1989.

Anderson, C. Anthony. 'Divine Omnipotence and Impossible Tasks: An Intensional Analysis,' *International Journal for Philosophy of Religion*, Vol. 15 (1984), 109–124.

Augustine. *City of God, Great Books of the Western World*, Vol. 18, Raymond Hutchins (ed.). Chicago: Encyclopedia Britannica, 1952.

Aquinas, Thomas. *Summa Theologica*, Vol. I. Translated by the Fathers of the English Dominican Province, rev. by Daniel Sullivan, *Great Books of the Western World*. Chicago: Encyclopedia Britannica, 1952.

Barth, Karl. *Church Dogmatics*, Vol. I.1. Translated by G. T. Thomson. Vol. II.1. Edited by G. W. Bromiley and T. F. Torrance. London: SCM Press, 1936.

Black, Max. 'Probability,' *The Encyclopedia of Philosophy*, Vol. 6, Paul Edwards (ed.). New York: The Macmillan Company, 1967.

Botterill, George. 'Falsification and the Existence of God: a Discussion of Plantinga's Free Will Defense,' *The Philosophical Quarterly*, Vol. 27, No. 107 (April, 1977), 114–134.

Carnap, Rudolf. 'On Inductive Logic,' *Probability, Confirmation, and Simplicity*, Marguerite Foster and Michael Martin (editors). New York: The Odyssey Press, Inc., 1966.

Copleston, Frederick. *A History of Philosophy, Medieval Philosophy*, Vol. 2, Part II. New York: Doubleday and Company, 1962.

Craig, William Lane. *The Only Wise God: The Compatibility of Divine Foreknowledge and Human Freedom*. Grand Rapids: Baker Book House, 1987.

Evans, C. Stephen. *Philosophy of Religion, Thinking about Faith*, Downers Grove: InterVarsity Press, 1985.

Fischer, John Martin (ed.). *God, Foreknowledge, and Freedom*. Stanford: Stanford University Press, 1989.

Flint, Thomas P. 'Hasker's *God, Time, and Foreknowledge*,' *Philosophical Studies*, Vol. 60 (1990), 103–115.

Fredosso, Alfred J. (trans.). Luis De Molina, *On Divine Foreknowledge* (Part IV of the *Concordia*). Ithaca: Cornell University Press, 1988.

Geach, P. T. 'An Irrelevance of Omnipotence,' *Philosophy*, Vol. 48 (October, 1973), 327–333.

Geach, P. T. 'Omnipotence,' *Philosophy*, Vol. 48, No. 183 (January, 1973), 7–20.

192   *Bibliography*

Geach, P. T. *Providence and Evil*. Cambridge: Cambridge University Press, 1977.

Gellman, Jerome. 'Omnipotence and Impeccability,' *The New Scholasticism*, Vol. LI, No. 1 (Winter, 1977), 21–37.

Gellman, Jerome. 'The Paradox of Omnipotence and Perfection,' *Sophia*, Vol. 14 (October, 1975), 31–39.

Griffin, David Ray. *God, Power, and Evil: A Process Theodicy*. Philadelphia: The Westminster Press, 1976.

Grim, Patrick. 'Plantinga's God and Other Monstrosities,' *Religious Studies*, Vol. 25, No. 1 (March, 1979), 91–97.

Hartshorne, Charles. *The Divine Relativity*. New Haven: Yale University Press, 1948.

Hasker, William. 'Foreknowledge and Necessity,' *Faith and Philosophy*, Vol. 2, No. 2 (April, 1985), 121–157.

Hasker, William. *God, Time, and Knowledge*. Ithaca: Cornell University Press, 1989.

Hasker, William. 'Response to Thomas Flint,' *Philosophical Studies*, Vol. 60 (1990), 117–126.

Hick, John. 'Coherence and the God of Love Again,' *The Journal of Theological Studies*, Vol. 24, No. 2 (October, 1973), 522–528.

Hick, John. *Evil and the God of Love*. First and revised editions. London: Macmillan, 1st ed., 1966, rev. ed., 1978.

Hick, John. *Faith and Knowledge*, 2nd ed. Ithaca: Cornell University Press, 1966.

Hick, John. 'Freedom and the Irenaean Theodicy Again,' *The Journal of Theological Studies*, Vol. 21, Part 2 (October, 1970), 419–422.

Hoffman, Joshua. 'Can God do Evil?' *The Southern Journal of Philosophy*, Vol. XVII, No. 2 (Summer, 1979), 213–220.

Hoffman, Joshua. 'Mavrodes on Defining Omnipotence,' *Philosophical Studies*, Vol. 35, No. 3 (April, 1979), 311–313.

Hoffman, Joshua. 'Pike on Possible Worlds, Divine Foreknowledge, and Human Freedom,' *The Philosophical Review*, Vol. 88, No. 3 (July, 1979), 433–442.

Hoffman, Joshua and Rosenkrantz, Gary. 'On Divine Foreknowledge and Human Freedom,' *Philosophical Studies*, Vol. 37, No. 3 (April, 1980), 289–296.

Hume, David. *Dialogues Concerning Natural Religion*, Norman Kemp Smith (ed.). New York: The Bobbs-Merrill Co., 1947, also *Hume Selections*. C. Hendel (ed.). New York: Charles Scribner's, 1955.

Kane. G. Stanley. 'The Concept of Divine Goodness and the Problem of Evil,' *Religious Studies*, Vol. 11 (March, 1975), 49–71.

Kane, G. Stanley. 'The Failure of Soul-Making Theodicy,' *International Journal for Philosophy of Religion*, Vol. VI, No. 1 (Spring, 1975), 1–22.

Kane, G. Stanley. 'Soul-Making Theodicy and Eschatology,' *Sophia*, Vol. 14 (July, 1975), 24–31.

Kane, G. Stanley. 'Theism and Evil,' *Sophia*, Vol. IX (March, 1970), 14–21.

Kenny, Anthony. *The God of the Philosophers*. Oxford: Clarendon Press, 1979.

Khamara, E. J. 'In Defence of Omnipotence,' *The Philosophical Quarterly*, Vol. 28, No. 112 (July, 1978), 215–228.

Kielkopf, Charles F. 'Emotivism as a Solution to the Problem of Evil,' *Sophia*, Vol. IX, No. 2 (July, 1970), 34–38.

Lackey, Douglas. 'The Epistemology of Omnipotence,' *Religious Studies*, Vol. 15, No. 1 (March, 1979), 25–30.

La Croix, Richard R. 'Swinburne on Omnipotence,' *International Journal for Philosophy of Religion*, Vol. VI, No. 4 (Winter, 1975), 252–255.

La Croix, Richard R. 'The Hidden Assumption in the Paradox of Omnipotence,' *Philosophy and Phenomenological Research*, Vol. XXXVIII, No. 1 (September, 1977), 125–127.

La Croix, Richard R. 'The Impossibility of Defining 'Omnipotence',' *Philosophical Studies*, Vol. 32 (1977), 181–190.

Leibniz, G. W. *Theodicy*. Austin Farrer (ed.), E. M. Huggard (trans.). New Haven: Yale University Press, 1952.

Leslie, John. *Physical Cosmology and Philosophy*. New York: Macmillan Publishing Company, 1990.

Lewis, David K. *Counterfactuals*. Cambridge: Harvard University Press, 1973.

Loux, Michael J. (ed.). *The Possible and the Actual*. Ithaca: Cornell University Press, 1979.

Lucas, J. R. *The Future*. Oxford: Basil Blackwell, 1989.

Mackie, J. L. 'Evil and Omnipotence,' *God and Evil*. Nelson Pike (ed.). Englewood Cliffs: Prentice-Hall, Inc., 1964, pp. 46–60.

Mackie, J. L. *The Miracle of Theism*. Oxford: Clarendon Press, 1982.

Madden, Edward H. and Hare, Peter H. *Evil and the Concept of God*. Springfield: Charles C. Thomas Pub., 1968.

Matson, Wallace I. *The Existence of God*. Ithaca: Cornell University Press, 1965.

Mavrodes, George I. *Belief in God*. New York: Random House, 1970.

Mavrodes, George I. 'Defining Omnipotence,' *Philosophical Studies*, 32 (1977), 191–202.

Mavrodes, George I. 'God and Verification,' *The Logic of God: Theology and Verification*. Indianapolis: Bobbs-Merrill, 1975.

Mavrodes, George I. 'Is the Past Unpreventable?' *Faith and Philosophy*, Vol. 1, No. 2 (April, 1984), 131–146.

McCloskey, H. J. *God and Evil*. The Hague: Martinus Nijhoff, 1974.

Mitchell, Basil (ed.). *The Philosophy of Religion*. Oxford: Oxford University Press, 1971.

Morris, Thomas V. (ed.). *Divine and Human Action*. Notre Dame: University of Notre Dame Press, 1989.

Morris, Thomas V. *The Logic of God Incarnate*. Ithaca: Cornell University Press, 1986.

Nash, Ronald H. *The Concept of God*. Grand Rapids: Zondervan Publishing House, 1983.

Orlebeke, Clifton J. and Smedes, Lewis, B. (editors). *God and the Good*. Grand Rapids: William B. Eerdmans Pub. Co., 1975.

Padgett, Alan. *God, Eternity and the Nature of Time*. London: The Macmillan Press Ltd., 1992.

Paterson, R. W. K. 'Evil, Omniscience, Omnipotence,' *Religious Studies*, Vol. 15, No. 1 (March, 1979), 1–23.

Peterson, Michael. *Evil and the Christian God*. Grand Rapids: Baker Book House, 1982.

Pike, Nelson. 'Divine Foreknowledge, Human Freedom and Possible Worlds,' *The Philosophical Review*, Vol. LXXXVI, No. 2 (April, 1977), 209–216.

Pike, Nelson. 'Omnipotence and God's Ability to Sin,' *Readings in the Philosophy of Religion*, Baruch A. Brody (editor). Englewood Cliffs: Prentice-Hall, Inc., 1974.

Pike, Nelson. *God and Evil*. Englewood Cliffs: Prentice-Hall, 1964.

Plantinga, Alvin. *Does God Have a Nature?* Milwaukee: Marquette University Press, 1980.

Plantinga, Alvin. *God and Other Minds*. Ithaca: Cornell University Press, 1967.

Plantinga, Alvin. *The Nature of Necessity*. Oxford: The Clarendon Press, 1974.

Plantinga, Alvin. 'The Probabilistic Argument from Evil,' *Philosophical Studies*, Vol. 35, No. 1 (January, 1979), 1–53.

Puccetti, Roland. 'The Loving God – Some Observations on John Hick's *Evil and the God of Love*,' *Religious Studies*, Vol. 2, No. 2 (April, 1967), 255–268.

Reichenbach, Bruce. *Evil and a Good God*. New York: Fordham University Press, 1983.

Reichenbach, Bruce. 'Mavrodes on Omnipotence,' *Philosophical Studies*, Vol. 37, No. 2 (February, 1980), 211–214.

Reichenbach, Bruce. 'Must God Create the Best Possible World?' *International Philosophical Quarterly*, Vol. XIX, No. 74 (June, 1979), 203–212.

Ross, James F. 'Analogy as a Rule of Meaning for Religious Language,' *Inquiries into Medieval Philosophy*, James F. Ross (editor). Westport: Greenwood Publishing Company, 1971.

Ross, James F. *Introduction to the Philosophy of Religion*. London: The Macmillan Company, 1969.

Rowe, William L. 'On Divine Foreknowledge and Human Freedom: A Reply,' *Philosophical Studies*, Vol. 37, No. 4 (May, 1980), 429–430.

Rowe, William L. *Philosophy of Religion*. Encino: Dickenson Pub. Co., 1978.

Salmon, Wesley. 'Religion and Science: A New Look at Hume's Dialogues,' *Philosophical Studies*, Vol. 33, No. 2 (February, 1978), 143–176.

Schilling, S. Paul. *God and Human Anguish*. Nashville: Abingdon, 1977.

Schlesinger, G. 'On the Possibility of the Best of All Possible Worlds,' *The Journal of Value Inquiry*, Vol. IV, No. 3 (Fall, 1970), 229–232.

Smart, Ninian. 'Omnipotence, Evil, and Supermen,' *Philosophy*, Vol. XXXVI, No. 137, 188–195.

Stalnaker, Robert C. 'A Theory of Conditionals,' *American Philosophical Quarterly, Monograph Series*. Nicholas Rescher (ed.). Monograph 2. Oxford: Basil Blackwell, 1968, pp. 98–112.

Swinburne, Richard. *The Coherence of Theism*. Oxford: Clarendon Press, 1977.

Swinburne, Richard. *The Existence of God*. Oxford: Clarendon Press, 1979.

Swinburne, Richard. *Responsibility and Atonement.* Oxford: Clarendon Press, 1989.

Tomberlin, James E., and van Inwagen, Peter (editors). *Profiles: Alvin Plantinga.* Dordrecht: D. Reidel Publishing Company, 1985.

Urban, Linwood and Walton, Douglas (editors). *The Power of God.* New York: Oxford University Press, 1978.

van Inwagen, Peter. *An Essay on Free Will.* Oxford: Clarendon Press, 1983.

van Inwagen, Peter. *Material Beings.* Ithaca: Cornell Univeristy Press, 1991.

Walton, Douglas. 'Some Theorems of Fitch on Omnipotence,' *Sophia,* Vol. XV, No. 1 (March, 1976), 20–27.

Ward, Keith. 'Freedom and the Irenaean Theodicy,' *The Journal of Theological Studies,* Vol. 20, Part 1 (April, 1969), 249–254.

Wierenga, Edward. *Nature of God.* Ithaca: Cornell University Press, 1989.

Wisdom, John. 'God and Evil,' *Mind,* Vol. XLIV (January, 1935), 1–20.

Woods, Michael. 'What is a Counterfactual Conditional?' (unpublished paper).

Yandell, Keith. *Basic Issues in the Philosophy of Religion.* Boston: Allyn and Bacon, Inc., 1971.

Yandell, Keith. *Christianity and Philosophy,* Grand Rapids: William B. Eerdmans Publishing Company, 1984.

Yandell, Keith. 'Ethics, Evil, and Theism,' *Sophia,* Vol. VIII, No. 2 (July, 1969), 18–28.

Yandell, Keith, (ed.). *God, Man, and Religion.* New York: McGraw-Hill, 1973.

Yandell, Keith. 'The Greater Good Defense,' *Sophia,* Vol. XIII, No. 3 (October, 1974), 1–16.

Yandell, Keith. 'A Premature Farewell to Theism,' *Religious Studies,* Vol. V, No. 2 (December, 1969), 251–255.

Yandell, Keith. 'The Problem of Evil and the Content of Morality,' *International Journal for Philosophy of Religion,* Vol. 17 (1985).

Yandell, Keith. 'Theism and Evil: A Reply,' *Sophia,* Vol. XI, No. 1 (April, 1972), 1–7.

Zagzebski, Linda Trinkaus. *The Dilemma of Freedom and Foreknowledge.* New York; Oxford University Press, 1991.

Index

Abelard, Peter, 54
actualization
  strong and weak, 30, 106–11
Adam, 146, 148, 152, 153, 155, 157,
  163, 186n72, 189n34, 190n39,
  198, 199
Adams, Robert Merrihew, 37,
  166n20, 184n37
Ad hominem argument, 6, 18,
  165n13
Ahern, M. B., 16–17, 168n3, 168n46
almightiness, 32
Alston, William P., 172n54
Ambrose, 145
analogia entis, 53, 73n87, 175n100
analogical attribution, 51
analogy
  of proportion and attribution,
  52–3
Anselm, 147, 189n34
angels
  fallen, 182n3
Aquinas, Thomas, 53, 57–9, 75,
  147, 151, 163, 173n74, 175n100,
  176n7, 179n60, 189n34
Aristotle, 137
atemporal eternity, 171n47
atonement, 147, 148–50, 189n25
  and supralapsarianism, 150–1
  as ransom or 'payment,' 149–50
  consequent necessity of, 147–8
  hypothetical necessity
    of, 147–8
  infralapsarianism, 150–1
  repentance, 149–50
Augustine, 48, 174n80, 57, 145, 147,
  149, 151, 163, 187n5, 188n17,
  189n34
Augustinian, 133, 134, 139, 145, 150,
  151, 152
axioms of character theory,
  129, 132–3
Ayer, A. J., 170n26

Barth, Karl, 174n88, 175n100,
  179n61
Bayes' Theorem, 10–14, 167n35
  conditional probability, 10–14
  'forward probabilities,' 10–14
  'prior probabilities,' 10–14
belief
  as person-relative and person-
    variable, 4–5
Berkhof, Louis, 150, 189n26, 189n32
Bertocci, Peter, 165n14
best of all possible worlds, 57–65
  BPW_1, 58, 59, 63
  BPW_2, 58, 59, 63
  bens of good, 58
  'best' as 'perfect,' 62, 176–7n22
  best of all possible world-kinds,
    60
  best universes, 60–61, 121–2,
    184n50
  'compossible goods,' 58
  the divine *ménage a trois*, 63
  greatest conceivable being,
    176n13
  Substitution Argument, 62
  Subtraction Argument, 62
Bettenson, Henry, 184n31
Beza, 151
Black, Max, 10, 167n32
Boethian, 38
Bonhoeffer, Deitrich, vi
Botterill, George, 48, 174n85,
  184n41
Brightman, Edgar Sheffield, 179n61
Broad, C. D., 170n26
Brunner, Emil, 174n88

Calvin, John, 48, 151, 174n81
Carnap, Rudolf, 8, 10, 166n22
Cartesian, 20, 34, 59, 66
Castenada, Hector-Neri,
  44
causally necessary, 66